THE FALL OF A

THE FALL OF A CAROLINGIAN KINGDOM

LOTHARINGIA, 855–869

CHARLES WEST

UNIVERSITY OF TORONTO PRESS
Toronto Buffalo London

© University of Toronto Press 2023
Toronto Buffalo London
utorontopress.com

ISBN 978-1-4875-4509-3 (cloth)   ISBN 978-1-4875-4518-5 (EPUB)
ISBN 978-1-4875-4516-1 (paper)   ISBN 978-1-4875-4519-2 (PDF)

All rights reserved. The use of any part of this publication reproduced, transmitted in any form or by any means, electronic, mechanical, photocopying, recording, or otherwise, or stored in a retrieval system, without prior written consent of the publisher – or in the case of photocopying, a license from Access Copyright, the Canadian Copyright Licensing Agency – is an infringement of the copyright law.

Library and Archives Canada Cataloguing in Publication

Title: The fall of a Carolingian kingdom : Lotharingia, 855–869 / Charles West.
Other titles: Lotharingia, 855–869
Names: West, Charles, 1979–, author.
Description: Includes bibliographical references and index.
Identifiers: Canadiana (print) 2023023691X | Canadiana (ebook) 20230236936 | ISBN 9781487545161 (paper) | ISBN 9781487545093 (cloth) | ISBN 9781487545192 (PDF) | ISBN 9781487545185 (EPUB)
Subjects: LCSH: Lothair II, King of Lorraine, approximately 825–869 – Divorce – Sources. | LCSH: Theutberga, Queen, consort of Lothair II, King of Lorraine, active 855–869 – Divorce – Sources. | LCSH: Divorce – France – Lorraine – History – To 1500 – Sources. | LCSH: Carolingians – History – Sources. | LCSH: Lorraine (France) – Kings and rulers – Biography – Sources. | LCSH: Lorraine (France) – History – Sources. | LCSH: France – History – To 987 – Sources.
Classification: LCC DC655.2 .W37 2023 | DDC 944/.38014 – dc23

Cover design: Alexa Love
Cover image: The Stuttgart Psalter (Württembergische Landesbibliothek Stuttgart, Cod.bibl.fol.23), folio 58r.

We welcome comments and suggestions regarding any aspect of our publications – please feel free to contact us at news@utorontopress.com or visit us at utorontopress.com.

Every effort has been made to contact copyright holders; in the event of an error or omission, please notify the publisher.

We wish to acknowledge the land on which the University of Toronto Press operates. This land is the traditional territory of the Wendat, the Anishnaabeg, the Haudenosaunee, the Métis, and the Mississaugas of the Credit First Nation.

University of Toronto Press acknowledges the financial support of the Government of Canada and the Ontario Arts Council, an agency of the Government of Ontario, for its publishing activities.

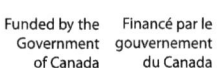

Contents

List of Figures vii

Foreword ix

Acknowledgments xi

Abbreviations xiii

Key Individuals xv

Introduction 1

Documents 11

1 King Lothar II Grants Winebert an Immunity, November 12, 856 11
2 A Coin of King Lothar II (undated) 16
3 The Quierzy Letter, November 858 19
4 The *Liber Memorialis* of Remiremont "Royal Entry," December 861 46
5 The Council of Aachen, April 29, 862 52
6 The Summit at Savonnières, November 862 85
7 Bishop Adventius of Metz Writes to Archbishop Theutgaud of Trier, Early 863 99

8 King Lothar II Grants a Church to the Convent of St-Pierre in Lyon, May 18, 863   102
9 Bishop Adventius Reforms the Monastery of Gorze, June 863   105
10 Eberhard and Gisela Make a Will, c. 863   112
11 Bishop Adventius of Metz Writes to Pope Nicholas I, Early 864   121
12 The Bishops of Lotharingia Write to the Bishops of West Francia, c. 865   129
13 King Lothar II Grants Queen Theutberga Lands, January 17, 866   134
14 Pope Nicholas I Writes about Waldrada to the Bishops of Gaul, Germany, and Italy, June 13, 866   140
15 Queen Ermentrude's Coronation, August 25, 866   146
16 Pope Nicholas I Writes to King Charles the Bald, January 25, 867   153
17 Bishop Adventius Organizes Prayers against the Northmen, May/June 867   163
18 The Metz Oath, c. 868   167
19 King Lothar II Writes to Archbishop Ado of Vienne, July 869   170
20 Pope Hadrian II Writes to the Aristocrats of Lothar's Kingdom, September 5, 869   174
21 The Sacramentary of Metz, c. 869   179
22 Emperor Louis II of Italy Writes to Emperor Basil I of Byzantium, Early 871   182

Conclusion   201

Bibliography   205

Index   223

Figures

1 Map of the Frankish kingdoms in 855   4
2 Lothar II's family (simplified)   6
3 Lothar II's charter for Winebert   16
4 Lothar II coin from the Pilligerheck hoard   19
5 *Liber Memorialis* of Remiremont   51
6 Lothar II's charter for Theutberga   139
7 Sacramentary of Metz   181

Foreword

This book analyzes the history of an early medieval kingdom, from its origin to its collapse, on the basis of a selection of translated sources. It is written in part for those who cannot read these sources in the original Latin or directly access the multilingual modern historiography, an audience including university students, researchers working in other fields, and interested general readers. It is also, however, intended to offer something to those who can read the original texts and the wider historiography. Despite much important corrective work, Frankish history after Charlemagne is still often smoothed into the master narrative of a declining empire, and I hope the material and arguments the book presents will help to restore some of the contours. It is my conviction that the topic to which this book is devoted not only is methodologically stimulating but also constitutes a crucial moment in European history, and I trust what follows bears this out.

The translations in this book tend more toward the literal than the idiomatic, partly in order to obscure as little as possible the thoughts and arguments in the texts, and partly with the aim of aiding and encouraging those readers with a little Latin to consult the original texts, which are for the most part freely available on the website of the *Monumenta Germaniae Historica* (www.dmgh.de). A translation is only ever a guide to the original, since many Latin words have slightly different connotations from their nearest English equivalent, and this book is intended as a gateway to, rather than a substitute for, these original works.

For quotations taken from the church fathers and other Latin sources, I have generally consulted, and given references to, modern English translations where these are available. For biblical quotations, I have drawn on the Douay Rheims English translation of the Vulgate. Readers should note that the names of many of the people mentioned in what follows are spelled differently across the international historiography (especially for women: e.g., Angilberga/Engelberga/Angelberga; Engeltrude/Ingiltrude/Ingeltrude; Theutberga/Teutberga/Theutberge), reflecting the unstandarized orthography of the time; I have used what seem to me to be the most common modern forms.

In interpreting these sources, I have highlighted English-language research, given the main audience for this book. However, all readers need to be aware that much of the best work on Frankish history, both in the past and in the present day, is written in other languages, especially in German, French, and Italian, and this is engaged with where appropriate in what follows.

Acknowledgments

I am grateful to Natalie Fingerhut at the University of Toronto Press for shepherding this book through to print, to Emily Reiner for her careful copy editing, and to the reviewers of the proposal and the draft manuscript for their advice and comments. Thanks, too, to those who read the manuscript in full or in part, gave suggestions, or otherwise assisted or encouraged, especially Tom Brown, Claire Burridge, Simon Coupland, Oren Falk, Clemens Gantner, Alice Hicklin, Julia Hillner, Emma Hunter, George Litchfield, Simon Loseby, Conor O'Brien, Martha Rampton, Laury Sarti, Mark Stephenson, Rachel Stone, and Marlene Wessel, as well as the indefatigable Cuthbert. Any errors that remain are my own. I have relied on the holdings of several libraries, in particular the university libraries in Cambridge and Sheffield and the National Library of Scotland. Finally, my thanks to the history students at the University of Sheffield for asking difficult questions about King Lothar II's divorce, and who in doing so inspired the writing of this book.

Abbreviations

Adventius, *Letters*	Adventius of Metz. *Epistolae ad divortium Lotharii regis pertinentes.* Edited by Ernst Dümmler. *Epistolae Karolini aevi* 4. MGH Epistolae 6, pt. 1, 205–40. Berlin: Weidmann, 1902.
Charles, *Reg.*	*Die Regesten Karls des Kahlen, 840 (823)–877.* Lieferung 2, Abschnitt 1, *849–859.* Edited by Irmgard Fees and Yanick Strauch. Mainz, 2022.
King Lothar II, *Charters*	*Die Urkunden Lothars I und Lothars II.* Edited by Theodor Schieffer. MGH Diplomata Karolinorum 3, 367–464. Hannover: Hahn, 1966.
MGH	Monumenta Germaniae Historica.
Nicholas, *Letters*	Nicholas I. *Epistolae.* Edited by Ernst Perels. *Epistolae Karolini aevi* 4. MGH Epistolae 6, 267–690. Berlin: Weidmann, 1925.
Nicholas, *Reg.*	Herbers, Klaus, ed. *Die Regesten des Kaiserreiches unter den Karolingern,* 751–918. Band 4, Papstregesten 800–911, Teil 2, 844–872. Lieferung 2, 858–867 (Nicolaus I). Vienna: Böhlau, 2012.

Key Individuals

Adventius, bishop of Metz (855–75) and adviser to Lothar II
Angilberga, empress, wife of Louis II and coruler of northern Italy
Charles of Provence, king of Provence, younger brother of Lothar II
Charles the Bald, king of West Francia, uncle of Lothar II
Engeltrude, wife of Count Boso of Italy, cousin of Lothar II
Ermentrude, queen of West Francia, first wife of Charles the Bald (842–69)
Gunthar, archbishop of Cologne (850–63) and adviser to Lothar II
Hadrian II, pope (867–72), successor to Pope Nicholas I
Hincmar, archbishop of Reims (845–82) and adviser to Charles the Bald
Lothar II, king (855–69)
Louis II of Italy, emperor and ruler in northern Italy, elder brother of Lothar II
Louis the German, king of East Francia, uncle of Lothar II
Nicholas I, pope (858–67)
Theutberga, queen and wife of Lothar II
Theutgaud, archbishop of Trier (847–63)
Waldrada, queen and wife of Lothar II
Walter, count and adviser to Lothar II

Introduction

The empire established by the Frankish ruler Charlemagne (†814), and ruled after him by his heir Louis the Pious (†840), encompassed most of western Europe. In 843, this empire fragmented into a constellation of independent kingdoms, each led by one of the emperor's male descendants and his spouse. For this reason, the history of Carolingian Francia is conventionally seen through the prism of a decaying empire, as Charlemagne's descendants strove and ultimately failed to maintain the huge polity he had created.[1] Yet it was also a time of energetic, sometimes frantic political and cultural creativity, as new models for legitimate authority were pioneered and tested, and the inherited resources of Late Antiquity were ingeniously invoked to new ends by competing kings and their courts.

This book opens up the dynamics of this period through a case study: the fate of the realm that was ruled by King Lothar II, Charlemagne's great-grandson, between 855 and 869. This kingdom stretched from the Alps to the North Sea, and its approximately 110,000 square

---

1 See de Jong, "The Empire That Was Always Decaying"; Nelson, "The Carolingian Moment"; and for a wider view, Burbank and Cooper, *Empires in World History*, 80–7 (emphasizing the empire's short life). There are two recent book-length overviews in English: Costambeys, Innes, and MacLean, *The Carolingian World*; and Airlie, *Making and Unmaking the Carolingians*. For a book-length study of a Carolingian king that engages trenchantly with the theme of decline, see MacLean, *Kingship and Politics in the Late Ninth Century*.

kilometers of territory (roughly the size of modern England) encompassed lands now in France, Germany, the Netherlands, Belgium, Luxembourg, and Switzerland. Lothar II's kingdom proved short-lived and did not outlast its ruler. Moreover, because Lothar II's court circle did not produce a full historical narrative in the form of a chronicle or set of annals, the kingdom's brief history is often told from the point of view of its better-documented neighbors. Nevertheless, the study of how this kingdom rose and fell in such a short time has much to tell us about the play between politics and culture in early medieval Europe in general, and in Carolingian Francia in particular. That is because the fate of this kingdom, known later as Lotharingia (from the Latin *Lotharii regnum*, meaning simply "Lothar's kingdom," as contemporaries called it), was shaped by the most extraordinary scandal of the Carolingian period.[2]

The origins of the story lie in a scramble for inheritance. When Emperor Louis the Pious, Charlemagne's heir, died in 840, his sons fought over their share of the Frankish empire. In 843, they agreed to divide his empire into three. To King Charles "the Bald" went a western realm, to King Louis "the German" an eastern realm, and to Emperor Lothar I, the eldest son, went a middle realm, the largest and most important of the three, which stretched from Frisia in the north to Tuscany in the south.[3] When Lothar I himself died on September 29, 855, the process of fragmentation repeated itself, as once again, three sons each sought their share of their father's lands.[4] The eldest son, Louis II of Italy, had already been crowned as coemperor and ruler in Italy in 850, and he staked a claim to the whole inheritance. In the event, however,

---

[2] The history of Lothar II's reign has been assessed many times. Key introductory readings in English are Airlie, "Private Bodies and the Body Politic"; Heidecker, *The Divorce of Lothar II*, published in 2010, and based on his *Kerk, huwelijk en politieke macht*, published in 1997; and d'Avray, *Papacy, Monarchy and Marriage*, 48–62, together with the companion volume of sources, *Dissolving Royal Marriages*, 11–43. An excellent and up-to-date German summary is provided by Dohmen, *Die Ursache allen Übels*, 181–241. Stone and West, *The Divorce of King Lothar and Queen Theutberga*, offers a translation with lengthy introduction to a key treatise by Hincmar of Reims.

[3] The epithets "the Bald" and "the German" were not used at the time, but I have kept them to help differentiate these kings from other rulers with the same names.

[4] On Emperor Lothar I, Lothar II's father, see Screen, "The Importance of the Emperor," as well as the major German study by Schäpers, *Lothar I*.

Emperor Lothar I's two other sons managed to assert their own rights as kings. Charles, who was the youngest son and sickly, ended up with a small kingdom based around the Rhône valley (for which reason he is usually called Charles "of Provence"). Meanwhile, Lothar II, the middle son who at this point was in his late teens, took the bulk of the lands north of the Alps, including the prestigious imperial palace of Aachen, with the support of his uncle, Louis the German.[5] Despite his grand imperial title, Louis II therefore had to content himself, for the moment, with the kingdom of northern Italy, though as we shall see his aspirations remained much larger.

It was to secure his fragile position that in the autumn of 855, Lothar II hastily entered into a marriage with a woman named Theutberga, whose kin group, known to modern scholars as the "Bosonids" after the male name Boso that ran in the family, was highly influential.[6] Theutberga's brother Hubert was a key figure in the Alpine frontierlands of Lothar II's kingdom and may have played a major role in helping Lothar II become king. As an adolescent, however, Lothar II had already struck up a relationship with a woman named Waldrada, with whom he seems to have formed a powerful emotional bond, strong enough for some to suspect the work of love magic.[7] It is also likely that as a king, he felt trammeled by Theutberga's powerful relatives and wished to free himself from their influence. As soon as Lothar II grew confident in his position, he decided to oust Theutberga from the royal bed, and her brother from his inner circle. In 857, probably in December, Lothar II simply dismissed Theutberga. Such an informal and unceremonious process proved unpopular, and in 858 "King Lothar was forced by his own people to take back the wife he had put aside."[8] In early 860, Lothar II tried again, this time compelling Theutberga to confess publicly to an array of terrible sins.[9]

---

5 Lothar II is generally assumed to have been born around 835 or a little later: see Airlie, "Private Bodies and the Body Politic," 8; and Heidecker, *The Divorce of Lothar II*, 51.
6 Bouchard, "The Bosonids or Rising to Power in the Late Carolingian Age."
7 See Rampton, "Love and the Divorce of Lothar II," and now Rampton, *Trafficking with Demons*, 351–8.
8 *Annals of St-Bertin*, trans. Nelson, 87. "Forced by his own people" (*cogentibus suis*) refers to Lothar II's elite followers, rather than the kingdom's populace as a whole, as noted by Heidecker, *The Divorce of Lothar II*, 64n7.
9 On the confessional and penitential aspects of the case, see Firey, *A Contrite Heart*, esp. 9–60.

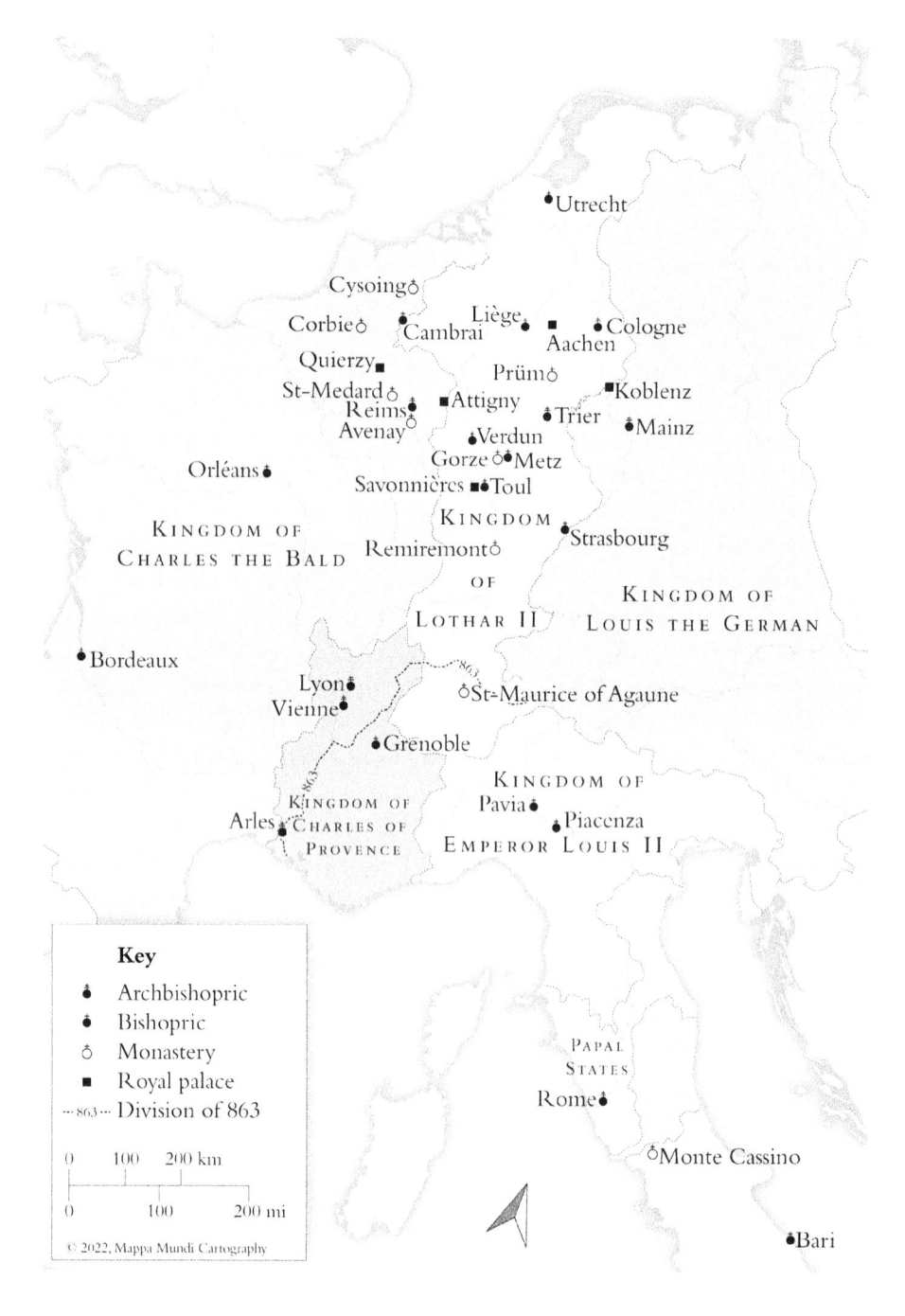

Figure 1. Map of the Frankish kingdoms in 855 (map by Mappa Mundi Cartography)

Rather than meekly submit to the fate of a lifetime's confinement, however, Theutberga fled to the court of the western Frankish king, Lothar II's uncle Charles the Bald, from where she launched appeals to the pope in Rome. Undaunted, Lothar II continued to work with the elites of his kingdom, especially his bishops, to build a consensus around his relationship with Waldrada. Yet the scandal only grew, and as it did, so too did questions over the king's fitness to rule. In the summer of 863, a council held in the city of Metz triumphantly confirmed Lothar II's new marriage to Waldrada, but in the autumn of that year the pope, Nicholas I, dramatically quashed this council's decisions. Despite his obvious reluctance, in 865 Lothar II was compelled to accept Theutberga back at his side as his queen, while Waldrada was summoned to Rome (though she refused to go). Lothar II never lost his determination to make Waldrada his queen, and as we shall see, he and his advisers came up with various inventive solutions to meet the unprecedented challenges they faced. But his opponents were equally inventive and proved better players of the fast-moving Carolingian political game than the inexperienced young king. When Lothar II died in 869, he was still married to Theutberga, and his kingdom was swallowed up by his powerful uncles.

After its collapse, attempts were made to revive Lothar II's kingdom, not least by the son he had with Waldrada, Hugh (or Hugo), but the kingdom of Lotharingia is now largely forgotten, though its name survives in transmuted form as the eastern French region of Lorraine (perhaps the only area of Europe named after a king).[10] Nevertheless, the collapse of the kingdom, which Lothar II's scandalous divorce catalyzed, had enormous long-term significance for European history. The political vacuum it created at the heart of Francia indirectly helped consolidate regnal communities to the west and the east; the lands between remained contested territory all the way down to the twentieth century. None of this later history was set in stone by Lothar II's divorce, but it is difficult to resist the conclusion that the map of Europe, and perhaps even the laws of Christian marriage, could have looked very different had Lothar II found a way through his difficulties.

---

10 On the memory of the kingdom, see MacLean, "Shadow Kingdom: Lotharingia and the Frankish World." For an overview aimed at a wider public, see Winder, *Lotharingia: A Personal History*. In 2016, Lorraine became part of the Grand Est region of France.

Emperor Louis the Pious
m. (1) Ermengard
   (2) Judith

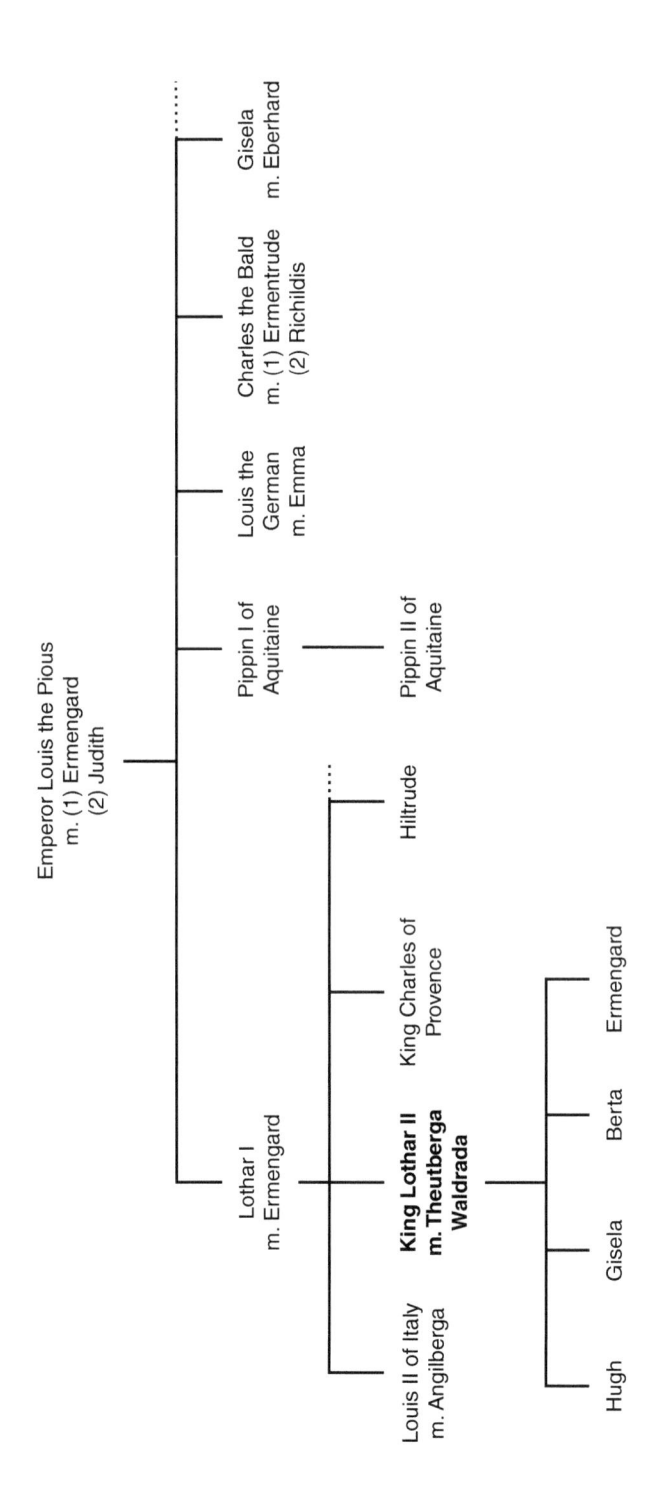

- Lothar I m. Ermengard
  - Louis II of Italy m. Angilberga
  - King Lothar II **m. Theutberga / Waldrada**
    - Hugh
    - Gisela
    - Berta
    - Ermengard
  - King Charles of Provence
  - Hiltrude
- Pippin I of Aquitaine
  - Pippin II of Aquitaine
- Louis the German m. Emma
- Charles the Bald m. (1) Ermentrude (2) Richildis
- Gisela m. Eberhard

Figure 2. Lothar II's family (simplified)

What lay behind this failure? For the chronicler Regino of Prüm, writing a generation later, Lothar II's kingdom collapsed because it had been cursed by the pope.[11] Modern historians have sought more mundane explanations. Arguing against a venerable tradition of analyzing the divorce case in narrowly legal terms, Karl Heidecker suggested in an excellent book that the swelling crisis that engulfed Lothar II's reign was driven primarily by *Realpolitik*. In this reading, Lothar II's marital controversies were expertly leveraged by his political opponents – most notably his uncles Kings Charles the Bald and Louis the German, whose neighboring kingdoms loomed over his – in pursuit of their own interests. Heidecker's emphasis lay on uncovering the unscrupulous machinations at work in Lothar II's divorce case, and how contemporaries instrumentalized norms and principles. As he put it, "The ultimate winner and losers in this affair would be determined by the ability to mobilize political power."[12]

This book, however, centers a somewhat different perspective. Its premise is that early medieval struggles for power did not take place independently of religious and legal frameworks but rather were refracted through them. As Costambeys, Innes, and MacLean put it, "The rulers of this generation cannot be seen simply as land-grabbing despots dragging the [Carolingian] empire into terminal political chaos, for they were part of a political order defined by strong codes of personal and political propriety."[13] The ruthlessness of Lothar II's opponents highlighted by Heidecker is a crucial part of the story, and a vital corrective to earlier interpretations, but we should remember that the crisis of Lothar II's kingdom was conceivable only in the context of the religious and legal frameworks that had been developing in Carolingian Francia around kingship on the one hand, and marriage on the

---

11 Regino of Prüm, *Chronicle*, trans. MacLean, 189; cf. 43–4.
12 Heidecker, *The Divorce of Lothar II*, 8; cf. "… the prohibition against divorce was used to eliminate a political opponent," 186. Böhringer, "Das Recht im Dienst der Machtpolitik?" proposes some nuances to Heidecker's argument.
13 Costambeys, Innes, and MacLean, *Carolingian World*, 407. Cf. Staubach, *Das Herrscherbild Karls des Kahlen*, 119–20: "For as long as one tends to place law and morality on the one side and politics on the other as two sharply separated, opposed, and contradictory fields, then in the event that they touch or even overlap, one must react with mistrust and the suspicion of insincere or hypocritical dressing up of self-interest" (my translation).

other.[14] No previous ruler in the Roman or post-Roman world in the West had seen their attempts to obtain a divorce spiral into a full-blown political crisis that threatened their survival.[15] Equally, it would have been utterly unthinkable for a contemporary ruler in, for instance, the Islamic world to have become so enmeshed in a drawn-out struggle over remarriage: no matter how pitiless his opponents, "the problem would never have arisen in the first place."[16] Moreover, the process of the divorce had its own momentum and dynamics, to which all involved had to respond as nimbly as they could.[17]

In these ways, the divorce case of Lothar II brilliantly illuminates the fluid interaction between political priorities and shifting norms, and it is this interaction that makes it a superb case study in late Carolingian political culture. The divorce case reveals the sophistication of this culture, as kings and their advisers, clerical and lay, sought to shape opinion and steer the course of events through the strategic and tactical employment of the written word, material culture, public assemblies, and military force, thereby setting parameters for the exercise of kingship in later European history. It shows how they made intelligent use of the material and intangible resources at their disposal to project their authority, build consensus, and meet emerging challenges, whether in the form of papal intervention, dynastic conflict, internal dissidence, or viking raids. And perhaps most importantly, it points to how very delicate and difficult this balancing act was. If late Carolingian kingship was in some ways like a game, it was a very complex one, with constantly changing rules, and in which the potential gains were enticing, but losing came with terrible costs.

---

14 For an overview of these norms from one important perspective, see Joye, "Family Order and Kingship according to Hincmar."
15 For a wide-ranging study of medieval marriage, with a focus on the patristic background, see Reynolds, *Marriage in the Western Church*. For the divorce around 370 of the Roman emperor Valentinian I from his wife Severa so that he could marry Justina, a woman who came from a more important family, see Woods, "Valentinian I, Severa, Marina and Justina." For the contemporary resonance of this case in the context of Lothar II's divorce, see Vocino, "Framing Ambrose," 140–1.
16 Cook, "Comparing Carolingians and Abbasids," at 219. Cf. d'Avray, *Papacy, Monarchy and Marriage*, 2–4.
17 For emphasis on this negotiation and contingency, see Patzold, "Verhandeln über die Ehe des Königs."

To illustrate these points, and to enable its readers to form their own informed judgment on the causes of the collapse of King Lothar II's kingdom, this book traces decisions as they were taken, as this is the best way toward a historical understanding of events. It examines the kingdom's emergence and destruction through a study of twenty-two sources that bring its history to life. These sources, selected from a much wider set of material, vary in genre and in origin, and they include conciliar acts, secret letters, formal charters, liturgical rites, and public statements, as well as visual and material sources. Some were direct products of the divorce case, while others relate to it more indirectly but help us understand essential context. Whereas much early medieval political history can be analyzed only in its broad outlines, the surviving evidence for the fate of Lothar II's kingdom is detailed and diverse enough to allow us to track, year by year, and even month by month, the dramatic unfolding of the crisis. We start with Lothar II at the promising beginnings of his kingship.

Documents

1. KING LOTHAR II GRANTS WINEBERT AN IMMUNITY, NOVEMBER 12, 856

As already mentioned, Lothar II's ascent to the throne after the death of his father Emperor Lothar I in the autumn of 855 was not entirely straightforward.[1] By late 856, however, his position seemed more secure, in part thanks to his marriage to Theutberga as well as an agreement over the succession with his brothers, King Charles of Provence and Emperor Louis II of Italy, known as the Treaty of Orbe.[2] This meant Lothar II could concentrate on carrying out the duties that early medieval kingship required. Most historians have understandably focused on his unprecedented marriage problems, but we should not forget that in many aspects, Lothar II acted as an entirely traditional Carolingian king.

One way of exploring how he did so, as Linda Dohmen has suggested, is by examining the writings known as royal charters, or diplomas.[3]

---

[1] See the introduction, pp. 2–3. Emperor Lothar I died on September 29, 855; Lothar II's scribes dated the beginning of his reign to some point between this date and November 6.

[2] The precise terms of this treaty do not survive, but there is a description of its outcome in *Annals of St-Bertin*, trans. Nelson, 83.

[3] Dohmen, "Der König und die Seinen." Koziol, *Politics of Memory*, 17–62, offers a useful summary of the nature and historiography of royal charters in this period.

Royal charters were legal documents written on single sheets of parchment in a highly stylized script or handwriting, and in a very formulaic Latin, which conveyed privileges and grants of different kinds. Thirty-six genuine charters issued by Lothar II survive as originals or as copies; another eleven are known to have been lost. This is only a fraction of the number issued by his uncle King Charles the Bald (with 354 surviving genuine documents), but it is enough to give us an insight into the king's rulership.

Lothar II, in his late teens on his accession, had been given a short moral treatise tailored to his age, so we can assume that, like many members of the Carolingian lay elite, he could read.[4] Writing, though, was a quite different skill, and the king's charters were drafted by experienced scribes. Some of these charters may have been produced by the recipients of the grants, but most were written by notaries working for the king. Lothar II had inherited a chancery staffed by several experienced notaries who had already served his father, Lothar I, and who thus constituted an important strand of administrative continuity.

Most surviving early medieval charters are about property, but the charter translated here is not, or at least only indirectly. In this charter, Lothar II confirms that a man named Winebert is exempt from public duties, including military service, as a consequence of Winebert's donation of his own property to the monastery of St-Arnulf in the city of Metz. The charter was written by the royal notary Rodmund (or Hrodmund), who had worked for Emperor Lothar I from 843, and who would continue to write charters for Lothar II (see Document 13).[5] We can imagine that there would have been some kind of ceremony at which the charter was handed over to Winebert before an audience of courtiers.

Winebert is not otherwise known and was probably of relatively undistinguished social status, though he was presumably free and

---

4 The short treatise was written by the elderly Hraban Maurus, archbishop of Mainz, for Lothar II around the time he became king. It eclectically covers the nature of the soul, the four virtues, the five senses, and extracts from the Roman writer Vegetius on military matters. The text seems designed to capture the imagination of a young ruler. There is no complete modern edition. For the engagement of Carolingian lay elites with written intellectual culture, see the studies in Nelson and Wormald, *Lay Intellectuals*. Queen Theutberga was also literate, receiving a book of medicine as a bequest: see Document 20, note 1.

5 See King Lothar II, *Charters*, 31–6, for Theodor Schieffer's summary of Rodmund's scribal activity; and Worm, *Karolingische Rekognitionszeichen*, 65–6, for more detail.

evidently owned land. In contrast, the "faithful minister Walter" who interceded with the king to secure the grant on Winebert's behalf, and who was presumably Winebert's patron, was a powerful figure who appears elsewhere in the sources for Lothar II's reign, described as one of the king's "special favorites."[6] Walter was a count, probably in the area around Metz, and it seems that he was a close adviser to Lothar; this access to the king's ear would have given him a great deal of influence and ability to help his clients and friends. In charters from October and November 855, we see Hubert, Queen Theutberga's brother, interceding for others in a similar way, but by late 856 Hubert's star at Lothar II's court had already waned.[7]

The blurring between religious and secular forms of authority, and the strongly interpersonal character of the relationships on display in sources such as this, has led some historians to question whether "state" is really the right word to characterize the apparatus of rule in early medieval Francia.[8] Be that as it may, the public duties for which Winebert and his family were liable as free Franks in Lothar II's kingdom were significant enough for him to prefer to place himself under the protection of a monastery in order to avoid them.[9]

Charters such as this one, in which kings alienated their own rights to the benefit of religious institutions, used to be seen as signs of weakness, diminishing the long-term capacity of the kingdom in pursuit of short-term political advantage. However, as this charter illustrates, and as Barbara Rosenwein has argued more generally, the reality was more complex.[10] The monastery that benefited from Winebert's grant was dedicated to St Arnulf, a seventh-century bishop of Metz who was

---

6 "One of the special favorites" (*maximi ... familiares*): *Annals of St-Bertin*, trans. Nelson, 102 (862) and 134 (866). See Heidecker, *The Divorce of Lothar II*, 71. Walter visited Rome for discussions with the pope on Lothar II's behalf in 861 and 866: see Nicholas, *Reg.*, 533 and 818.
7 King Lothar II, *Charters*, nos. 1 and 2, 384–5.
8 *Der frühmittelalterliche Staat*, ed. Pohl and Wieser, is a useful resource on this question, including several important English-language contributions. A recent theoretical contribution is provided by Carvajal Castro and Tejerizo-García, "The Early Medieval State."
9 On Carolingian military service, see Halsall, *Warfare and Society*, 71–110; and now Haack, *Die Krieger der Karolinger*.
10 Rosenwein, *Negotiating Space* (concentrating on immunity charters granted to monasteries).

widely considered as a holy ancestor of the Carolingian dynasty; it was also where Lothar II's grandfather, Emperor Louis the Pious, was buried, alongside other relatives. Like other Carolingian kings, Lothar II did not reside at a "capital" but rather moved between palaces and churches located throughout his kingdom. Among these, Aachen was preeminent because of its associations with Charlemagne.[11] Yet the monastery of St-Arnulf was also and unquestionably an important site for the king, because of its role in his dynasty's memory.

So, by making this grant, Lothar II helped cement his own association with this key site, publicly reaffirming his position within the Carolingian dynastic tradition.[12] Moreover, monasteries such as St-Arnulf were themselves integrated into circuits of royal power: they could be relied upon to serve as land banks from which to reward the king's loyal supporters, and even to contribute to military expeditions, as well as to offer prayers for the king and his family. In short, through this 856 charter the king lost the services of Winebert and his family, but he gained in various other, more intangible ways.

The charter survives in the original in the city archives of Metz in eastern France, with its wax seal still attached.[13] It is by no means a grand charter (indeed, it lacks certain scribal formalities), but it is significant as a unique surviving example of a Carolingian king exempting an individual from military service.[14] Of course, there may have been many other similar documents that have not been preserved. For unlike charters that transferred or confirmed title to property, which tended to be carefully looked after, a text like this was of limited value for monks in later centuries, on whose archives we entirely depend. The charter does not even identify which lands Winebert had brought with him to St-Arnulf. It was dismissively annotated by a later medieval monk as a *carta inutilis*, a "useless charter," and seems to have survived only by the proverbial skin of its teeth.

---

11 Lothar II is known to have resided at several palaces, including Gondreville, Marlenheim, and Nimwegen, as well as numerous monasteries, but nearly a third of his surviving documents were issued at the palace of Aachen.
12 The critical importance of dynasty for the Carolingian ruler is the focus of Airlie, *Making and Unmaking the Carolingians*.
13 On Lothar II's seal, see Kornbluth, "Seal of Lothar II."
14 The charter unusually lacks a notarial subscription, which would normally be in the space to the left of the seal (compare with the much grander charter discussed in Document 8).

Translation[15]

In the name of the almighty Lord and our Savior Jesus Christ, Lothar, king by divine clemency.

Let it be known to all the faithful people of the holy church of God and of ourselves, present and future, that our faithful minister Walter brought to our most serene ears how in the time of Drogo, the former Archbishop of Metz,[16] a certain man named Winebert gave his property to the church of St-Arnulf of Metz, on the condition that he and his children should be made immune from all public exaction and military expedition.

Therefore, so that the church of St-Arnulf may more firmly be able to obtain these properties, and so that Winebert and his sons, that is Teudoin and Beringar, may be absolved from all public exaction, that is from paying the *stofa*[17] and from military expedition, and that they and their successors may more securely hold and possess these properties for the agreed payment, that is three pennies worth of wax,[18] we have ordered this charter to be made.

Through it, we insistently command and in every way confirm that no count or any minister of judicial authority or traveling royal envoy shall demand any public service from this Winebert and his sons and their heirs. Through this document of Our Piety, let them and their successors be free at all times from all exactions, and firmly hold and possess these properties with the agreed payment, without any disruption or contestation.

And so that this true authority of our absolution and confirmation shall be trusted and maintained more firmly, we have ordered it to be sealed below with our ring.

---

15 Edition: King Lothar II, *Charters*, no. 6, 391–2 (http://www.mgh.de/dmgh/resolving/MGH_DD_Lo_I._/_DD_Lo_II._S._391).

16 Drogo, an illegitimate son of Charlemagne. Note that he is here termed archbishop; after Drogo's death, Metz had only the status of a bishopric. See Glansdorff, "L'évêque de Metz et archichapelain Drogon"; and Gantner, "A King in Training?" at 165–6. Given Drogo had died only in December 855, Winebert's grant could have been quite recent.

17 The nature of the *stofa*, which is a vernacular word, is mysterious but must refer to some presumably irregular tax or due.

18 That is, Winebert's annual payment to the monastery, in exchange for which he was allowed to continue living on the lands he had formally handed over to the monastery. The wax was used for candles to light the church.

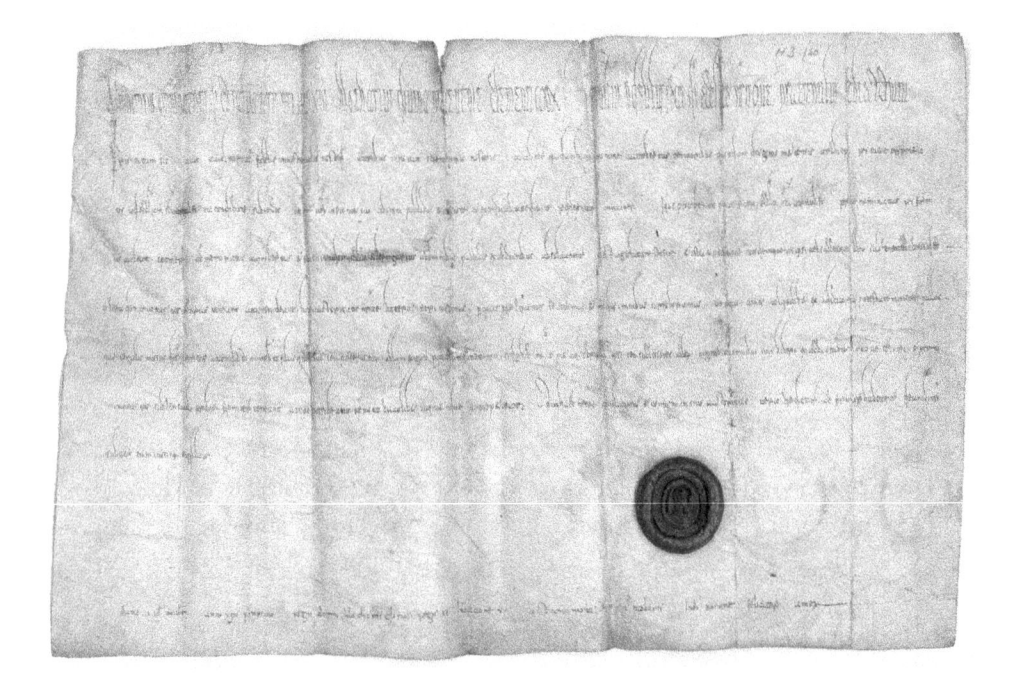

Figure 3. Lothar II's charter for Winebert (Metz, Archives départmentales de la Moselle, H3 20)

On the second of the ides of November [November 12] in the second year of the rule of the glorious lord King Lothar, fifth indiction. Enacted at the monastery of St Nabor, in the name of God, Amen.[19]

2. A COIN OF KING LOTHAR II (UNDATED)

Most of the sources for Lothar II's reign are texts, but one form of material evidence that does tell us something about this king is his coinage.[1]

---

19 "St-Nabor," whose name evolved over time to the modern town of St-Avold, was a monastery some twenty miles east of Metz. Not much is known of its history in the ninth century; this is the only occasion Lothar II is known to have visited it.

***

1 Thanks to Simon Coupland for advice, and to Stefan Wittenbrink for providing the image of the coin.

Lothar II followed the tradition that reached back to Charlemagne of minting small, flat silver pennies about two centimeters in diameter.[2] In line with that tradition, the coin of Lothar II depicted below is inscribed in Latin with +*Hlotharius rex* ("King Lothar") on one side, and +*Viridunum civi[ta]s* ("the city of Verdun") on the other. These inscriptions accompany images of a simple cross on the obverse (front), and a stylized church decorated with a cross on the reverse (back), similar to those found on Lothar II's other surviving coins. These inscriptions and images made the coin into a small portable token reminding those who handled it of Lothar II's legitimacy and authority. A coin such as this would have been enough to buy a dozen large loaves of bread in the ninth century, representing roughly the daily earnings of an unskilled laborer. It was a relatively valuable object, but not out of reach of the peasantry.

Lothar II is known to have issued coins from episcopal cities at Verdun (such as this coin), Cologne, Trier, Strasbourg, Metz, and Cambrai, as well as (probably) the frontier settlement of Mouzon and the palace at Aachen. In this he was following in the footsteps of his father, who had issued coins from most of these places, though Emperor Lothar I's coins had usually made reference to his imperial title and were also minted in northern Italy.

However, although Lothar II minted coins in traditional places, he seems to have issued coins on a scale far smaller than had his father. Many hundreds of coins issued by Lothar I survive, but only a score or so of Lothar II's have yet been found. This could be coincidental, but the pattern seems consistent. Medieval coins are discovered both as individual finds, when they were accidentally dropped and lost, and as hoards, when they were buried deliberately for safekeeping and for whatever reason never retrieved. Lothar II's coins are rare in both contexts. Just half a dozen of his coins have been reported as single finds, and only around twenty or so have been found as part of coin hoards.[3]

This particular coin comes from an enormous hoard found in 1955 in Pilligerheck near Koblenz, now in Germany but at the time part of

---

2 For a wide-ranging study of early medieval silver coins, see Kuchenbuch, *Versilberte Verhältnisse*; for a historiographical overview, see Screen, "Coining It?"

3 The precise number of the king's coins found in hoards is uncertain because the hoard of Lothar II's coins found at Niederlahnstein included seventeen coin fragments, which represent an unknown number of broken coins in addition to the five intact. See Coupland, "Denare Lothars II," 182.

Lothar II's kingdom.[4] The hoard contained around 2,500 coins, making it one of the largest Carolingian coin hoards ever discovered. Of all these coins, just five (including the one pictured) were issued by Lothar II, all struck at Verdun. The Pilligerheck hoard was probably hidden early in Lothar II's reign, which would help explain why there were so very few of his coins present. But another coin hoard found in 2015 at Bassenheim (again near Koblenz) presents a similar picture, though it is much smaller: of the twenty coins buried there, only one bears Lothar II's name.[5] Just one hoard has been found that was made up wholly of Lothar II's coins: a little set of five coins (plus some coin fragments) minted at Cologne, found at Niederlahnstein in the Rhineland in 2015.[6]

Why Lothar II minted so few coins compared to his father is mysterious. The great trading settlement at Dorestad in the lower Rhine, which lay in Lothar II's kingdom and which had flourished earlier in the ninth century, had by the 850s all but vanished, which may have affected the king's ability to obtain silver for his coins.[7] Yet it is not clear how the economic activity at Dorestad, a center for long-distance trade, affected the wider Frankish economy, or whether its collapse would have had a significant impact on royal revenues, not least because the settlement had essentially been under the control of Northmen from the 840s. In any case, as we shall see, in 864 Lothar II was able to demand and obtain great quantities of pennies from the people in his kingdom to buy off the Northmen, which suggests there was not a general shortage of coin.[8] It is possible that Lothar II did not attempt to replace the coinage of his father but was content to let it circulate, simply topping it up little by little. Perhaps he was making a subtle point about continuity: that he was ruling in line with his father's traditions and customs, and therefore there was no need for the coinage to change.

---

4 The hoard is discussed and cataloged in *Der karolingiche Münzschatzfund von Pilligerheck*, ed. Petry and Wittenbrink.
5 Coupland, "Der Karolingerschatz von Bassenheim."
6 Coupland, "Denare Lothars II."
7 On Dorestad, see Coupland, "Boom and Bust."
8 *Annals of St-Bertin*, trans. Nelson, 112.

Figure 4. Lothar II coin from the Pilligerheck hoard (Trier, Rheinisches Landesmuseum, Inventar-Nr. 197, Photo: Peter Ilisch/Stefan Wittenbrink)

3. THE QUIERZY LETTER, NOVEMBER 858

In the late summer of 858, one of Lothar II's uncles sought to rip up the political arrangements that had been established by the Treaty of Verdun in 843, which had divided the Frankish empire into three. On the invitation of disaffected aristocrats in the realm of King Charles the Bald, King Louis the German of East Francia dramatically invaded West Francia. Setting off in mid-August, Louis marched right across Lothar II's kingdom, traveled through Ponthion, Châlons, and Sens, and penetrated as far west as Orléans on the river Loire. He then invited the bishops of West Francia to a council at Reims, near his winter base at the palace of Attigny, where on December 7 he issued a charter dated to the first year of his rule in West Francia.[1]

King Charles was caught unawares and fled south into Burgundy. The West Frankish bishops, however, met for discussions at the palace of Quierzy. Refusing Louis's invitation, they instead sent him an extended letter that offered some frank advice. King Louis, they warned,

---

1 This charter, no. 94 in the standard MGH edition, is available in French translation with commentary in Glansdorff, *Diplômes de Louis le Germanique*, 241–8. For general context, see Nelson, *Charles the Bald*, 187–91; Goldberg, *Struggle for Empire*, 250–62; Costambeys, Innes, and MacLean, *Carolingian World*, 395–6; and Staubach, *Herrscherbild*, 101–17.

should examine his conscience and be wary of his counselors, bearing in mind the fate of his father Emperor Louis the Pious, who had been betrayed by his own followers. But the bishops went further. They developed the letter into a practical treatise on good Carolingian kingship, with a uniquely revealing list of the things a good Christian king ought to do.[2] This included working for peace and defeating the Northmen, rather than bringing about disruption; protecting the church and looking after monasteries; organizing his court as a model for everyone; appointing royal officers, counts, and envoys (*missi*), who were suitable for the task; and managing his royal estates and their residents effectively. Louis had come to West Francia promising to be a good king: the Quierzy Letter defined what that meant, and challenged him – and indeed all Carolingian kings – to measure up to it.

By offering critical advice at a distance, rather than joining his court at Attigny, the West Frankish bishops signaled their lack of support for King Louis's invasion. Their refusal to back Louis doubtless played a role in the king's retreat east to his own kingdom early in 859, as support for Charles built up again. Peaceful if not friendly relations were gradually restored between the two brothers through envoys, culminating in a meeting of the kings at Koblenz in June 860, though there remained tensions between them.

Lothar II was not directly involved in Louis the German's invasion; indeed at the time of the invasion, Lothar II was himself in West Francia, helping Charles besiege a group of Northmen.[3] Not long beforehand, probably in the early summer of 858, in a bid to resolve concerns around his abrupt removal of his wife Theutberga, Lothar II had subjected her to a trial by ordeal on spectacular charges of incest and abortion. These charges were designed to shame Theutberga and her family, while leaving his own reputation unscathed.[4] Theutberga's champion, however, passed the ordeal, so Lothar II had to accept her back as his

---

[2] For an overview of the parameters of early medieval kingship, with references to this letter, see Nelson, "Kingship and Royal Government." On this letter as critique, see West, "'And How, If You Are a Christian, Can You Hate the Emperor?'"

[3] On the siege at *Oscellus* (possibly Oissel), which lasted for several weeks, see *Annals of St-Bertin*, trans. Nelson, 88; Charles, *Reg.*, 913.

[4] For more details on this event, and Theutberga's perhaps surprising success at proving her innocence in 858, see Stone and West, *The Divorce of King Lothar and Queen Theutberga*.

queen. His visit to West Francia in August 858 may have been partly inspired by the wish to shore up support after this humiliation; perhaps he also wanted to avoid Theutberga.

Though an observer rather than a participant in the 858 invasion of West Francia, Lothar II would have seen at close quarters the fragility and instability of the Carolingian political order that it illustrated. Despite his political alliance with Charles, reflected in their joint military expedition against the Northmen, Lothar II seems to have quickly recognized Louis as the new ruler of West Francia in December 858, before turning his support back to the resurgent Charles in February 859. Meanwhile, the position of the bishops reflected in the Quierzy Letter showed the high standards to which kings could be held accountable, as well as the practical consequences of being judged as failing to meet them. Yet it seems that Lothar II failed to draw the right lessons from the invasion. It is noticeable that queens and marriage barely feature in the Quierzy Letter; Lothar II's marriage crisis would soon turn them into critical issues.

The Quierzy Letter was a collective work, written in the name of all the bishops concerned, but in large part it was probably composed by the archbishop of Reims, Hincmar, drawing on the decisions of recent Frankish councils.[5] The letter is preserved in transcriptions of a now lost manuscript from Beauvais, and in Paris, Bibliothèque nationale de France, MS Lat. 5095, a ninth-century manuscript linked to Laon, where it is copied on folios 130r–137v.

Translation[6]

The chapters that follow were sent by the bishops of the provinces of Reims and Rouen from the palace of Quierzy, where they were meeting, to King Louis at the palace of Attigny, via Archbishop Wenilo of Rouen and Bishop Erchenrad of Châlons, in the year of the Lord 858, in the

---

5 On Hincmar, see Stone, "Introduction: Hincmar's World."
6 Edition: *Die Konzilien der karolingischen Teilreiche 843–859*, ed. Hartmann, 408–27 (http://www.mgh.de/dmgh/resolving/MGH_Conc._3_S._408). I am grateful to Richard Gilbert, Robert Heffron, and Harry Mawdsley, who worked on an initial draft of this translation with me as part of a Latin translation group. It also draws on Jinty Nelson's unpublished partial translation, which she kindly made available, and has benefited greatly from her suggestions.

month of November.[7] To the glorious king Louis, we bishops of the provinces of Reims and Rouen who could be present send greetings.

Chapter 1. [*The bishops send their apologies for the meeting*]

Some of us have the letters of Your Dominance, in which you ordered that we should meet you on the seventh kalends of December [November 25] at Reims, so that you might discuss with us and with your other faithful followers the restoration of the holy church and the state and wellbeing of the Christian people.[8] But we were not able to come to the meeting, on account of the inconvenience and the shortness of time, and the unsuitability of the place, and – which is more grievous – because of the confusion and disorder that has arisen.

And according to the divine laws (which with your brothers you told us that you would observe),[9] it makes good sense that, just as archbishops should not dare to do anything without the agreement of the suffragan bishops, so neither should suffragan bishops act without the agreement or order of archbishops, except about matters that concern their own dioceses. And, in such a short time, we were unable to arrange letters for the archbishops for an assembly. Therefore, let Your Excellence know that Our Humility has not disregarded your command, but as has been said long before us, "whoever orders the impossible makes himself ridiculous."[10]

Chapter 2. [*The bishops emphasize that their advice comes from God*]

But we could have more justly and reasonably had a discussion about the restoration of the holy church of God, and about the state and

---

7 The Paris manuscript has a slightly differently worded version of this preface: "Copy of the letter of the bishops from the synod held at Quierzy to King Louis, sent through Archbishop Wenilo and Bishop Erchenraus."
8 These letters do not survive. "Your Dominance" (*vestra dominatio*) was a common formal term of address for kings. For Louis the German's justification of his invasion, see *Annals of Fulda*, trans. Reuter, 42.
9 Probably a reference to a joint declaration issued by the Carolingian kings at Meerssen in 851, a few years previously.
10 The origin of this proverb is unknown, but Hincmar of Reims quoted it on other occasions too: it may have been a Frankish saying or proverb.

wellbeing of the Christian people – which discussion you now say you want to have with us – if with concern for heavenly matters you had wished to obey our advice: or rather God's advice, recommendations, and entreaties. For we did not write, advise, and say our own thoughts, but rather what we found in the holy pages, spoken by Love, which is God, and what we found to be innate in nature.[11] Those things which have been and are being done, contrary to what we have written, advised, and said, are known even by the less wise to be a disease of the natural law and a vice.

In this regard, let any sensible person come to his senses, and understand how greatly God is offended when a sin is committed intentionally in such great and open matters. About this it is written, *They go down alive into hell* [Ps. 54:16], that is they slip knowingly into sin. Such things happen by divine permission in the suffering world on account of our shared sins, that is sins of the pastors and of the flock, and on account of the failings of the king and the kingdom. For as it is written, *These things are sent through evil angels. The Lord made a way for the path to his anger* [Ps. 77:49]. But, as Truth avers, this will not take place without incurring an avenging anger, nor without the staff of the Lord's wrath. Thus we have read, thus we have heard, thus we have seen and certainly will soon see. For although we are sinners, we are repentant and have strong faith in divine mercy, and have received the sacred ministry by the working of the Holy Spirit, without which we cannot administer the sacraments. And we know what was truthfully said to us by Truth: *it is not you who speaks, but the spirit of your father, who speaks in you* [Matt. 10:20].

Chapter 3. [*The bishops remind Louis that he has not listened to their advice before*]

Although Your Dominance knows very well those things which we say have been written, advised, and said, yet it is not irrelevant if we recall them now to your memory. You have sufficiently heard those things which are fitting to salvation, firstly through the venerable bishop Hildegar [of Meaux] in writing and in speech, secondly through

---

11 A reference to previous communications with the king, now lost. The bishops emphasize that they are not saying anything novel or original.

the honorable bishop Aeneas [of Paris] in letters and speech, again through Aeneas orally, then through Hincmar and Wenilo archbishops of Reims and Rouen, and again through those people with the others whom you summoned.[12] This was when we requested, as we did before, that your brother [Charles] and all his faithful followers might come before you and your faithful followers at a suitable time and place for reasonable discussions, so that what had been done badly might be amended, with your counsel and aid and with God's help. We fear greatly for those who do not obey all of what was said, as it is said: *if they have kept my word, they will keep yours also* [John 15:20], and the rest of the Lord's admonition.

And if these things have not been heard before, then it can be supposed that neither will those things be heard that you say you wish to seek and to hear from us now. It seems to some people that, just as the Lord wanted to signal something different when he cursed the fig tree because he wanted a fig, although the Gospels say it was not the season for figs, so in a similar way they might be able to infer some different sense in a meeting so hasty and inconvenient, saving the sincerity of Your Dominance, about which we wish to imply nothing against innocence.[13] And because the blessed Peter warns every bishop that he must be prepared to [give] an account to the satisfaction of all [who are] asking him, we are faithfully giving to Your Dominance such counsel as we now perceive to be timely.

Chapter 4. [*The bishops call on Louis to examine his conscience, comparing the situation with the rebellions against Louis the Pious, and urging suspicion of his lay advisers*]

Firstly, consider your arrival into this kingdom in [your] heart of hearts, before the eyes of the Lord, to whom according to the Psalms, *the thoughts of man are confessed* [Ps. 75:11], and weigh up the scales of justice. And whatever your encouragers and advisers and flatterers are saying to you, *return to your heart* [Isa. 46:8]. And whatever you can find and

---

12 All these documents are lost; they were presumably attempts to slow Louis's invasion.
13 Here the bishops are implying that Louis had a hidden intention in summoning them to Reims: perhaps a plan to compel them to crown him as king?

say to justify and recommend your arrival, examine your conscience: and judge whether you wish to keep doing those things which you are doing.

And place before your mind's eye that hour – of which you can be certain, since in no way can you escape it – when your soul will depart your body, and will leave behind the whole world and all power and all riches and the body itself, and will go forth naked and desolate, without the help of a wife or children, and without the support and company of your retinue [*drudores*] and vassals [*vassi*], and will leave unfinished whatever it thought about and decided to arrange: for as scripture says, *In that day all their thoughts will perish* [Ps. 145:4]. And your soul will see and feel all its sins, watching as devils constrain and compel it. And whatever it thought, spoke, and did against love and the faith owed on this earth, and has not made up for through the worthy fruits of penance, it will have before its eyes for ever, and will wish to escape, and will not be able to. For it is certain that devils come to all men when they leave their body, both to the just and to sinners; and [the devil] even also came to Christ himself, in whom he found nothing [of] his own, as it is written: *The prince of this world comes, and has nothing in me* [John 14:30]. And truly believe us, o king who we wish always to be good and Christian, that this hour is not far away, but near enough to you, and nearer than is hoped.[14]

Therefore do not let those things that you see seduce you. Indeed in the time of your father [Louis the Pious], we saw things begun and initiated by some people, which we see in this time to be brought about by those who do this, and they will be completed by others.[15] And just as they laugh now when they obtain from you what they want in the moment of their desire, so they will laugh when the hour of your death comes to you, and they will ask how they might hold through someone else what they have obtained from you. And it is possible that some are asking this while you are still alive. And unless they do worthy penance, they too will go miserably to that hour of their death, just like those

---

14 Despite this gloomy prediction, Louis the German lived for nearly another twenty years, dying in 876.
15 The precise meaning of this cryptic statement is not clear, but the bishops are evidently drawing connections between events in Emperor Louis the Pious's reign (814–40) and contemporary actions.

went who abandoned your father with your brother [Lothar I].[16] For just as those organized sedition against paternal reverence, so these are inciting you against fraternal love, in the name of peace and the state of the church and the salvation and unity of the people. And "the poison was hiding under the honey."[17]

And the words of the psalmist were fulfilled in those people, and are being fulfilled in these: *Those who speak peace with their neighbor, but have evil in their hearts* [Ps. 27:3], and the rest which follows. And what they received in this world is well known, and what they will receive in the next world will be known in full in the Judgment. And seeing their fate [of the rebels against Louis the Pious], these [followers of Louis the German] should have feared their deeds, and they should act as if the Lord looks down at them, he who looks down and protects the small and the humble; and so *once the wicked man is scourged*, as it is written, the child *will be wiser* [Prov. 19:25]. And they will understand that the Lord will neither spurn nor forget his people in the end; since *it is because of the misery of the needy and the groans of the poor that I will now arise* [Ps. 11:6], said the Lord. Besides, just as then he said to them, so now the Lord says to these: *I was silent, but can it be that I will always be silent? I will shout out as if giving birth* [Isa. 42:14]; *my hour has not yet come* [John 2:4], but now *it is your hour, when darkness reigns* [Luke 22:53]; and *if you, even you, had only known on this day what would bring you peace – but now it is hidden from your eyes, because the days will come upon you* [Luke 19:42–3].

Invite yourself, we beseech you, to some place where you are able to concentrate, to read the homily of St Gregory on the reading of the Gospel: *Jesus, seeing the city, wept over it* [Luke 19:41].[18] We beseech you, lord, that you may have before your mind's eye that day when your soul will receive back its own body along with all other men, and you will come before the face of the eternal Judge in the sight of all angels and men; on which day, just as St Paul said, the Lord will judge everyone, not through another's testimony, but through everyone's hidden thoughts that either accuse or defend them, when everyone

---

16 A reference to the "Field of Lies" in June 833, when Emperor Louis the Pious's supporters deserted him in favor of his son Lothar I (father of Lothar II).
17 A slightly edited quotation from Jerome, *Letters*, trans. Fremantle, letter 15, 19. Note that Hincmar is suggesting that Louis's advisers were encouraging the king through appeal to key Carolingian ideals.
18 Gregory the Great, *Forty Gospel Homilies*, trans. Hurst, homily 39, 359–69.

receives their own body, according to his deeds, whether good or bad. And at that time, the words that we have written will not be despised by those who now hold them in contempt, when without doubt they will be repeated as evidence in that terrible Judgment. And none of those people will help you then. If they continue in this fashion, doing such things as we hear about and experience and lament, they will not even be able to help themselves, but will go into the eternal fire, while the just, who now suffer unjustly, will go into the life eternal.

Chapter 5. [*The bishops call on Louis to help improve the situation, not worsen it*]

We have heard that many cruel and abominable things have happened in the dioceses on the routes through which you came, some of which we have experienced and some of which we fear to experience, and we lament with those who have experienced and are experiencing them.[19] These things are worse than the calamity and misery that we suffer from the pagans,[20] since they are carried out by Christians against Christians, by kin against kin, by a Christian king against a Christian king, by a brother against a brother, against all divine and human laws.

The church, already afflicted by pagans, proclaims against these things, *And they have added to my grief of my wounds* [Ps. 68:27]; and all of us have patiently supported peace, and it has not come. And we sought good things, and behold – disorder. So prohibit, restrain, and calm these things, because your palace ought to be sacred, not sacrilegious.[21] For the palace of the king is so called on account of the rational people residing there, and not on account of walls or bricks that are incapable of feeling. And the king [*rex*] is so called from "ruling" [*regendo*], so that under God he rules himself, and with God he rules the good in purity of heart, truth of lips, and firmness of stability – and he sets the wicked right from their wickedness, and guides them in righteousness. And if you have to come to amend those things that have been done badly,

---

19 Here the bishops are criticizing the conduct of Louis the German's army as it moved into the kingdom of West Francia.
20 A reference to the vikings or Northmen.
21 On this concept of the "sacred palace," see de Jong, "Sacred Palace." For its use in Lothar II's kingdom, see Document 5, p. 56.

then you ought not to bring with you the worse things that we have seen done by Christians against Christians. And if you have come to make peace, then you should obtain peace peacefully from the Author of peace.

And if you have to come to dispel discord and to restore love, then you should show that which Christ taught through Paul. For he says, *Love is not ambitious, it does not act wrongly, it does not seek its own things, it does not rejoice in iniquity, it rejoices in truth* [1 Cor. 13:4], truth which works through love and not through power or excessive greed. As it was written, *without any love, even if he has surrendered his body to be burned, it can do no good* [1 Cor. 13:3]. The Lord gave a sign to all people, that they may know if someone is a Christian and if he will enter the Kingdom of God or not, saying: *in this, all men will learn that you are my disciples, if you have love for one another* [John 13:35]. For they who in the beginning of the faith were called disciples are now called Christians. And love itself is the wedding garment, and they who do not possess it at the heavenly wedding banquet in the future Judgment will be thrown into the outer darkness and into the eternal fire, and there they will weep and gnash their teeth.

Chapter 6. [*The bishops call for Louis to drive away the Northmen*]

Let that love stir you up against the pagans. Although some who had and still have generous honors[22] were not at that time thus moved to a proper sense of obligation [*pietas*] to accompany us against the pagans – and if they had done it and had unanimously wished it, inflamed with righteous zeal, the pagans could with God's help have been expelled or destroyed[23] – now, through your command and with whatever motivation, the holy church may be liberated from the pagans' domination, and the kingdom which is being ransomed from them may be rescued from an unjustified tribute.[24]

---

22 Honors (Latin: *honor*, or *honores* in the plural) was a term used by writers in Carolingian Francia to indicate important rewards such as titles and grants of land.
23 Perhaps a reference to Charles's unsuccessful siege of a group of vikings at *Oscellus* in July/August 858, recorded in *Annals of St-Bertin*, trans. Nelson, 87–8.
24 Frankish kings were often prepared to pay large sums of money to the Northmen to persuade them to leave, a tactic which irked the bishops, who usually footed some of the bill, described here as a *tributum indebitum*.

And may those who have fled from the pagans find a peaceful refuge when they come to those regions you are staying in, rather than so much depredation that the inhabitants cannot live, let alone offer support to those who have fled. For now, as our sins demand, it is coming to pass what was formerly said through the prophet: *He will flee from the face of the lion and will run into a bear, and when he enters a house and leans against the wall, a snake will bite him* [Amos 5:19]. *And when they flee weapons of iron, they shall run into a bronze bow* [Job 20:24]. For in every region, the wretched – alas! – find affliction.

Chapter 7. [*The bishops call on Louis to protect the church, and give the example of Charles Martel as a warning*]

If you seek to restore the church of God, just as you wrote to us, then guard the privileges due to bishops and to the churches entrusted to them, as is divinely constituted. Take care to preserve the rights and immunities and the honor of these churches, as your grandfather and your father kept them. And what your brother, our lord [Charles], who received part of the kingdom by paternal gift and with the mutual undertakings of you and your faithful men, has done for the cult and honor of the churches, you should similarly maintain.

And cherish the leaders and pastors of the church as fathers and vicars of Christ, just as the holy scripture orders, saying: *Treat the priests of God as holy*, and *bow your head to a great man* [Eccles. 7:31; 4:7]. And obey their spiritual counsel, as the scripture says again: *Ask your father and he will tell you*, ask *your elders, and they will tell you* [Deut. 32:7]; and similarly: *Ask* my *priests* my *law* [Hag. 2:13]; and the Lord through the prophet Malachi: *The lips of the priest shall keep knowledge, and they should seek the law from his mouth, because he is the messenger of the Lord's flock* [Mal. 2:7]. And do not trouble them at an unsuitable and unfavorable time,[25] but allow them to carry out the sacred ministry, to which they were appointed, for the salvation of the people; and do not stir up those subject to them in domestic care, and do not permit them to dishonor or oppress the bishops.[26]

---

25 Cf. p. 41.
26 These *domestica cura subiecti* were presumably members of the bishops' households.

Make sure that the fitting honor and owed rights, which the canons and the capitularies[27] of your grandfather and father decreed, are preserved for the priests. Command that bishops shall have the peaceful freedom to travel through their diocese, preaching, confirming, and correcting. Ensure that, if the bishops order it, an envoy of the state [*res publica*], that is an officer of a count, goes with them to compel incestuous freemen to come to the bishop's court, if they are not willing to come to the bishop through the admonition of priests.[28] Establish an officer for this purpose through whom, if a bishop tells you about some ecclesiastical necessity for which his messenger has come, he may obtain what he reasonably seeks in your palace, just as the count of the palace acts in the matters of the realm.[29] Make sure that they are able to have provincial synods with other bishops in peace, and specific synods with priests.[30] Do not allow church properties and goods, which are the offerings of the faithful, the price of sins, and the stipends of the male and female servants of God, to be plundered and separated from the churches,[31] but instead bravely resist and defend them, as a Christian king and *alumnus* of the church.

Concerning that property consecrated to God, which the freemen serving the churches possess through the disposition of the leaders of those churches, the successors of the apostles established this arrangement: that because the offerings of the faithful grew and the wickedness of the unfaithful grew even more, the armed forces of the kingdom might be augmented through the dispensation of the church to resist the wickedness of evil men, so the churches may have defense and peace, and Christendom [*christianitas*][32] may have

---

27 Capitularies were a kind of royal edict. For an introduction to the problems of defining capitularies as a genre, see Pössel, "Authors and Recipients of Carolingian Capitularies"; and the *Capitularia Project* website, https://capitularia.uni-koeln.de/en/project/definition/.

28 In other words, counts were to help bishops enforce norms against incestuous marriage.

29 Cf. Hincmar's comments in *On the Governance of the Palace*, trans. Dutton, *Carolingian Civilization*, 524–5.

30 A reference to two different kinds of synod: ones that brought together several bishops from the same ecclesiastical province, and diocesan synods in which a bishop brought together the priests in his diocese.

31 A quotation from Julianus Pomerius, a Late Antique author often cited in Frankish councils.

32 Here *christianitas* seems to have a territorial meaning: "Christendom." On other occasions, however, it seems more to mean the ensemble of Christian practices ("Christianity").

tranquility.³³ Therefore, just as the goods and properties from which the clerics have a livelihood are under the consecration of immunity, so too are those goods and properties from which vassals owe military service; and they ought to be defended with equal protection by royal power for the requirements of churches.

For indeed, the prince Charles [Martel], father of King Pippin, was the first among all the kings and princes of the Franks to separate and distinguish the property of the churches from the churches themselves: because of this alone, he is certainly doomed forever.³⁴ For the holy bishop Eucherius of Orléans, who rests in the monastery of St-Trond, was seized while kneeling in prayer and taken to another world, and among other things that the Lord showed him, he saw Charles being tortured in deepest hell.³⁵ When Eucherius asked the angel leading him about it, the angel replied that it was by the judgment of the saints, who will judge in the future judgment with the Lord, and whose property Charles took and divided up. In front of that judgment, he was condemned in soul and body to eternal punishments, and he receives these punishments not just for his own sins but also for the sins of all those who gave their goods and properties in the honor and love of the Lord to the places of the saints, for the lighting of the divine cult and for the sustenance of the servants of Christ and the poor, for the redemption of their souls. When Eucherius returned to himself, he summoned holy Boniface and Fulrad, abbot of the monastery of St-Denis and the high chaplain of King Pippin. He explained what he had seen to them, and gave as proof that they should go to Charles's tomb, and if they did not find his body there, they should believe that what he said was true. And they went to the aforementioned monastery where Charles's body was buried, and they uncovered and looked at his tomb, and suddenly a dragon emerged, and the whole interior of the tomb was found to be blackened, as if it had been burned. We ourselves saw people who lived

---

33 The bishops here discuss the arrangement by which church property was temporarily allocated to secular aristocrats, to increase military resources.
34 Charles Martel (†741), ruler of the Franks and grandfather of Charlemagne, and thus a direct ancestor of King Louis the German.
35 Bishop Eucherius of Orléans died around 738 (before Charles Martel!). For this famous story about Charles Martel's empty tomb, and its place in the myths around this ruler, see Fouracre, *The Age of Charles Martel*, 123–5; and Blanc and Naudin, *Charles Martel et la bataille de Poitiers*, 123–6.

up to our time and who were involved in this matter, and they attested truthfully to us in person what they had heard and seen.

Once aware of this, his son Pippin brought together a synod at Estinnes,[36] of which George the legate of the apostolic see was in charge along with St Boniface – and we have [the records of] that synod – and he took care to return to the churches as much as he could of those churches' properties that his father had taken. And since he did not prevail in restoring all the properties to the churches from which they had been taken, on account of the conflict which he was having with Waifar, the prince of Aquitaine, Pippin thereafter asked for *precaria* grants to be made by the bishops and decided that ninths and tenths [of the revenues] were to be given to the restoration of the roofing, and with regard to each holding, twelve pence were to be given to the church from which the properties, were [held as] benefices, as it is recorded in the book of the capitularies of the king, until these properties could be returned to the church.[37]

And the lord emperor Charles [Charlemagne] established a decree valid till now in the royal name, that neither he nor his sons nor any of his successors would attempt to do things of this kind. He confirmed this with his own hand, of which [confirmations] we have very many, and there is an excerpted chapter in the book of his capitularies, which anyone who has that book and wishes to read it will be able to find.[38] We have this account in writing, and some of us also heard the emperor Louis [the Pious], your father, talk about this in person.

And the holy canons, written by the Holy Spirit, reckon those who plunder ecclesiastical property and unduly usurp ecclesiastical estates for themselves to be similar to Judas, the betrayer of Christ. And the saints in heaven, who reign with God in heaven and glitter with miracles on earth, will exclude them from the threshold of the church and from the heavenly kingdom, like murderers of the poor. About these sacrilegious people, there is a prediction in the prophecy of the

---

36 The Council of Estinnes (or Les Estinnes), held in 743.
37 This text, setting out how churches would be compensated for the enforced loan of their lands (the so-called *precaria* grants), is not in Ansegis's collection of capitularies but in the capitulary collection of Benedict Levita, bk. 1, ch. 3. See Ubl, "Der Entwurf einer imaginären Rechsordnung im 9. Jahrhundert."
38 Probably a reference to Ansegis, *Collectio capitularium*, bk. 1, ch. 77, ed. Schmitz, 475–6. On the collection of Ansegis, see Airlie, "'For It Is Written in the Law.'"

psalmist, who said, *My God, send them whirling this way and that, like straws before the wind. And, as the fire burns up the forest and its flames scorch the mountains, so you shall pursue them in your tempest, and trouble them in your wrath. Fill their faces with shame* [Ps. 82:14–17].

Chapter 8. [*The bishops call on Louis to support the monasteries, and remind him of his previous pledges*]

Restore the religious monasteries to their deserved privileges, especially those of canons and monks and nuns which from ancient times have been under a male or female leader in religious clothing,[39] when your parents held the primacy of the kingdom and even when St Remigius with God's help converted the Franks to the Lord and when he baptized their king.[40] These are the monasteries that your brother [Charles], our lord – partly on account of his youth, partly from weakness, and partly from some people's cunning suggestion and even from the necessity of threats, since those petitioners said that unless he gave them these holy places, they would fall away from him and, deserted by them, he would lose his kingdom through you (as now transpires) or through your brother [Emperor Lothar I] – has committed to such people.

For the same brother of yours, having been warned by the inspiration of God, and the refutations of the bishops, and also by the apostolic see, had corrected to a certain degree what he has wrongly done; he has often asked, groaning, how he can amend those things that are still not corrected. May it not happen that you, who have come here for the restoration of the holy church, should either worsen those things that he has amended and so offend just as he offended, nor that you permit to go unamended whatever he has not yet been able to amend. As we are your witnesses, you have often warned your brothers about these matters, and in every summit which you have jointly held, you have argued about it very eagerly: just as with your brothers you accepted the capitularies (which we have) at the place by Thionville which is called

---

39 A criticism of the royal practice of appointing people as titular or lay abbots who were not themselves monks, thereby giving them access to monastic resources, as a way of rewarding supporters. See de Jong, "Carolingian Monasticism," 634–6.
40 Remigius baptized King Clovis around 500 (the precise date is contested).

Yutz,[41] and which you confirmed with your own hand in a chirograph at Meerssen.[42] If perhaps anyone should act against this, you will therefore not be immune if you do not take care to carry out what you swore and confirmed, with the Lord as witness: far from it! It helps no one to criticize other people's wicked deeds unless he beware his own, as Paul demonstrates saying, *Do you think, o man, that you will escape the judgment of God, you who do the same thing which you* point out? [Rom. 2:3].

Chapter 9. [*More about monasteries*]

Firmly and resolutely order the leaders [*rectores*] of the monasteries, to whom you have committed the monasteries, that they carefully and responsibly arrange that, according to the order and the habit and the sex in which the residents are constituted, the male and female servants of the Lord should live according to the appropriate order, and have the necessary stipend in food and clothing and everything else, and that they provide housing and servants as is fitting, as religious leaders in clothing and manner of life.[43] Let them in no way disregard the reception of guests and paupers. And we shall not state that unsuitable people and things that are not befitting to religion should not be introduced into the monasteries, since we are not unaware that religious leaders should take the foresight and care that is needed.[44]

Chapter 10. [*About guesthouses for pilgrims*]

Maintain the hostels of the pilgrims such as those of the Scots [Irish], which were constructed and established in the time of your predecessor

---

41 A reference to the meeting of the three Carolingian rulers (Charles the Bald, Louis the German, and Lothar I [father of Lothar II]) at Yutz/Thionville in 844.
42 A reference to the meeting of the three Carolingian rulers (Charles the Bald, Louis the German, and Lothar I) at Meerssen in 847. In later centuries a chirograph was a particular kind of document, but here the bishops probably just mean a document personally signed by the kings, not just their scribes. The original signed document itself does not survive, but some copies do, and the text of the agreement is edited in *Capitularia regum Francorum*, ed. Boretius and Krause, 2:68–71.
43 For Carolingian ideas about monastic life, see Kramer, "Monasticism, Reform, and Authority."
44 The Latin here is a little hard to construe, but the meaning is that keeping *inconvenientes personae* away from monasteries is something that goes without saying.

kings, so that they are kept for what they were assigned to do, and are regulated and guarded by God-fearing leaders, lest they are ruined. And command the leaders of the monasteries and the guesthouses, that is hostels, that as the canonical authority teaches and the capitularies of your father and your grandfather command, they should be subject to their own bishops, and they should rule the monasteries and hostels committed to them with the bishops' counsel, because the bishops will want to bestow fatherly concern upon them according to their ministry.

And since in frequent announcements you, along with your brothers, have often granted the appropriate law and justice to each in their order, let ecclesiastics and religious men and women of the habit and pilgrims and the poor, in whom Christ is specially received, know that your grant is always still in force.

Chapter 11. [*The bishops remind Louis of his responsibilities*]

And since you wish, as you wrote to us, to discuss the condition and salvation of the Christian people, start first of all with yourself, you who ought to correct others, as is written, *Physician, heal thyself* [Luke 4:23]. And the hand which tries to clean others' dirt ought itself to be clean from dirt. And whatever you ought to correct in others, no one should be able rightly to reprehend in you. For however many people that you are raised above in the pinnacle of the realm, for so many you should serve their behavior, and like a lamp placed on a candlestick, demonstrate an example of goodness, since the eyes of all rest upon you.[45] And for however many people you destroy by your bad example, people who ought to have been built up in goodness by you, under so many it will be necessary for you to be tormented in punishment in the future world.

For this reason, it is right that you, who are king and are called lord, should always with raised heart admire him, from whom, that is to say from the King of kings and the Lord of lords, you have borrowed the name of king and lord. And, just as he *orders the globe of the earth according to justice* [Ws 9:3], and to this end, as it is said in the Book of Wisdom, created man so that he should act similarly: so if you wish to rule with

---

45 Cf. a similar argument in Hincmar, *On the Divorce*, trans. Stone and West, Appendix Responsio 1, 284.

him, imitate him, because *whoever claims to abide in Christ ought to walk in the same way in which he walked* [1 John 2:6], who said *you must be perfect, just as your heavenly Father is perfect* [Matt. 5:48].

And if you say: "How can I be perfect, when in another part of scripture it says: if he who does not offend in word is a perfect man, he who does not sin in malice or greed does not fall from perfection?" *The just man falls seven times and rises again; the impious fall down into evil* [Prov. 24:16], but the just man, *when he falls, will not be bruised, for the Lord catches him in his hand* [Ps. 36:24]. However it may be, in truth none can better point out to someone that he is sinning, through the will of his greed or the necessity of his weakness, than can his own conscience, which cannot deceive the eyes of its watcher.

Therefore, it is necessary for you to live, judge, and act, even in secret, as if you were always in public; for often someone will praise you in words while in his heart he bitterly blames you; and often those things about you that he praises to you, he will judge to be blameworthy in front of others.[46] Thus with the help of God you will be able to live, judge, and act as we say, if private affection does not incite you; if the greed for glory, riches, possessions, and power does not inflame you; if you do not lend more trust to someone else's tongue than to your own conscience; if the maggot of flattery does not gnaw at you; if the envy of another's happiness does not burn you; if the neglect of the soul and love of the flesh does not vex you; if you believe Christ died not for himself, that is to say not for his own necessity, but for us, so that we who were dead may live. And you, o king, may take care to live more for the salvation of others than for your own desires, if you know that you will die and you believe that you will render account to God for your own deeds, and that what you worthily receive [at the Day of Judgment], you will have without end or any change.

Chapter 12. [*Advice on how to run his court and kingdom*]

Nourish, rule, and arrange your domestic household in such a way that when the people of the kingdom assemble before you, they may see in you and in your retainers how soberly, how justly, how piously, and

---

46 For a discussion of the conceptualization of the public here, see Staubach, "'Quasi semper in publico.'"

with how much humility and chastity, they ought to nourish, arrange, and govern their household too; for, as a certain wise man once said, the family will be protected according to the habits of its master. And that is why the king's household is called a school, that is, a *disciplina*, not so much because there are scholars there, that is, disciplined and well-corrected people, like others; but rather it is called a school, by which we mean a *disciplina*, that is, a correction, because they correct others in behavior, progress, in word and deed, and in the preservation of all goodness.[47]

And unless you are supported by the God of virtues, you will be like a peg which is not secured, and you will fall, and those hanging from you will slip. So therefore, as God when he was being tempted taught to render to those constituted under authority, *what is of Caesar to Caesar and what is of God to God* [Matt. 22:21], likewise you, who are under God and above men, should render to God what is of God, and like a just Caesar, render to the subjects what belongs to them. Render to God a pure and immaculate faith and a most sincere observance regarding priests, the privileges of the churches, the holy places, ecclesiastical men and women, the defense of the church and of Christianity [*christianitas*]; the equity and justice of the Christian people; the support, peace, and consolation of all the needy, as we set out above. Render to God a daily payment in daily prayer, in just and assiduous alms. Give to him your devotion in holy gifts and profuse tears according to the size and number of your daily sins. Render to your subjects judgment with mercy, justice with equity. Take care to exalt the humble and God-fearing, and to subdue and humiliate the proud. Try to be more loved than feared by the good. Take care that the wicked fear to do evil things, if not on account of God, then out of fear of you. Let not a lying tongue, a full hand, or unearned subservience be worth more to you than truth, equity, and sincerity, knowing that it is written, *he who draws his hand back from every bribe will dwell in the heavens* [Isa. 33:15]. This must be understood aptly: the gift is no different from the spoken favor, from the hand's donation, or from the subjection of unearned subservience.[48]

---

47 The Latin here is hard to construe (and there are slight variations in the transmission), but the meaning is clear: the court is like a school because its residents receive moral instruction.

48 This approach to bribery is based on ideas that Pope Gregory the Great developed in the late sixth century. On Carolingian corruption, see Fouracre, "Carolingian Justice."

Appoint officers of the palace who know, love, and fear God; who take the greatest care that the needy coming to the palace run to see you, their father and consoler, when you pass through them, and do not – which we say unwillingly – flee while groaning and cursing.[49] Appoint counts and officers of the state [*res publica*] who do not love gifts, who hate avarice, who detest pride; who neither oppress nor dishonor the men of the countryside; who in no way devastate their harvests, vineyards, meadows, and woods; who do not seize or plunder their cattle or pigs or whatever they have, nor take it away through violence and trickery; who do things that are of God and fitting to Christianity [*christianitas*], by the counsel of the bishops; who hold courts not to acquire profit, but so that the houses of God and the orphans and people may have justice; who take more care to bring the litigants to peace, with justice preserved, than to commit them [to legal action] so that they can draw some profit from it. But if they cannot placate them, then, as is just, let them make a just judgment with great care, knowing that it is written, *I shall show you, o man, what is good*, that is doing justice and judgment, and *walking carefully with your God* [Mic. 6:8]. So that what pleases him also pleases you and you carry it out, but what is displeasing to him is displeasing also to you, and you do not carry it out.

But if you do such a thing through weakness, do not stubbornly or obstinately persevere in your wicked deed, but at once pull back your foot as if from a hot iron, and tread in the path of the Lord's will. And, as it is written that there are paths which seem good to men and lead to the abyss, do as scripture orders you as a man: ask for the right path and walk in it. For as it is said in the Gospels, the path that leads to perdition is broad, and many go along it; and the path that leads to life is restricted and narrow, and few come upon it. Since you are a man, listen to the prophet and pray with him: *Set before me for a law the way of thy justifications, o Lord: and I will always seek after it*, and *Lead me into the path of thy commandments*, and *Remove from me the way of iniquity: and out of thy law have mercy on me* [Ps. 118:33, 35, 29]. For as the prophet Jeremiah says, *The path is not man's, nor is it in a man to decide where to walk and direct his steps* [Jer. 10:23] – *but his steps are directed by the Lord, and he will like his way* [Ps. 36:23].

---

49 An insight into how royal power could be perceived.

Let the counts similarly, as far as they can, appoint as their officers those who similarly fear God and love justice, and who, when they see their lords acting kindly and affably to their countrymen, attempt according to their measure to imitate them in all goodness and justice.

Chapter 13. [*The bishops call on Louis to help bring the excommunicated to repentance*]

Call back to the path of justice and law those men and powers of the world who among these seditions flee the yoke of the law and the justice of equity, and who commit deeds for which they have deserved ecclesiastical and episcopal excommunication. And order or compel that they humbly go to their bishops, as is required of them. And advise or with royal power command that they either do satisfaction to the churches against which they have sinned, with justified and necessary humility, or that they humbly and truthfully explain themselves, so that they can be absolved by the Lord through the episcopal ministry.

And if perhaps you, or someone else from their company and association, is infected by and condemned for communicating with them, let whoever it is reexamine himself and do penance. For by the witness of sacred authority, no one can be absolved from his own sins who is damnably weighed down by external sins, as the holy prophet David showed when he prayed to the Lord and said, *Cleanse me from my secret sins, Lord, and spare your servant from those of others* [Ps. 18:13–14].

Chapter 14. [*Advice on managing royal estates*][50]

And, finally, appoint stewards [*iudices*] of the royal estates who are not greedy, and who neither love avarice nor usury nor carry it out; nor let them give royal money or their own money as loans, nor let their subordinates be usurers: all these things you should hate and flee even more than your officers do. And do not let the stewards oppress the royal servants [*servi*], nor demand more from them than they used to give in the time of your father, nor afflict them with carting duties

---

50 Cf. Campbell, "The *Capitulare de villis*." Carolingian kings did not generally impose taxes, so revenues from royal lands (sometimes known as the fisc) were extremely important for maintaining their rule.

at inconvenient times. Nor let them condemn free tenants [*coloni*] through deceit or tricks or unsuitable loans. For if through such deeds or others you acquire a weight of silver or gold in the treasure chest, greater and heavier will be the weight of sin which you will have on your conscience and soul.

Let the stewards develop your estates with modest buildings, so that there should be the necessary decency and the staff [*familia*] should not be unduly burdened; let them work and farm the lands and vineyards at the appropriate time with the solicitude that is owed. Let them preserve and distribute the products with faithful discretion; let them produce the appropriate and necessary foodstuffs; let them guard the woods which provide foraging; let them defend and farm the meadows which provide grazing. In this way, it will not be necessary for you for whatever reason and on whosoever's advice to travel through the properties of bishops, abbots, abbesses, or counts, nor to demand more hospitality than reason requires, nor to burden the church's poor and the farmers [*mansuarii*] of your faithful men by demanding carting and traveling duties contrary to what is owed,[51] nor to pile up sin on your soul through consuming these resources that are not due.

Nor should you strive to demand more from the counts and your faithful men from what they take from the Franks than was the law and custom in the time of your father. You should rather have enough so that you can live sufficiently and honestly with your domestic household and receive legates coming to your palace and, as is written, enough so that you can give what is necessary to those who are enduring righteous labors.[52] For the king ought to be generous, and what is given ought not to have been acquired from injustice or iniquity.

The stewards [*iudices*], however, should discipline the free tenants [*coloni*] of the estates, so that they do not oppress the ecclesiastical men or the poorer Franks, or other servants by means of royal privilege, and so that they do not devastate the woods or property belonging to others which are in their neighborhood. For a just king, who should seek justice, should not have impious or unjust officers or tenants [*coloni*]; but he should demonstrate to everyone a worthy model in himself and

---

51 On royal regulation of labor services in Carolingian Francia, see West, "Carolingian Kingship and the Peasants of Le Mans."
52 Probably a reference to Ephesians 4:28.

in his followers. Because if he himself loves God, all good men will love him, and if he himself fears God, all evil men will fear him. And the king as well as his officers should perform good deeds through love of God, and should teach everyone else to perform good deeds, and they should shun evil through fear of God, and should instruct everyone else to shun evil. Appoint envoys of such a kind throughout the kingdom, who know how the counts and other officers of the state [*res publica*] administer justice and judgment to the people, and just as they are placed over the counts, so they should surpass them in knowledge, justice, and truth.[53]

Chapter 15. [*The bishops again warn Louis of the fate of those who attack the Lord's anointed, while declaring that unlike some secular advisers, they are chiefly interested in peace*]

So, because you have shown through your letters that you wish to discuss with us the restoration of the holy church and the state and welfare of the Christian people, we have taken care to reply to Your Dominance in writing, though we cannot come into your presence on account of the inclemency of the weather and the inconvenience of the time, and because it is nearly Christmas. In the meantime, do what you can with those faithful to you in our absence.

And when a time comes which is more suitable and appointed by the sacred canons, and if the infestation of the pagans and the excessive confusion of most wretched uproar, looting, and pillaging allows us, if God wills, to celebrate a synod with the lords, brothers, and co-provincial archbishops and co-bishops, we shall discuss the remaining issues with them as with masters and fathers, and we shall strive to give to Your Lordship the counsel that is owed. And if God decrees that the integrity and safety of the church and the kingdom will come together and prosper in your hands, then we shall take care to act under the rightful regime of your service as seems to suit divine dispositions, with our archbishops and co-bishops.[54] For God, to whom things are possible

---

53 King Charles the Bald seems to have taken the letter's advice, issuing detailed instructions in 860 to the royal emissaries (*missi*) traveling throughout his kingdom.
54 Here the bishops hold out the possibility of coming over to Louis's rule.

that men judge impossible, is capable of turning a less good start into a perfectly good end.

If Your Wisdom judges it appropriate to speak and discuss with the neighboring king [Lothar II][55] and his faithful men, while our lord, that is your brother [Charles], has left this part of the kingdom, it is all the more fitting for us to await the canonical time so that we may speak with our brothers and co-provincial archbishops and bishops, since a general matter looms over the whole of the cisalpine church.[56]

And it is especially necessary for us to speak with those archbishops and bishops who, with the consent and will of the people of this kingdom, anointed our lord your brother as a king with the sacred chrism by divine gift, and whom the holy apostolic see, our mother, took care in apostolic writings to honor and to confirm as the king.[57] Read the Book of Kings, and you will see with what reverence the holy Samuel, whose place in the church we hold though unworthy, thought it appropriate to treat Saul, who had been accused and cast out by the Lord. And pay attention to how serious David considered it was to lay hands on the Lord's anointed, though he was elected and anointed in his place by the Lord.[58] Even though Saul was not only from another family but from another tribe, and David recognized that he [Saul] was rejected and he [David] was elected by the Lord, still David took no forceful action against Saul, but gave him great assistance and devoted service. And he did not attempt to take his kingdom from him by war, nor to seize it by a trick. And although he had many advising and assisting him in this direction, he accepted no gold to attempt it, even though he had very often experienced many persecutions and death threats from him. Moreover, you know well what David ordered about the person who, although he was lying, claimed that he had laid hands on the Lord's anointed. If there is anyone who does not know, we shall tell him: he ordered him to be killed by the sword.

---

55 King Lothar II indeed visited Louis the German while he was residing at Attigny, and made an agreement with him, though its details have not survived: see *Annals of St-Bertin*, trans. Nelson, 88.

56 That is, the church north of the Alps. Cf. Hincmar's calls for a general synod of the Frankish church in *On the Divorce*, trans. Stone and West, Response 3, 122, and Appendix Responsio 1, 284.

57 This seems to be a reference to earlier papal letters to Charles the Bald that have not survived. Charles had been anointed as king in 848.

58 A reference to 1 Kings 24.

Thus, if anyone faithlessly and contumaciously lays a hand on any of the Lord's anointed, he despises Christ the Lord of the anointed, and without doubt he will perish in his soul through the hostility of the spiritual sword.[59] We say this not to seek to pile up inflated arguments against Your Dominance, but so that we may more clearly show what should be revered in your brother by us, for the quality of our ministry and with the faith and benevolence that is owed.

We must not and we do not wish to think of you as someone who wishes to expand your kingdom at the cost of your soul, nor that you wish to accept us to help with ecclesiastical direction and governance, with such disgrace that we would lose the priesthood. For we shall be deprived of that priesthood if we hurry to hand over ourselves and our churches to you, against God and against the authority of reason. For the churches committed to us by God are not like benefices or a sort of king's property, that someone can give or take them without consideration and according to whim.[60] For all that belongs to a church is consecrated to God. And whoever cheats a church of something, or takes it away, knows that he has committed sacrilege according to the holy scripture. And we bishops consecrated to the Lord are not such men that, like secular men, we should commend ourselves in vassalage to someone, but we commit ourselves and our churches to the defense and to the assistance of governance in the ecclesiastical regime.[61]

Nor should we have to carry out any oath-swearing, which the evangelical and apostolic and canonical authority forbids us to do.[62] It is abominable that any hand anointed by sacred oil, which makes the flesh and sacrament of the blood of Christ from bread and a mixture of wine and water through prayer and the sign of the cross, whatever it may have done before ordination, should after ordination to the bishopric in any way touch a secular oath. And the tongue of a bishop, which through the grace of God is made the key of heaven, becomes

---

59 In other words, the bishops are protecting the life of the anointed king, Charles the Bald.
60 In other words, clerical offices should not be treated like secular offices.
61 Here the bishops contrast their acknowledged obligations, to help defend the *ecclesiasticum regimen*, with the secular practice of vassalage (*vassalliticum*).
62 The bishops here justify their refusal to swear Louis an oath (*sacramentum*) of loyalty, which would have involved a promise and some kind of hand gesture. On the importance of oaths to the Carolingian rulers, see Nelson, "Carolingian Oaths."

wicked when, just like a secular person, the bishop swears an oath in the name of the Lord upon a holy object, and by the invocation of the saints. Unless perhaps (may it not happen) a scandal to his church should occur against him; and then he should act with moderation, just as, with the Lord guiding, the leaders of the church decreed by synodal discussion. And if at any time, the oaths, having been demanded and performed by the bishops, are against God and ecclesiastical regulations, which by the Holy Spirit's dictation were confirmed by the blood of Christ, then they are declared invalid by the pages of the holy scripture, and thereafter those who are demanding and performing [these oaths] require the medicine of salutary penance.

So wait patiently, my lord, like a Christian prince and a son of the church, and honor the leaders of the holy church, so that he might honor you who said, *He who listens to you, listens to me; and he who rejects you, rejects me* [Luke 10:16], and *I will honor those who honor me, and those who despise me will be unworthy* [1 Kings 2:30], and *he who touches you touches the pupil of my eye* [Zech. 2:8], and, in the psalm: *Do not touch my anointed ones, nor malign my prophets* [Ps. 104:15] *for they who malign* – that is, who do evil things – *shall be cast out, while those who wait upon the Lord shall inherit the land* [Ps. 36:9] – that is, the kingdom of God. And when the time and place come, as we said above, we shall speak with our brothers, and, whatever we shall discern by the righteous dispositions of the Lord, no doubt we shall act accordingly.

And there is no reasonable cause which should provoke you against what we are asking for. For we are not the kind of men who, once we have understood the Lord's will, would wish or feel that we ought to answer back in any way, or ought to stir up, nourish, or hold on to fights and quarrels or seditions, which the common people call "wars."[63] For the Lord wished to appoint [us] as preachers and advocates of peace, and appointed [us] to bewail and heal our sins, and those sins [of the people] committed to us, and indeed of the whole people. And he ordered us to be at war with vices and to have peace with our brothers. We want and seek peace and tranquility, not quarrels and war. For as the Apostle [Paul] says, *For the weapons of our warfare are not carnal* but spiritual *and mighty in God* [2 Cor. 10:4], *by which our feet are shod in the*

---

63 *Werras*, a word taken from the vernacular. This is its first known occurrence.

preparation of the Gospel of peace, bearing the breastplate of justice and the shield of salvation, girding our loins in truth, carrying the shield of faith and the sword of the Holy Spirit [Eph. 6:14–17]. *For our wrestling is not against flesh and blood; but against principalities and power, against the rulers of the world of this darkness, against the spirits of wickedness in the high places* [Eph. 6:12]. And we fight not for the earthly king but for the heavenly king, for the salvation of ourselves and of the earthly king and of the whole people committed to us. Our office is to harm nobody, to act faithlessly toward no one, and to wish to be of use to everyone.

Nevertheless, our lord king, do not listen to those speaking against God and your soul, who perhaps say to you, "Don't worry, king, about what those felons and ignoble people tell you. Do what we tell you, since your ancestors held the kingdom with our ancestors, not with theirs." We beg Your Dominance that you listen rather [to us], if you are a Christian king, as by the grace of God you are, and if you trust in him and wish to reign through him, through whom as it is written, *kings rule* [Prov. 8:15], and to whom belongs the kingdom, indeed the orb of the world and its plenitude. For that God who came in the flesh, and who alone could be both king and priest, when he ascended into heaven divided his kingdom, that is the church, between the pontifical authority and the royal power for its guidance.[64] And he did not choose the wealthy and the noble for this, but the poor and the fishermen, and as it is written, *He chose the ignoble and the despicable of the world, so that he might confound the strong* [1 Cor. 1:27]. And it may be that the people who say these things to you, if perhaps they speak to you fearing God less than is necessary, are those with whose ancestors the devil, who is according to scripture *the king over all the children of pride* [Job 41:25], disturbed the kingdom of Christ, which is the church, and now keeps those ancestors in his kingdom, which is hell, and will keep them with him forever.

Know for certain that Christ the King of kings conquered, expanded, and ruled his kingdom with our ancestors, that is with the apostles. And

---

64 The notion that the world was arranged into two complementary orders (*ordines*) was developed during the reign of Louis the Pious, using Late Antique texts such as a letter from Pope Gelasius (d. 496), most notably at the Council of Paris in 829. This might seem to modern readers like a division between "church and state," but it is better thought of as a division of responsibilities within a single framework, the *ecclesia*. For this "Paris model," see Patzold, *Episcopus: Wissen über Bischöfe*, esp. 149–83; and de Jong, "Ecclesia and the Early Medieval Polity," 129–31.

through us and with us – may it not be for our judgment that we say this! – the same Lord Jesus Christ every day conquers, expands, and governs that church which is his kingdom. As is said by the Lord of the church through the prophet: *Your sons are born for your fathers* [Ps. 44:17], that is, he created bishops for you in the place of apostles, who rule and teach you. With the church committed to us by God, o Christian lord king, as you ordered in your letters, we will take care to stir up and alert the Lord, the great helmsman on the boat of the holy church floating on this sea, that is the shipwrecking world, who is sleeping for our common sins, and to pray for you. So that he may quickly wake for his own ineffable piety, and command the winds and waves, that is the diabolical storms and the disturbances of secular men, and some little tranquility may return, by the grace and mercy of our Lord Jesus Christ, to whom belongs the power and the honor and the glory and the rule, for ever and ever, Amen.

4. THE *LIBER MEMORIALIS* OF REMIREMONT "ROYAL ENTRY," DECEMBER 861

As we have seen, the ordeal by boiling water that Lothar II compelled his wife Queen Theutberga to endure in the early summer of 858 did not go as planned. The queen, or rather her unnamed champion, passed the ordeal, and since the ordeals were supposed to represent God's direct legal intervention, this meant Theutberga's name was cleared. However, Lothar II had evidently made up his mind that he wanted to dissolve the marriage, and in any case, he risked losing face if he changed course. So in the new year of 860, while Frankish politics was still dominated by the fallout from Louis the German's invasion of West Francia, Lothar II arranged for two councils to be held at the palace of Aachen. There, Theutberga "voluntarily" confessed to having committed incest with her own brother and requested permission to retire to a convent; the assembled bishops agreed, thereby effectively ending her and Lothar II's marriage.[1] In pursuing this approach, Lothar II and his

---

1 For further discussion of these 860 events, see Stone and West, *The Divorce of King Lothar and Queen Theutberga*.

advisers were creatively adapting the tradition of public penance that had played such a critical role in Frankish politics in the 830s, when first Emperor Louis the Pious and then his main accuser, Archbishop Ebbo of Reims, had been compelled to make public confessions of their sinfulness.[2]

Not everyone in his kingdom was supportive of Lothar II's efforts. It may not be a coincidence that in 860, a leading cleric, Eigil, abbot of the wealthy monastery of Prüm in the Eifel region near Trier, defected to Lothar II's uncle Charles the Bald, who rewarded him by making him abbot of a monastery in West Francia, Flavigny, and later archbishop of Sens.[3] Moving as abbot from one monastery to another was unusual, especially from a community as important as Prüm. Eigil had been personally involved in the 860 council, and we may wonder whether he disliked Lothar II's strategy and voted with his feet.[4] Charles also provided a refuge for Theutberga, who fled to his protection in 860. We do not know whether Lothar II willingly let her go because she was no longer of any importance after her public humiliation, or whether, as may be more likely, she staged an escape.[5]

Charles and Lothar II had confirmed alliances in 857 and again in 859, but it is clear that relations between the uncle and nephew had now deteriorated.[6] Lothar II's response to Charles's perceptible and growing coldness in the face of his continuing marital controversies was to turn to his other uncle, Louis the German, to deepen the ties between them.[7] In December 861 the two kings wrote a joint letter to the pope, complaining about Charles, whom they accused of maneuvering to

---

2 For the public penance imposed on Louis the Pious in 833 and its subsequent interpretations, see Booker, *Past Convictions*; for a direct comparison between the public penances imposed on Archbishop Ebbo in 835 and on Theutberga in 860, see van Doren, "*De Divortio* and *de Resignatione*."
3 Heidecker, *The Divorce of Lothar II*, 74n9; and Goldberg, "'A Man of Notable Good Looks,'" 371. Eigil had close links with western Frankish monasteries, which perhaps eased the move.
4 For other cases, see Airlie, "Unreal Kingdom," 342–3.
5 The *Annals of St-Bertin*, trans. Nelson, 92, record that she had been "shut away in a convent" before she fled. Cf. the escape engineered by Judith, the daughter of Charles the Bald, who eloped with Count Baldwin in 862 (see Document 6, p. 91).
6 The two had agreed a pact (*firmitas*) in March 857 at St-Quentin and again in February 859 at Warcq. See Charles, *Reg.*, 883 and 945.
7 As noted in *Annals of St-Bertin*, trans. Nelson, 93.

invade the kingdom of Lothar II's sickly brother, Charles of Provence.[8] It is likely that this joint letter was preceded by a face-to-face meeting between the kings, arranged to cement their entente.

The image below might present us with a snapshot of this very meeting, which is not otherwise attested in any source. It is a page from the so-called *Liber Memorialis* or "commemoration book" of Remiremont, an old and rich convent in the Vosges mountains.[9] Seven books of this kind survive from early medieval continental Europe, beginning from the late eighth century.[10] They are liturgical books made up chiefly of lists of names. The book would be placed on an altar during Mass, and the officiant would refer to it in his prayers, knowing that God could read all the names inside. The commemoration book of Remiremont, initiated by Abbess Theuthild perhaps in 861, is a typical example, containing literally tens of thousands of names.[11] Since people in this period generally had only a single name, with neither surname nor nickname, it can be hard to identify who these individuals were. What is more, names were added into the book at different periods, over several decades, and sometimes long after their bearers had died, creating a fearsomely difficult – and visually confused – historical source.

Sometimes, however, names were entered as groups, as in the case of this page, which gives historians something to work with. If one looks closely, one can see at the top right and the top left two sets of names, written in a light brown ink.[12] It seems these names were written by the same scribe, on a page that was at the time blank. Years later, the rest of the page was filled in with other unrelated names in different inks,

---

8 The *Annals of St-Bertin*, trans. Nelson, 96, claim that Charles had been invited.
9 For a recent study of Remiremont, with a bearing on Lothar II's divorce case, see Vanderputten and West, "Inscribing Property, Rituals, and Royal Alliances."
10 See Butz and Zettler, "The Making of the Carolingian *Libri Memoriales*"; and McKitterick, *History and Memory*, 156–73.
11 The dating of the manuscript is contested. It is conventionally thought to have been started in 821, but Gaillard, *D'une réforme*, at 49–54, has suggested that in its current form it may have been begun in 861, though including pages taken from a slightly older necrology. In this case, assuming Schmid's arguments in "Ein karolingischer Königseintrag" about the list's dating hold, the royal entry could have been initially part of this earlier necrology, or it was added very early into the new book.
12 The names are edited in *Liber Memorialis von Remiremont*, ed. Hlawitschka, Schmid, and Tellenbach, 1:93.

sometimes written by very inexperienced scribes, who squeezed them into blank spaces as the book was gradually filled out.

The original set of names on the left begins with kings: *Domnus Lotharius rex*, "the lord king Lothar," *Domnus Hludowicus rex*, "the lord king Louis." In a groundbreaking article in 1968, the German historian Karl Schmid focused on this royal entry, or *Königseintrag*. He argued that these kings were none other than Lothar II and Louis the German, whose names are followed by Louis's sons (confusingly also named Louis and Charles, in line with dynastic tradition), and then Lothar II's brother, Charles of Provence. One of Louis the German's sons, Karlman, is not listed; Schmid thought this was because he was at this moment in revolt against his father, an event that Schmid used to date the list to December 861.[13]

After a gap, another list of names follows in the same ink, written sequentially rather than in a column: Berta, Rotrude, Hugh ("Uhgo"), Emma, a name that has been erased, Waldrada, Doda, Ermengard ("Irmingart"), and another Ermengard. Most of these are female names, and Schmid argued that these were the two kings' wives and daughters, though it is not possible to be much more precise: for instance, both Louis the German and Lothar II had a sister called Rotrude, and we cannot tell which of these two is listed here. For our purposes, however, the key point is that Lothar II had brought Waldrada with him as an acknowledged part of his family, on par with Emma, Louis the German's wife.[14] With Waldrada came their son Hugh, whose presence in this otherwise female section of the list suggests he was still a baby.

At the top right, in the same light brown ink, we see a list of fifty or so men's names, beginning with *Teudhericus, Reginar, Sicricus*, which continues in a second block on the bottom left. These names are written less ceremonially than those of the kings, and unlike the kings, there is little attempt after the first line to Latinize the Frankish names. These men may have been the aristocrats, clerical and lay, who accompanied Louis the German and Lothar II at their meeting.[15] Most of these individuals cannot be identified, but some four lines down, we can see

---

13 Schmid, "Ein karolingischer Königseintrag."
14 On Emma, see Goldberg, "*Regina nitens sanctissima Hemma.*"
15 Butz, "Von Namenlisten zu Netzwerken?"

Uualther, Walter, who is probably the same follower of Lothar II that we met before.[16]

Schmid thought it was possible that the kings and their households and retinues met in person at Remiremont itself in December 861, or visited it after their business was concluded. The monastery was located in the Vosges mountains, which were excellent hunting grounds, and there was an important royal palace there.[17] In any case, it seems that the kings' alliance found spiritual expression in this list: a God's-eye group photograph of the kings' inner circle, recorded for eternity. Lothar II's new family, Waldrada and Hugh, were conspicuously included. So too, incidentally, was his stepmother Doda, an unfree woman whom in 851 the newly widowed Emperor Lothar I had freed and taken as a concubine, and who after Lothar I's death seems to have joined Lothar II's household. Lothar II, after all, would have been the last person to exclude someone from the family on grounds of marital irregularity.

As mentioned above, Remiremont was a convent, an institution for aristocratic women who had taken the veil, so it is possible that these names were written by one of the nuns there, though the Remiremont community may not have been consistently well disposed to Lothar II.[18] Regardless of who wrote it, though, the list shows us Lothar II's court at a confident and forward-looking moment, including his new wife and young heir, meeting as equals with his older uncle. Naturally, Theutberga is not listed; she would not have been present and was now written out of the family.

Things did not quite turn out as Lothar II might have hoped in December 861. It seems that the list itself shows traces of these later developments, for it has been visibly altered at some later stage. A name in the list of royal women has been erased and replaced by an unidentified "Gerolt." More curiously still, the name Waldrada has apparently been reinked, that is, written over again, with the word *dōma*, an abbreviation for *domina*, "Lady," a title not accorded to any of the other women in the list, inserted directly before it. As we shall see, Waldrada

---

16 See Document 1, p. 13.
17 On the importance of hunting, see Goldberg, *In the Manner of the Franks*.
18 Although Lothar II himself and his followers were named in the *Liber Memorialis* in this entry, Abbess Theuthild in particular seems to have regarded the king coolly, omitting his name in a separate catalogue of kings. See Vanderputten, *Dark Age Nunneries*, 56–9.

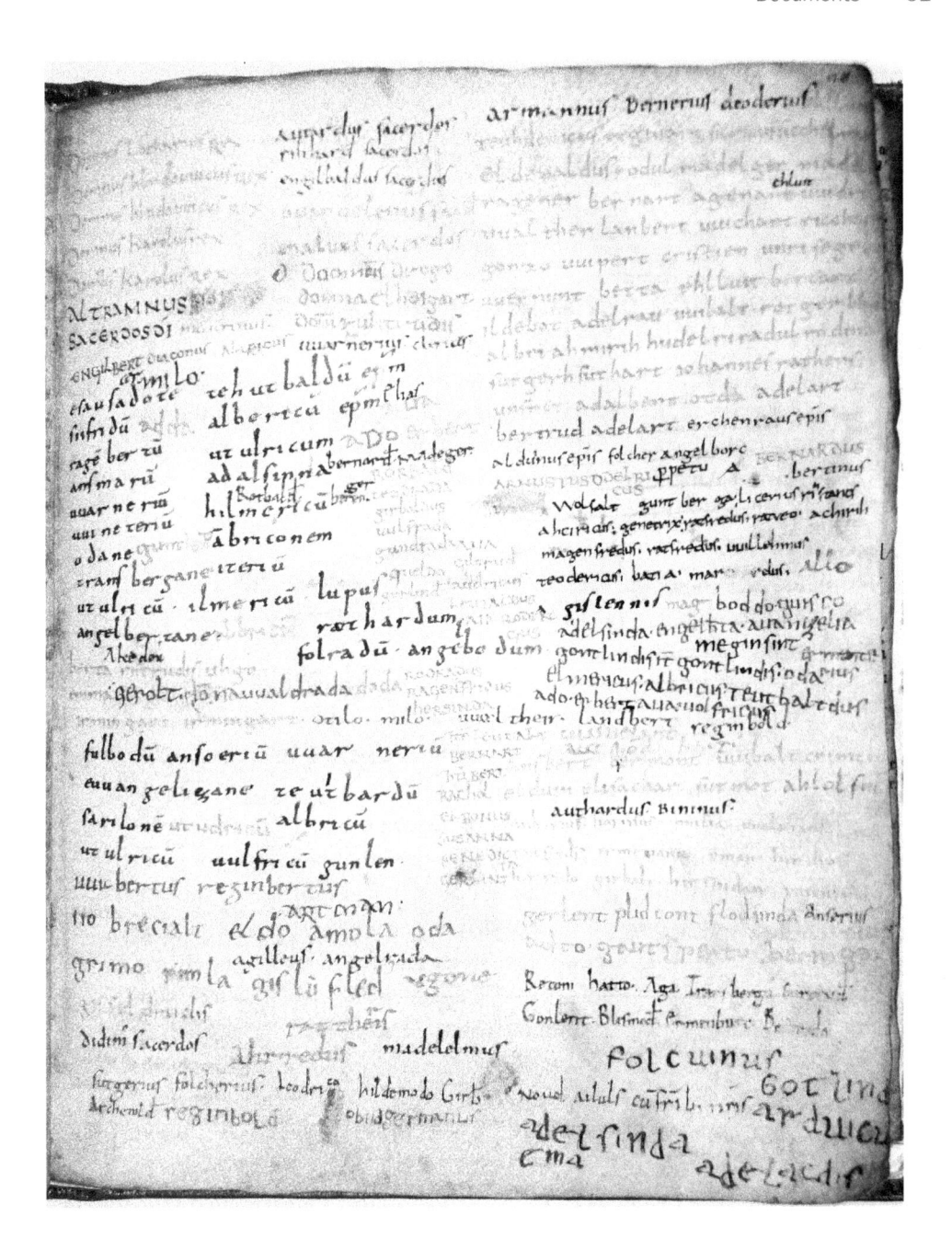

Figure 5. *Liber Memorialis* of Remiremont (Rome, Biblioteca Angelica, MS 10, fol. 48r, 43r in old foliation, by concession of the Italian Ministero della Cultura)

would end up back at Remiremont when Lothar II's kingdom collapsed in 869. Might this have been the occasion for one of the nuns to revisit this list of names and accord Waldrada the respect that she had tragically failed to secure in her worldly life?

5. THE COUNCIL OF AACHEN, APRIL 29, 862

By the spring of 862, Waldrada was living at Lothar II's court, but their marital status still needed to be regularized. It is possible that she was pregnant, which would have conferred some urgency to the question.[1] So in April, perhaps emboldened by the support of his uncle Louis the German, Lothar II convened another council of bishops at the royal palace of Aachen.

Whereas Theutberga had been the focus of attention of the previous two councils in 860, now it was Lothar II who took center stage. The king turned up to the meeting barefoot to demonstrate his repentant state of mind. In a remarkable text, labeled a "booklet of complaint" (Text B below), Lothar II threw himself on the bishops' mercy, pleading with them to help him, not as a king but as a young man necessarily separated from his wife but incapable of celibacy, and to grant him permission to take a new wife. Once again, we see Lothar II drawing on the discursive machinery of the "penitential state" that Mayke de Jong has shown developed during the rule of Lothar II's grandfather, Emperor Louis the Pious.[2] Lothar II had already experimented with this daring strategy of advertising his own male weakness in order to compel episcopal support in 860, though that had not prevented him, or some of his supporters, from simultaneously, and somewhat inconsistently,

---

1 *Annals of St-Bertin*, trans. Nelson, 102. The marriage seems to have taken place before the Council of Savonnières in November 862: see Document 6, pp. 85–98. For the possibility of Waldrada's pregnancy at this time, see Dohmen, *Ursache allen Übels*, 235–6.

2 De Jong, *The Penitential State*, esp. 267–70. On Carolingian masculinity, see Stone, *Morality and Masculinity*, with Lothar II's speech discussed at 305–6; Stone is preparing a more detailed study of penitential Carolingian rulers.

expressing representations of royal authority that placed kings above bishops.[3]

The bishops assembled at Aachen did as expected. They confirmed that King Lothar II and Queen Theutberga were separated, and they moreover permitted Lothar II to remarry; later in 862, Lothar II took Waldrada as his queen.[4] However, a precise understanding of how the council unfolded is complicated by the existence of two alternative versions of the council's acts or minutes (Texts A and C below). The two versions agree on the basics of what happened at the council.[5] But looking more closely, there are some subtle differences between them, for instance over the question of Lothar II's penance. One version of the acts of the 862 council may have been compiled by Bishop Adventius of Metz, the other by Gunthar, archbishop of Cologne since 850 and probably Lothar II's most influential adviser.[6] The earlier 860 Council of Aachen had also produced two distinct versions of its decisions.[7] This was unusual, because Carolingian councils were usually preserved in only a single version.[8] This repeated double transmission could reflect a deliberate tailoring to appeal to different audiences, or it could reflect a long-standing lack of consensus among Lothar II's senior clerical elites over the best strategy to take in representing the king's actions.

---

3 This alternative representation of kingship is recorded in Hincmar, *On the Divorce*, Appendix Question 6, 298, with commentary at 73. The contrasting, perhaps competing, representations of Lothar's kingship are perhaps already visible in the two versions of the January 860 council: see this document, note 7. Independent evidence for this conception of Carolingian kingship is provided by the contemporary monk Radbert of Corbie, who criticized an unnamed bishop for claiming "that the king is subjected to no authority" and did not live in any single diocese (quoted by Ubl, *Inzestverbot und Gesetzgebung*, 326).

4 The precise date of this move, which Staubach, *Herrscherbild*, 145, characterized as "an over-hasty step," is uncertain. Waldrada received a blessing on Christmas Day 862, but there could have been a prior ceremony: see Staubach, *Herrscherbild*, 447–9.

5 Heidecker, *Kerk, huwelijk en politieke macht*, 133, notes that they avoided – perhaps deliberately – quotations from the forged Pseudo-Isidorian Decretals.

6 West, "Dissonance of Speech, Consonance of Meaning." Cf. also Heidecker, *Kerk, huwelijk en politieke macht*, 231; and on Adventius more broadly, Gaillard, "Un évêque et son temps." On Gunthar, see Böhringer, "Gunthar Erzbischof von Köln."

7 It may be that these same two bishops had also been responsible for the two versions of the first 860 council, partially copied in Hincmar's *On the Divorce*. For the differences between the two accounts, see Firey, *Contrite Heart*, 16–29.

8 For a wide-ranging discussion of Carolingian councils, see Kramer, "Order in the Church."

Two other texts have also been associated with the events at Aachen in 862, because they are copied next to the council records in a medieval manuscript. These are two erudite treatises on the question of marriage. One is sadly fragmentary – the manuscript breaks off – and is not translated here. The other survives in full and is translated below as Text D. It is a long text, but it rewards attention because it constitutes a major (and rather neglected) Carolingian work on marriage, which demolishes the arguments Lothar II had made up to this point. It focuses on two questions. In the first place, was it possible for a man to remarry after putting away his wife for fornication or adultery? The author goes systematically through the biblical texts related to the question, then turns to the patristic interpretation of these texts, in the process demonstrating the depth of Carolingian expertise on scripture and its exegesis. The treatise works through the tensions and contradictions before concluding that no, it was not possible for a man to remarry in these circumstances. Then it turns to the question of incest, which Lothar II had accused Theutberga of committing prior to their marriage. What did it matter, its author asks, whether or not Theutberga had committed incest before marriage? Marriage represented a fresh start; as long as she had done nothing blameworthy since then, there was no case to be made against her.

Although this treatise is often considered as part of the 862 Aachen council, it was quite clearly written afterward, as a response to the council. Karl Heidecker suspected it was written by "political outsiders with a really thorough knowledge, who reacted to the [council] with a brilliant exposé."[9] There is now good reason to suppose that it was written by a monk of Corbie in West Francia, perhaps Ratramnus or Paschasius Radbert.[10] Whoever the author might be, we may imagine

---

9 Heidecker, *The Divorce of Lothar II*, 107n46. At 43n27, he suggests it was by "some unnamed bishops."
10 For an identification of the author with Ratramnus, see Hoffmann and Pokorny, "Ratramnus von Corbie," at 11, building on a suggestion by Ubl, *Inzestverbot und Gesetzgebung*. However, the text also has considerable overlap with Radbert's commentary on the Gospel of Matthew, as noted by Gerda Heydemann in "Bibelexegese und rechtlicher Diskurs," though the text also uses some sources that Radbert tended not to, so the matter is not clear-cut. I am grateful to Dr Heydemann for her advice.

that someone harboring doubts about the council had canvased a learned monk for his thoughts, just as someone in 860 had approached Archbishop Hincmar, leading him to write his treatise on Lothar II and Theutberga's marriage.

The arguments laid out in Text D would have horrified Lothar II's court, demonstrating as they did that the line Lothar II had taken so far was not going to work. Nor was this text isolated. The divorce case had sparked a renewed interest across the Frankish world in the rules around remarriage, particularly in the Gospel of Matthew's apparent loophole permitting remarriage on grounds of adultery, and the fragility of the legal and theological arguments developed by Lothar II's court was becoming more evident.[11] At the subsequent Council of Metz, held in June 863, Lothar II accordingly moved the argument for divorce away from Theutberga's incest and toward his prior relationship with Waldrada, a relationship that he now argued had really been a prior marriage.[12] In other words, scholarly argument seems to have driven a shift in royal policy.[13]

Text A comes from a now lost manuscript associated with Bishop Adventius of Metz, preserved through an early modern transcription in the Biblioteca Vallicelliana in Rome, where it is shelved as manuscript I 76.[14] Texts B, C, and D are all from a ninth-century manuscript now in the Vatican, Biblioteca Apostolica, shelved as Pal. Lat. 576, where they are copied in sequence on folios 36v–46 (followed by the other incomplete treatise, not translated here).

---

[11] For this revival of interest in the exegesis of Matthew, see Heydemann, "Bibelexegese und rechtlicher Diskurs." For traces of scholarly interest in Irish circles, see Vocino, "A *Peregrinus*'s Vade mecum," esp. 112–17; and Tessera, "Milano, gli Irlandesi e l'impero carolingio."

[12] See Document 9, p. 105. The change of emphasis may have taken place already later in 862; Nicholas, *Letters*, no. 11 (Nicholas, *Reg.*, 589), a text written late in 862 or early in 863, suggests that Lothar II was emphasizing a preexisting relationship with Waldrada by this point (translated in d'Avray, *Dissolving Royal Marriages*, 18–19).

[13] Heidecker, *The Divorce of Lothar II*, 131, suggests that what changed Lothar II's argument was Theutberga's flight; but she had left Lothar II's court in 860, according to *Annals of St-Bertin*, trans. Nelson, 93.

[14] On this manuscript, see most recently West, "Knowledge of the Past."

Translation[15]

A. Acts of the Council (Bishop Adventius's version?)

Chapter 1. In the year 862, tenth indiction, on the third kalends of May [April 29], on the summons of the most glorious lord king Lothar [II], the archbishops and their fellow bishops met at Aachen, that is Gunthar, archbishop of Cologne and archchaplain of the sacred palace; and Theutgaud, archbishop of Trier; Adventius, bishop of Metz; Hatto, bishop of Verdun; Arnulf, bishop of Toul; Franco, bishop of Liège; Bishop Hunger [of Utrecht]; and Rathold, bishop of Strasbourg.[16]

This was so that with the assistance of divine clemency, they might be able to intervene faithfully and healthily with the already mentioned most serene ruler, for the utility and necessity of the holy mother church. For in our dangerous times, the pastoral trumpet should sound out even belatedly, according to prophetic admonition, where it is said, *Cry, cease not, lift up thy voice like a trumpet* [Isa. 58:1].[17]

So, faithfully thinking over many times God's judgments of the unfaithful and the dangers of the world as it grows old, and not without deep groans, we[18] called our most Christian ruler [Lothar II] to remember that he should not be unmindful of his vocation, and that what he is called by name he should fulfill in deed,[19] so that Christ the King of kings, who has made him the deputy of his name on earth, will return to him a worthy remuneration in heaven for the dispensation entrusted to him. To this, he [Lothar II], as a true worshipper of God,

---

15 Edition: *Die Konzilien der karolingischen Teilreiche 860–874*, ed. Hartmann, 71–8 (http://www.mgh.de/dmgh/resolving/MGH_Conc._4_S._71).

16 Together, these eight were the majority of the bishops of Lothar II's kingdom as it was in 862; absent were the bishop of Cambrai, Theoderic, who may have been too sick to attend (he died in August 862), and the archbishop of Besançon, Hartwig (or Arduicus). The names of Hunger and Rathold have been added in the margin of the surviving transcription of the text, but it is difficult to know what this signifies. Note that unlike the second Council of Aachen in 860, no bishops were present from other Frankish kingdoms.

17 Note that in this version of events, the council is described as convoked by Lothar II, implicitly to discuss his marriage dispute.

18 Here the text suddenly changes from "they" to "we."

19 The Latin word for king (*rex*) is linked to the Latin verb for ruling (*regere*). Cf. Document 3, p. 27.

purely and truthfully assented to Our Unanimity, promising irrevocably that he wished to obey our advice in all things and to comply with our reasonable admonitions. And as we said these things, so he adjusted his most gentle demeanor [*affectus*] along with us more than can be believed, so that it would be clear without doubt that in his heart he grasped the right hand of him in whose hands are the hearts of kings.[20]

Chapter 2. Meanwhile, regarding those salutary replies and spiritual advice that concerned the state of the holy church of God, and the utility of the realm and the salvation of the people committed to him, he reassured Our Unanimity. He affirmed that he was entirely ready in all matters, so that he would be a true helper and an indefatigable assistant of our order and of the whole of holy religion.

Chapter 3. After this, he humbly and devoutly sought pastoral advice, placing into the hands of our brothers a booklet of complaint and of his very serious necessity.[21] There he asked for divine and pastoral advice in appropriately mournful fashion, and with quavering voice he again talked of the causes of his weakness: how he had been deceived in a certain woman named Theutberga by the factional arguments of treacherous men. And indeed he unstintingly recalled that he had endured the sentence of separation by the judgment of the bishops. If she had been suitable for the marital bed and had not been defiled by the pestiferous pollution of incest, and publicly condemned by a spoken confession [Aachen 860], he would willingly have kept her. But he confessed that he was incontinent,[22] and asserted that he was not able to bear the ardor of his youth without conjugal union.

He repeated that it was beyond doubt we had declared to him that Theutberga was incestuous, and that we had ordered him to abstain from every concubine, and that it was extremely difficult for him to stay like this in his youth. Here Archbishop Theutgaud was a witness that, according to divine and his own counsel, if he [Lothar II] had done anything wrong with the concubine joined to him [i.e., Waldrada], he

---

20 In other words, Lothar II's outward *affectus* visibly showed his inward state of mind.
21 This is a reference to Lothar II's complaint, translated below as Text B. Note the distinction drawn in this version of the council between the advice given to him about the kingdom in Chapter 2 of this text and the advice then given about his personal affairs.
22 That is, incapable of celibacy: a reference to his relationship with Waldrada.

had healthily expunged it, assisted with ecclesiastical medicine and secret and constant tears and vigils and mortifications of spiritual continence, and moreover with donations of alms.[23] And to be brief about many things, if the joyful flesh had led him to sin, then we believe the afflicted flesh brought him back to pardon.

Chapter 5.[24] Therefore the concern of pastoral care and the examples of divine speech began to stir up the souls of our brothers about what should be done and arranged, and what should be reasonably decided about a proclamation and lament of this kind. And we were worried above all that – may it not happen – such a ruler might, after a worthy satisfaction and a very salutary reconciliation, incur an injury from weakness, and *returning [like a dog] to his vomit*, might *like a sow wallowing in mud* [2 Pet. 2:22] seek illicit embraces on several occasions.

Chapter 6. And so the pious Solicitude of our brothers decreed that it should be discussed again, how they had imposed the censure of ecclesiastical authority on the already mentioned woman Theutberga, as her public confession demanded.[25]

Chapter 7. A volume of several councils was brought out, and we had the fourth chapter from the Council of Lérida read out, where it is written:[26]

> About those who stain themselves in incestuous pollution. It was agreed that for as long as they persist in that detestable and illicit

---

23 That is, if Lothar II had sinned with Waldrada (which is not admitted), then he had already done penance for it, implicitly imposed by Archbishop Theutgaud, before the council had met. This addressed a point repeatedly made in 860 by Hincmar of Reims in his *On the Divorce*, that it was essential for Lothar II to perform penance. Note that Waldrada is termed a concubine in this 862 text, not a wife, as would later be argued.
24 There is no Chapter 4 in the only surviving manuscript. It seems most likely that at some point, a scribe made a mistake in the numbering (the alternative, that a chapter has been missed out, is less likely because of the similarities with Text C below).
25 In other words, the decision of Aachen 860 is reexamined and confirmed.
26 The Council of Lérida of 546 (in Visigothic Spain), ch. 4; here slightly garbled probably due to a copying error. The book in question could have been a copy of the Dacheriana collection of canon law, which contains this text at bk. 1, ch. 90. A ninth-century copy of this work is preserved in Cologne, Dombibliothek Cod. 122 (this canon at folio 44v). In reality, the text they quoted was about marriage between people who were related, not about the marriage of someone who had previously committed incest (see this document, pp. 81–2).

marriage of the flesh, they should only be admitted to the Mass of the Catechumens in the church. And as the Apostle commanded, it is not fitting for any Christians even to break bread with them.

Chapter 8. In addition to this, in the commentary of St Ambrose on the letter of St Paul the Apostle to the Corinthians, Chapter 33, it was said through the Lord's mouth to those who were joined in marriage, that[27]

> *the wife is not to leave her husband, and if she does leave him, she should remain unmarried* [1 Cor. 7:11]. This is the counsel of the Apostle, that if she leaves because of the bad way of life of the husband, she should remain unmarried, and that if she is not able to contain herself, because she does not wish to fight against the flesh, then let her be reconciled to her husband. For it is not permitted to the woman to marry if she has sent her husband away for the cause of fornication or apostasy, or if the husband has sought the use of his wife impelled by illicit lust.[28] For in no way does the inferior use the same law as the more powerful. If the man, however, apostatizes, let him not seek to pervert the use of his wife; the woman is not allowed to marry another, nor to return to him for the sake of fornication.[29]
>
> And let not the husband put away his wife [1 Cor. 7:11]. By implication, however: except for the cause of fornication.[30] And he [Paul] does not continue, as he did for the woman in saying, *But if she does leave, let her remain thus.* For it is permitted to the man to marry a wife, if he sent his sinning wife away. For a man is not constrained

---

27 This long quotation is taken from an exposition on the letter of St Paul to the Corinthians. Carolingian authors attributed it to St Ambrose, but it is now thought to have been written by another fourth-century author, known as Ambrosiaster. It is relatively unusual for biblical exegesis to be so prominent in a church council; it suggests that the council was short of authoritative sources. On Ambrosiaster, see Hunter, "The Significance of Ambrosiaster."
28 A reference to "deviant" (i.e., non-procreative) sexual practices.
29 That is, married Christians and apostates must separate.
30 Matthew 5:32 famously permits marital separation (but not, Carolingian writers argued, divorce) on grounds of fornication. Here Ambrosiaster brings St Paul into line, by suggesting that Paul simply took it for granted.

by the same laws as a woman.[31] For the man is the head of the woman.

For the rest I speak, not the Lord [1 Cor. 7:11]. He [Paul] says this to show what the Lord ordered through his own mouth and what he conceded by his authority, for the Lord spoke through him who said, *Do you seek proof that Christ is speaking in me?* [2 Cor. 13:3].

Chapter 9. From the Council of Agde, Chapter 62:[32]

We reserve no mercy for incestuous unions, unless they heal the adultery with separation. Incests [*incestos*] are not to be considered with the name of marriage, and even to label them as such is deadly.

And there after some other things, it is written

Those indeed to whom an illicit conjunction is forbidden will have the freedom of entering into a better marriage.

Chapter 10. For the rest, having clearly read these and other canonical sanctions of this kind, and the statements of the holy father Ambrose, we believe that she who was proven by a public (so it is said) confession to be marked by the incestuous crime of fornication was not a suitable or legitimate spouse, nor a wife prepared by God.

Therefore to our glorious ruler, for his most devoted affection in the divine cult and for his most victorious defense of the kingdom, and to whom not only we but truly canonical authority forbid an incestuous marriage, we do not deny the legitimate and suitable marriage conceded to him by God, according to the indulgence spoken by the Apostle: *It is better to marry than to burn* [1 Cor. 7:9].

---

31 This line of interpretation became increasingly unusual in Late Antiquity, which tended to argue that men and women were subject to the same rules.
32 For the (mis)interpretation of this key text, also quoted by Hincmar of Reims though in a slightly different form, see Stone and West, *The Divorce of King Lothar and Queen Theutberga*, 61–2, and this document, pp. 81–3. The decree was in fact issued by the Council of Epaon in 517 but was included under the Council of Agde of 506 in the influential Hispana collection of canon law.

B. The Booklet of Complaint of Lothar II

THE DECLARATION OF LOTHAR APPEALING TO THE BISHOPS ABOUT CONCEDING MARRIAGE TO HIM

O holy priests and venerable fathers, you who are placed as mediators between God and men, and to whom is committed the care of our souls, who provide medicine for the wounds of sin, who have the power of binding and loosing, and who are our doctors and leaders: to you I humbly appeal, and trustingly demand your kind and faithful counsel.[33]

Royal power should acknowledge the sublime authority of the sacerdotal dignity, by which two orders the church of the believers is ruled and guided by God's will.[34] But we know that one is as superior to another, as much as we rightly venerate the excellence of heavenly teaching which is closer to God. Therefore, we who offend or lightly or willfully stray through human weakness before God, we solemnly hasten back and flee to your pastoral dignity.

Recognizing my own errors by the inspiration of divine clemency, and frightened by and shuddering at the stains of such great sins, I myself seek the remedy of salvation from Christ through you, by suppliantly confessing and by demanding pardon. I trust greatly in your Piety, and I do not at all doubt that I shall be mercifully and measuredly accepted and treated with spiritual compassion, according to what the Apostle says: *Who is weakened, and I am not weakened?* [2 Cor. 11:29]. *For if someone is overtaken in some sin, let you, who are spiritual, instruct in the spirit of leniency, considering yourself, that you may not also be tempted* [Gal. 6:1]. And another scripture warns, *the bruised reed should not be crushed* [Isa. 42:3].

---

33 In this opening address to the bishops, Lothar speaks in the first person singular (I), though elsewhere in the text he uses the plural (we), perhaps to emphasize his personal contrition.

34 For this Carolingian notion of society as a single church (*ecclesia*) divided into two orders, the *auctoritas pontificalis* and the *potestas regia*, see Document 3, p. 45. Lothar II's following declaration, that sacerdotal authority is superior inasmuch as its heavenly teaching is closer to God, is unusually forthright. For background, see O'Brien, *Rise of Christian Kingship*.

As for the rest, fathers, we thank you very much, since you kept the faith owed to our lord father [Lothar I], and after his death you have been kind and faithful to us in all things. And since you generally and in many ways attended to our adolescence and unstable time of life, and also specially and diligently watched out for the deceit imposed on us through that so-called wife [Theutberga].[35]

About that business, we know that you have deeply in memory what was done by your advice.[36] For by your command we separated from ourselves that woman, who freely confessed to the terrible and incestuous contagion of fornication, according to the precept of St Paul, who said, *Do not keep company with fornicators* [1 Cor. 5:9]. Whatever I have done afterward in the weakness of incontinence, whether by necessity or by will, it is your duty to amend opportunely and rationally, and it is my duty willingly to obey.[37]

For you know that I was brought up from infancy and childhood among women, and that I desired to reach the harbor of legitimate marriage, for the good of chastity[38] and to avoid the wickedness of indecency. I am not unaware that whatever goes beyond licit union should be considered the wickedness of fornication and harmful pollution. I know that a concubine is not a wife, and I do not wish to have what is illicit, but what is licit.[39] You therefore, mindful of my youth,[40] consider what I should do, to whom neither is a wife conceded, nor a concubine permitted. It is known to you that the Apostle says, *I wish the younger ones to marry, to procreate children* [1 Tim. 5:14]. And *Who cannot contain himself, let him marry. For it is better to marry than to burn* [1 Cor. 7:9]. And again, *Let everyone have his own wife for fear of fornication* [1 Cor. 7:2]. And the Apostle Matthew: "God blessed marriage, and permitted love to rule in the bodies of men."[41]

---

35 *Nuncupata uxor*, which might mean "already-mentioned wife" but here probably means "so-called wife," since Lothar does not acknowledge in this text that Theutberga really was his wife. Thanks to Rachel Stone for this suggestion.
36 At the Councils of Aachen in 860.
37 Incontinence in the sense of inability to remain sexually inactive: an allusion to Lothar's relation with Waldrada.
38 Chastity in the sense of practicing only legitimate sexual activity (i.e., procreative and within marriage). Chastity is often conflated with celibacy today, but they were distinct in Late Antiquity and the early Middle Ages.
39 Lothar II's sharp distinction between a wife and a concubine is clear and striking.
40 Lothar was at this point probably in his mid-twenties.
41 This is taken from an apocryphal Life of St Matthew, not the Gospel.

Therefore I speak straightforwardly, and I confess that I am not at all able to endure without any conjugal union. And in truth I wish to be separated from all fornication *according to the inward man* [Romans 7:22]. And now, my dearest ones, we suppliantly beg your Sanctity and beg for the love of Him who redeemed us, that in the kindness of love and devoted fidelity, you will not delay from coming to the aid of our body and soul in peril, for the utility of the holy church of God and the kingdom committed to us: so that we may equally rejoice and exult in the Lord, both in our prosperity and in our most prompt devotion toward you.

C. Acts of the Council (Archbishop Gunthar's version?)

When we, archbishops and bishops from various provinces of the whole kingdom of the most serene king Lothar [II], had convened at the palace of Aachen and were discussing ecclesiastical rights with pastoral care and solicitude, the case of our ruler [*princeps*] was brought into our midst, whose marriage controversy we had touched upon before.[42]

Informed by the example and bolstered by the authority of the highest Lord Pastor, that is Jesus Christ, who *came into the world to save sinners* [1 Tim. 1:15], and knowing that we can and should threaten sinners with the fear of punishment if they do not come to their senses, and faithfully permit and concede mercy to them if they do, we bitterly grieved for the aforementioned king, given to us by God's disposition and deceitfully wounded in his inexperience of rule, as we discovered.

And we carefully and faithfully struggled to rescue him from the net in which he lamented he was caught, according to what the Apostle says: *If any of you err from the truth, and one convert him, he must know that he who causeth a sinner to be converted from the error of his way, shall save his soul from death* [James 5:19]. What we order to be bestowed upon all, in no way should we deny to our king and ruler, who humbly presented himself to our earlier meeting[43] and lamented that he had been horribly deceived in the name of marriage; and he added that he knew he was not able to continue without a consort for his youth. And he brought

---

42 Note that in this version, the council is presented as meeting independently of the king. Unlike the other version, the participants are not mentioned by name.

43 *Priori conventu nostro:* probably a reference to the Council of Aachen of 860.

forth a booklet of complaint which requested a path for his salvation, with divine inspiration.[44]

Pitying his grief and anxiety, as was fitting, we understood his attitude of pure devotion and demonstrated that he could remove previous sins through the remedy of penance, and could guard against future ones through the display of good works. He embraced this by necessity and willingly, according to our exhortation.[45] Gathering some of our colleagues, he set himself attentively to fasting, almsgiving, and other works pleasing to God for the whole of Lent, hoping to placate God with a fitting satisfaction, and he openly showed that he wished to deserve this by arriving barefoot.[46]

Then in this council too, he revealed the situation of his fragility, and usefully and praiseworthily sought advice from us for his salvation. Therefore, according to his petition and devotion, and most carefully upholding the form of humane piety and most vigilantly moderating the judgment of our ministry, we decreed that what we provided to him should be committed to memory.

We learned from many proofs that the woman [Theutberga] was more imposed upon him by wicked intention than legitimately joined to him in the name of a wife, and that she is not able to be a wife, which we clearly recognized by many attestations, or rather detestations, and finally by her spontaneous confession.[47] How could she be joined in marriage, whom by her own assertion her brother did not fear to defile? For as the Lord said to Moses, *Thou shalt not uncover the nakedness of thy sister* [Lev. 18:9], and as Moses himself terribly intoned by the Lord's inspiration, *Cursed be he that lieth with his sister, the daughter of his father, or of his mother* [Deut. 27:22]. And another scripture says, *he that keepeth an*

---

44 This is a reference to the booklet translated above as Text B. Here it is implied that it was delivered at the 860 council, which is unlikely (the other version of the 862 council clearly states it was given during the council itself).
45 Note that in this version of events, Lothar II is depicted as having been given penance by a council of bishops, unlike the more spontaneous impression indicated by the alternative version of events. Emphasis is placed on his unforced acceptance of it.
46 This penance would have been carried out not long before the council itself, given its April date. Christians were supposed to fast during Lent in any case (I am grateful to Rachel Stone for discussion on this point).
47 This is a reference to the Council(s) of Aachen in 860, which survive only in the extracts quoted by Hincmar of Reims in his *On the Divorce*.

adulteress, is foolish and wicked [Prov. 18:22]. And the Apostle: *he who is joined to a harlot, is made one body* [1 Cor. 6:16].

And about this it is said in the Council of Agde at Chapter 4,[48]

> It is agreed that those who stain themselves with the pollution of incest should be permitted only to the Mass of the Catechumens, for as long as they persevere in that detestable and illicit fleshly union. And as the Apostle commanded, it is not fitting for any Christians even to break bread with them.

And St Ambrose writes in the exposition of the first letter to the Corinthians, Chapter 34, after he [St Paul] spoke to the unmarried and to widows, addressing those who were joined in marriage, through the Lord's mouth:[49]

> *the wife is not to leave her husband, and if she does leave him, she should remain unmarried* [1 Cor. 7:11]. And that if she is not able to contain herself, because she does not wish to fight against the flesh, then let her be reconciled to her husband. For it is not permitted to the woman to marry if she has sent her husband away for the cause of fornication or apostasy, or if the husband has sought the use of his wife impelled by illicit lust.[50] For the inferior does not use the same law as the more powerful. If the man however apostatizes, let him not seek to pervert the use of his wife; the woman is not allowed to marry another, nor to return to him for the sake of fornication.[51]
>
> *And let not the husband put away his wife* [1 Cor. 7:11]. By implication, however: except for the cause of fornication.[52] And he [Paul] does not continue, as he did for the woman in saying, *But if she does*

---

48 What follows is actually a quotation from the 546 Council of Lerida, which is also quoted in the other version of the council, with some minor textual variants. The passage from the "Council of Agde" quoted in that version of the acts is omitted in this one. For a discussion of this confusion, see West, "Dissonance of Speech, Consonance of Meaning."
49 This long quotation from Ambrosiaster is the same as in the other version of the acts, with one small omission: "This is the counsel of the Apostle, that if she leaves because of the bad behavior of the husband, she should remain unmarried."
50 A reference to "deviant" (i.e., non-procreative) sexual practices.
51 That is, married Christians and apostates must separate.
52 See this document, note 65.

> *leave, let her remain thus.* For it is permitted to the man to marry a wife, if he sent his sinning wife away. For a man is not constrained by the same laws as a woman.[53] For the man is the head of woman.
>
> *For to the rest I speak, not the Lord* [1 Cor. 7:11]. He [Paul] says this to show what the Lord ordered through his own mouth and what he conceded by his authority, for the Lord spoke through him who said, *Do you seek proof that Christ is speaking in me?* [2 Cor. 13:3].

Perhaps someone will say to this among other things: *What the Lord has joined, let not man separate* [Matt. 19:6].[54] This is indeed excellent and most apt to be observed in those whom the Lord has joined, for the wife will be prepared for the husband by the Lord, as it is written elsewhere. But who would dare to say that this woman [Theutberga] was joined or prepared by the Lord, who according to so many and such important prohibitions of the Old and New Testaments should not be joined in union, but should rather be mourned and handed over to the death of the body, so that her spirit may be saved, as is shown by the confession of her own lips?[55] According to that sentence, *by thy words thou shalt be justified, and by thy words thou shalt be condemned* [Matt. 12:37]. And David at once ordered the man who boasted that he had killed Saul to be slain, saying *Thy blood be upon thy own head: for thy own mouth hath spoken against thee, saying: I have slain the Lord's anointed* [2 Kings 1:16].

And Pope Innocent wrote to the Toulousains, affirming that the person can in no way be absolved who pronounces a capital sentence against himself, whether in true confession or by false testimony, words that would be punished in another: "For everyone who is the cause of death to himself is a greater murderer."[56] And this is also shown very

---

53 See this document, note 31.
54 This section, justifying the bishops' decision, is not present in the other version of the council.
55 This seems to imply that Theutberga's life was in danger, but note that since 860 she was being sheltered with her brother in West Francia (*Annals of St-Bertin*, trans. Nelson, 93), so it was an empty threat. The intention may have been to suggest that she was morally dead, leaving Lothar II free to remarry. These threats are not present in the other version of the council.
56 The point seems to be that Theutberga's confession was so damning that it does not matter whether it was true or not. This is not in fact a letter from the fifth-century Pope Innocent I to the Toulousains, but a quotation from the fourth-century Council of Valence. This text is quoted by Hincmar of Reims in *On the Divorce,* trans. Stone and West, 180–1.

abundantly from the letter of Valentinus to the people of Fréjus, and in the African Council, Chapter 91.[57]

If anyone should presume to say that we have acted and decided irrationally and incautiously in this business, we who are neither tainted by sloth nor weakly supported by these and other instruments of divine eloquence: then let him know that unless he is cleansed of the stain of detraction and unjust accusation, he will have a harsh reckoning with us about these things, before the tribunal of eternal justice.[58] For let us proclaim before God that we have acted and spoken about this woman [Theutberga] motivated by neither any spiteful poison nor bitter zeal against her, nor led by the grace of any favor, but only according to what we found needed to be done, after most diligent examination and most studious inquiry, moderately and gently – saving the rule of canonical authority, which it is not permitted for anyone to violate – as it is right to recognize from the letters of our discussion written on this matter by us.

As for the ruler and our lord Lothar, after the recognition of his excesses and a fitting punishment with severe affliction for his errors, knowing that according to his declaration there is a law in his limbs warring against the law of his mind, we are not able to forbid him from marrying a wife and procreating children, lest he slip into worse things.[59] For as the Apostle says, *Who cannot contain himself, let him marry, only in the Lord; it is better to marry than to burn* [1 Cor. 7:2]. And again, *Let everyone have his own wife for fear of fornication* [1 Cor. 7:2], which of course is a concession of necessity, not of apostolic will, as he [Paul] says again, *I wish all men to be like me* [1 Cor. 7:7].[60] And so, therefore, we do not at all dare to prohibit these things, so worse things can more easily be guarded against, and every pretext of undue opportunity may be avoided with more solicitous custody.

It was commanded to two of our brothers separately to entrust to writing this chain of reasoning, which with the Lord's inspiration we

---

57 Not a letter of Valentinus, but a letter from the Council of Valence. This letter and the African Council are cited by Hincmar of Reims in *On the Divorce,* trans. Stone and West, 116. Did the author of this version of the council consult Hincmar's work?
58 Here the council defends itself against real or imaginary criticism.
59 The reference to procreation perhaps betrays the otherwise unmentioned matter of Lothar II's heirs.
60 That is, celibacy is a higher state than marriage.

all together discovered.[61] When each of them presented his text to the holy council in the early morning after the night, our whole company praised it as filled with a wonderful appropriateness of meaning, and we thanked the Lord for the concordant sentence. And so we decided to add this, that if the tenor of one of the texts, discrepant in words, reaches anyone's hands, let him not be disturbed by the dissonance of speech, but rather be compelled to trust by the consonance of meaning.

D. A Treatise on Marriage[62]

We have taken care to respond briefly and appropriately to the question which Your Reverence asked us, to tell you what could be seen in the little works of the fathers.[63] This is the heart of the question: if a man is permitted to put away his wife and marry another while the first is still alive.[64]

In the Gospel according to Matthew, it says:

> *And it hath been said, whosoever shall put away his wife, let him give her a bill of dismissal. But I say to you, that whosoever shall put away his wife, excepting for the cause of fornication,*[65] *maketh her to commit adultery: and he that shall marry her that is put away, committeth adultery* [Matt. 5:31–2].

Here the Lord attests that a wife can be put away, but only for the cause of fornication. He says there is no other reason why she can be put away. And after she is put away, unless if it was for fornication, she

---

61 This paragraph explains why there are two versions of the same council, and argues that they do not really differ in substance.
62 Although associated with the 862 council, this text is in reality a later commentary on a written account of the council.
63 Neither the commissioner nor the author of this text is named, though there is reason to suppose the author may have been a monk of Corbie (see this document, note 10).
64 That is, the core problem facing Lothar II.
65 This clause, about fornication (*fornicatio*), is not present in the other Gospels, as the treatise goes on to explore. On this so-called "Matthean exception," which appears to permit divorce on grounds of adultery, see Reynolds, *Marriage in the Western Church*, 173–226; and Bof and Leyser, "Divorce and Remarriage between Late Antiquity and the Early Middle Ages."

cannot marry someone else, and nor can she be taken in marriage by anyone else. For adultery would be recognized in both of them.

Whether the man who has put his wife away for the cause of fornication is able to marry another woman is not explicitly indicated in this passage. But it is more clearly expressed in another passage in this Gospel, when the Lord was questioned by the Pharisees,

> *Is it lawful for a man to put away his wife for every cause? Who answering, said to them: Have ye not read, that he who made man from the beginning, made them male and female? And he said: For this cause shall a man leave father and mother, and shall cleave to his wife, and they two shall be in one flesh. Therefore now they are not two, but one flesh. What therefore God hath joined together, let no man put asunder* [Matt. 19:3–6].

Thus it seems to be required that a wife should not be put away, since putting her away makes a division in the one flesh. When he says, *Therefore now they are not two, but one flesh,* he shows that whoever puts her away dissolves that one flesh, that is one body.

And he says more clearly below, *And I say to you, that whosoever shall put away his wife, except it be for fornication, and shall marry another, committeth adultery: and he that shall marry her that is put away, committeth adultery* [Matt. 19:9]. What he put in his previous speech obscurely, here he shows more clearly. For there he says, *whosoever shall put away his wife, excepting for the cause of fornication, maketh her to commit adultery,* noting the case of the woman if she marries and of the man who marries her, and not being explicit about the case of the man who put her away. But here he says, *whosoever shall put away his wife, except it be for fornication, and shall marry another, committeth adultery,* indicating that if he puts her away, it is not permitted for him to marry if he does not wish to be an adulterer. But he makes a point, which raises a question, by saying, *except for the cause of fornication.*

But let us see what the other evangelists say. In Mark, it is read, *Whosoever shall put away his wife and marry another, committeth adultery against her. And if the wife shall put away her husband, and be married to another, she committeth adultery* [Mark 10:11–12]. There is no mention of a cause, but it is simply instructed that a man, if he should *put away his wife and marry another,* is stained with adultery. And this matter is also similarly taken for the woman, that if she puts her husband away for any reason and marries another, she will be marked with adultery. We see that in this Gospel what was mentioned in Matthew and led to the question is excluded. That is, that the cause of fornication was mentioned, for if a woman was put away for fornication, he who put her away could marry another woman. But in the words of this testimony [from Mark], we recognize that if a woman is put away for adultery or any other reason, it is not at all permitted to the man to marry another woman, and that if he does so, he will not be immune from the blame of adultery.

Luke: *Every one that putteth away his wife, and marrieth another, committeth adultery: and he that marrieth her that is put away from her husband, committeth adultery* [Luke 10:18]. Gradually it is developed, and what was less explicit in one part becomes clearer in another. Matthew mentioned the cause of fornication, for which a wife was put away. Mark says that she should be put away for no reason, and if she is put away she should not be joined to anyone else. Luke in truth says that a woman can be put away, we may understand for the cause of religion or fornication, but that in no way can another woman be married. By all these we are taught that a wife cannot be put away by her husband except for the cause of fornication or religion,[66] and that if she is put away, then neither can the husband who put her away marry another woman, nor can she who was put away marry someone else, until either one, that is either he who put away or she who was put away, is widowed.

The Apostle Paul: *But to them that are married, not I but the Lord commandeth, that the wife depart not from her husband. And if she depart, that she remain unmarried, or be reconciled to her husband. And let not the husband put away his wife* [1 Cor. 7:10–11]. He clearly decides the case of the wife of the man putting her away, that *she remain unmarried, or be reconciled to her husband*. But whether the husband if he puts away his wife is constrained by the same law raises a question, because of what is read in the commentary of St Ambrose, which since you have it with you, we do not need to quote here.[67] But we say that Paul did not in any way dissent from the Gospel, nor teach anything other than what

---

66 That is, to join a religious community.
67 This commentary (in fact by Pseudo-Ambrose, or Ambrosiaster) was quoted in both versions of the acts of the 862 Council of Metz (this document, notes 27 and 49).
It argued that men could be treated differently from women in the case of adultery. The author of this treatise avoids discussing it.

Christ taught. And what the Gospels understand, the testimonies provided above clearly show. From this, what is less determined here by the Apostle about the condition of the husband who puts away his wife is given to be understood from earlier comments of this Apostle, and from the testimony of the Gospels. For when he says, *And if she depart, that she remain unmarried, or be reconciled to her husband,* he shows that she either should not depart, or that if she does depart, she should remain unmarried, or finally, at the end, be reconciled to her husband. When he adds, *And let not the husband put away his wife,* adding nothing more, it is implied from the earlier comments that either he should not send his wife away or if he does, he should not marry another woman, or finally, should be reconciled to his wife. This decision is confirmed as following the words of the Apostle and consonant with the Gospels.

Let us move on to the words of the doctors [of the church] on this passage. The venerable Augustine says on the sermon of the Lord according to Matthew,[68]

> For he who gave the commandment that a bill of dismissal should be given, did not give the commandment that a wife should be put away; but whosoever shall put away, says he, let him give her a bill of dismissal, in order that the thought of such a writing might moderate the rash anger of him who was getting rid of his wife. And, therefore, he who sought to interpose a delay in putting away, indicated as far as he could to hard-hearted men that he did not wish for separation. And accordingly the Lord himself in another passage, when a question was asked him as to this matter, gave this reply: Moses did so because of the hardness of your hearts. The Lord, therefore, in order to confirm that principle, that a wife should not lightly be put away, made the single exception of fornication; but enjoins that all other annoyances, if any such should happen to spring up, be borne with fortitude for the sake of conjugal fidelity and for the sake of chastity; and he also calls an adulterer that man who marries someone who has been divorced by her husband. And the Apostle Paul shows the limit of this state of affairs, for he says it is to be observed as long as her husband lives; but on the husband's death he gives permission to marry.

---

68 Augustine, *On the Sermon on the Mount*, bk. 1, ch. 14, trans. Findlay, 17.

This author says that a dissolution of a woman from a man is not to be done easily, and is possible only for the cause of fornication, and once the dissolution has been made, they should either be reconciled to one another, or neither should be joined in the law of marriage to another person.

In the commentary of Jerome on Matthew,[69]

> *And it hath been said, Whosoever shall put away his wife, let him give her a bill of dismissal* [discidium]. *But I say to you, that whosoever shall put away his wife, etc.* [Matt. 5:31]. In a later part, the Savior explains this passage more clearly: that Moses ordered a bill of dismissal to be given because of husbands' hardness of heart. He was not conceding dismissal, but removing murder. For it is much better to permit a deplorable separation than for blood to be shed through hatred.

This author leans on the authority of the Lord to prefer choosing a separation rather than for a murder to happen.[70] But he does not say whether the person who is dismissed can marry again while the other person is still alive.

In the same commentary:[71]

> It is fornication alone which conquers affection for a wife. Indeed, when she divides one flesh into another, and through fornication separates herself from her husband, then a husband does not have to keep her, so that she does not bring him under the curse, since scripture says, *He that keepeth an adulteress, is foolish and impious.* Wherever there is fornication and the suspicion of fornication, a wife can be freely put away. And since it could have happened that someone calumniated an innocent person, and for a second marriage accused the first wife of a crime, thus he orders the first wife to be put away, in such a way that he may not have a second wife while she is alive.

---

69 Jerome, *Commentary on Matthew*, bk. 1, ch. 5, trans. Scheck, 83.
70 As it was alleged that Frankish husbands sometimes resorted to: see Stone, *Morality and Masculinity*, 202–5.
71 Jerome, *Commentary on Matthew*, bk. 3, ch. 19, trans. Scheck, 216.

The blessed Jerome does not prohibit putting away a wife caught in adultery and, what is more, merely marked by the stain of suspicion of adultery, if the husband's wrath cannot be restrained in any other way. But he excludes the motive of marrying another wife in the zeal of casting aside one's own chastity, and says that he who was not willing to keep the first wife cannot marry a second one.

In the commentary of the Venerable Bede on Mark,[72]

> There is only one carnal reason, fornication, and one spiritual reason, the fear of God, for putting away a wife, as many are read to have done for the sake of religion. But there is no justification written in the law of God that says another woman can be married while the one who was put away is still alive.

Bede does not deny that a woman can be put away, whether for the reason of fornication or for religion. But following the authority of his elders, he does not agree that another woman can be married while the first is still alive.

St Ambrose in his exposition on the Gospel of Luke,[73]

> I think we must first speak of the law of marriage, so we can then deal with the prohibition of divorces [*divortia*].[74] Some people think that all marriage is of God, especially since it is written: *What therefore God hath joined together, let no man put asunder* [Matt. 19:6]. And if all marriage is of God, then no marriage ought to be dissolved. How then did the Apostle say, *If the unbelieving depart, let him depart* [1 Cor. 7:15]? In this, he marvelously both did not wish there to remain a reason for divorce among Christians, and he showed that not every marriage is of God. For by the authority of God Christians do not unite with gentiles, since the law forbids it.

From the words of this doctor, it is given to be understood that not every marriage is from God, and in what cases this should be understood: that is, if a Christian marries a nonbeliever or a Christian woman

---

72 Bede, *Marci euangelium expositio*, bk. 3, ch. 10.
73 Ambrose, *Commentary on the Gospel according to Luke*, bk. 8, ch. 2, trans. Ní Riain, 270.
74 *Divortium* is a term from Roman law, not found in the Vulgate Latin Bible.

marries a Jew, this kind of marriage should be dissolved, since it is not from God. But if a Christian man marries a Christian woman, and those things which should legally be done in marriage are completed,[75] then such a marriage cannot be denied to be from God.

Ambrose continues:[76]

> Therefore, do not put away your wife, since this would be to deny God, the author of your union. Indeed, if you must tolerate and amend the faults of others, this is especially so for your wife. Hear what the Lord has said: *whosoever shall put away his wife [...] maketh her to commit adultery* [Matt. 5:32]. Since it is not permissible for her to change her marriage while her husband is alive, the lust for sinning can creep its way in. And the man who is responsible for this slip is also guilty of the blame.

Here he declares that a wife should not be put away at all. For if after she is put away she marries or secretly corrupts herself, the blame will redound upon him, the author of the separation.

And he continues:[77]

> So, you put away your wife as if by law, without accusation, and you believe this is permitted because human law does not forbid it.[78] But the law of God forbids it. You obey men: fear God. Listen to the law of the Lord, to which those who enact the laws themselves defer: *What therefore God hath joined together, let no man put asunder.*

In this passage he touches on what customarily happens among secular men in putting away their wives. This is wholly prohibited by divine law, but human laws concede it. But blessed Ambrose says that divine laws ought to be followed more than human ones. And heavenly law is to be preferred to human law, the heavenly law to which those who establish earthly law are themselves subject.

---

75 Perhaps a reference to the gift of a dowry.
76 Ambrose, *Commentary on the Gospel according to Luke*, 271.
77 Ambrose, *Commentary on the Gospel according to Luke*, 271.
78 Roman law indeed permitted unilateral divorce: see Treggiari, *Roman Marriage*, 441–6.

And Ambrose continues:[79]

> I ask you, will you allow that during your lifetime your children live under a stepfather, or, while their mother is still living, live under a stepmother? Suppose the wife you have repudiated does not marry: should she have lost your regard when you were her husband, when she has kept faith to you, an adulterer? Suppose she gets married: this necessity is your fault, and what you thought was your new marriage is adultery. What difference does it make whether you commit adultery by openly displaying your fault or by pretending to be a husband, except that it is more serious to have committed an open crime than a secret theft?

Here he links together many issues which dissuade against separation, which is wicked and unjust. Wicked, if you have had children with the woman who is put away, and she marries and your own children grow up with a stepfather, which often happens when the children are driven out with their mother;[80] or if only the mother is driven away and the children remain, and the father marries again and the children lead an ignoble life under a stepmother. All these things openly declare an impiety. But if the woman put away is unwilling to marry, then her continence condemns her husband as an adulterer. And it is unjust to be put away as a chaste woman by an incontinent man. For if the man marries another woman, he is no less wicked, since he acts against the law of God, and therefore in this way he is also wicked. Ambrose therefore teaches that a woman should in no way be put away; that if she is put away, another woman should not be married; nor can there be said to be a free marriage or one without sin whenever there is a marriage against the laws of Christ, even if the law of the world seems to offer some protection.

Augustine discusses this more than adequately in his books *On Adulterous Marriages*. If someone reads these books carefully, his mind will not be able to entertain any hesitation about this question. From these books, we have taken care to annotate a few things in brief in this chapter, so that whoever either cannot or is unwilling to read the whole

---

79 Ambrose, *Commentary on the Gospel according to Luke*, 271.
80 An insight into Frankish expectations around child custody?

work in its fullness will be able to understand from a few parts what this Catholic author wishes to be held in this matter by Catholics. In the first book, after many things, he says:[81]

> Why is this? What if in his account Matthew did not relate the whole of what was said on the matter, but related a part of it in such a way that the whole is implicit in that part, whereas Mark and Luke, to make it evident, preferred to state it fully, so that the whole doctrine would be clear? We have no doubt to begin with that what we read in Matthew is true, *whosoever shall put away his wife, excepting for the cause of fornication, maketh her to commit adultery* [Matt. 5:31]. But we wanted to find out whether it is only the man putting away his wife when it is not for fornication who commits adultery by marrying someone else; or whether everyone who marries someone else after putting away his wife commits adultery, including the one who puts his wife away for committing fornication. Do we not have our answer in Mark? *Whosoever shall put away his wife and marry another, committeth adultery against her* [Mark 10:11]. Are we not also told in Luke? Why are you uncertain whether someone who puts his wife away for the reason of fornication and remarries is guilty of adultery? *Every one that putteth away his wife, and marrieth another, committeth adultery* [Luke 16:18].
>
> So, because it is not proper to say that when the evangelists use different words to speak about the same matter, they disagree in their understanding of the same doctrine, then the only alternative is to understand that Matthew intended the part to stand for the whole. The doctrine he held, however, was the same. Hence there cannot be the slightest doubt that it is not true that the man who puts away his wife and remarries is an adulterer, namely that man who puts her away not for fornication, while another man, who puts his wife away because of fornication, is not an adulterer. Rather, everyone who puts his wife away and marries again is guilty of adultery.[82]

---

81 Augustine, *Adulterous Marriages*, bk. 1, ch. 12, trans. Kearney, 150–1.
82 The passage is a little confusing to follow. Augustine's point is that one cannot draw a distinction between someone who remarries after separating from his wife on grounds of fornication, and someone who remarries after separating from his wife on other grounds: both men are adulterers.

> How can those next words in Luke be true? *He that marrieth her that is put away from her husband, committeth adultery* [Luke 16:18]. How is he guilty of adultery, if not because the woman he has married is still someone else's wife, as long as the man who put her away is still living. It clearly would not be adultery if the woman he is sleeping with now were his own wife and not someone else's. But it is adultery; therefore the woman he is sleeping with is someone else's wife. So if she is someone else's wife, namely the wife of the man who put her away, then she has not yet ceased to be the wife of the man who put her away, even if she was put away for the reason of fornication. On the other hand, if she has ceased to be his wife, then she is now the wife of this man she then married; and if she is his wife, then he cannot be considered an adulterer, but her husband. But since scripture does not call him her husband, but an adulterer, she is still the wife of the man who put her away, even if it was because of fornication. It follows also that anyone whom he himself takes as another wife after putting her away is also an adulteress, because she is sleeping with someone else's husband. If it is agreed then that he makes that woman he marries an adulteress, how can it be that he too is not an adulterer?

The venerable Augustine shows with many reasons that anyone who puts his wife away, whether for the reason of fornication or without it, and marries another woman, commits adultery. And that she who marries another man while her husband is still alive, whether she was put away for or without the reason of fornication, commits adultery. Nor are such weddings considered to be legitimate marriages by the laws of the church [*ecclesie leges*] since they are agreed to be dissolved by adultery.

And again in his second book:[83]

> I am speaking of course to Christian men, who listen with faith to the words, *the man is the head of the woman* [Eph. 5:23], and so acknowledge that they are the leaders and women their companions. It follows that in the way he lives a man must be careful not

---

83 Augustine, *Adulterous Marriages*, bk. 2, ch. 8, trans. Kearney, 170–1.

to go down any path where he is frightened his wife might follow by imitating him. The people we are speaking about, however, are not happy to have the same rule of chastity apply to husband and wife, but prefer to be subject to the laws of the world rather than those of Christ, because in the matter of chastity the laws of the courts do not seem to place the same restrictions on men as they do on women. However, let them read what the emperor Antoninus, certainly no Christian, decreed about this. A husband is not allowed to bring a charge of adultery against his wife, unless he himself in his conduct has given her the example of chastity. And if the hearing establishes that both alike have been unchaste, both will be convicted. Those are the words of that emperor, as we read them in the Gregorian Code:[84]

> My rescript will not prejudice the case in any way. If it was your fault that the marriage was dissolved and in accordance with the Julian law your wife Euphasia married, she will not be condemned for adultery because of this through my decree, unless there is proof that she committed it. They [the judges] will have it in their minds to investigate this, to see whether, while you yourself lived chastely, you also led her to cultivate good habits. It seems iniquitous to me that a man should demand from his wife chastity that he himself does not practice. This can be a reason for condemning the man too, and not allowing the case between them to proceed, on the ground that the two offences cancel each other, or extinguishing the grounds for the action.

If these are the rules that have to be observed for the honor of the earthly city, how much more must the heavenly homeland and the community of angels require chastity? This being so, is the shamelessness of men therefore less serious, rather than worse and more serious, because of their proud and licentious arrogance?

It is therefore shown by the authority of the present doctor [Augustine] that an equal fault of wife and husband is to be punished with the same

---

84 Augustine here quotes imperial Roman law.

penalty, and what is not allowed for a wife is not allowed for a husband. Just as she commits adultery by not keeping faith with her husband, so he is treated as an adulterer if he does not keep faith with his wife.

Now that these things have been briefly set out, let anyone who wants to know the opinion of this author [Augustine] on this matter more fully read the books which we have excerpted. And he will see that if a wife is put away, according to the Gospel teaching it is not possible to marry another, nor can such a union be called a marriage, but rather an adultery.

In the canons of the apostles:[85]

> If any layman drives away his own wife and takes another, or a wife put away by someone else, let him be deprived of communion.

In the African Council:[86]

> It was agreed that according to Gospel and apostolic teaching, neither a husband put away by his wife nor a wife put away by her husband can marry someone else. But let them remain thus until they are reconciled with each other. And if they despise this instruction, let them be brought to repentance. In this matter an imperial law should be requested to be promulgated.

In the decretal of Pope Innocent:[87]

> And this needs to be understood, why it is unfitting for communicant husbands to be with adulterous wives, when by contrast women can be seen to stay in relationships with adulterous husbands. The Christian religion condemns adultery in both sexes equally. But wives cannot easily accuse their husbands of adultery, and hidden sins cannot be punished. But husbands are accustomed to bring their adulterous wives before priests more freely, and so

---

85 *Canons of the Apostles*, ch. 47 (a set of decrees attributed to the apostles, though Carolingian writers were not certain of their authenticity).
86 From the Dionysio-Hadriana canon law collection.
87 Pope Innocent I, letter to Bishop Exuperius of Toulouse (JK 293), *Epistolae*, ed. Migne, col. 499–500.

communion is denied to the women when their crime is revealed. Since the acts of husbands are hidden, it is not straightforward to avoid someone on account of suspicions, although they will rightly be expelled if their crime is detected.

This chapter is interposed so that we can see that the penalty for the crime of adultery is the same for the man as the woman, although it is usually easier to punish the woman, not for an inequality in the case but in the absence of an accuser. These above two chapters agree with the sentences of the fathers provided earlier, that is that whether the man or the wife has been put away, they should either be reconciled with each other, or not marry anyone else.

Up to this point we have tried to show that he who this is about [i.e., Lothar II] should either remain celibate or should be reconciled to his wife [i.e., Theutberga], if he wishes to obey divine letters and the authority of the fathers. It is countered that this union was not a legitimate marriage, because she did not marry her husband as a virgin but as a corrupted woman, and this by her brother.[88] Whatever she was before she married, if she kept her faithfulness to her husband after she married by preserving her chastity, the previous corruption does not prejudice the subsequent chastity. Even if she had been a courtesan or a prostitute, or had been exposed to many corruptors, if she has kept the marital bond uncontaminated, then the later cleanliness washes away the stains of her former life. For the Apostle says, *And such some of you were; but you are washed, but you are sanctified, but you are justified* [1 Cor. 6:11].

And Augustine, writing to Pollens, says,[89]

> You think it is difficult for a husband or wife to be reconciled with the other partner after adultery. But it will not be difficult, if there is faith. In fact, why do we still call them adulterers, when we believe they have been either cleansed by baptism or healed by penance?

---

88 This was the accusation made against Theutberga in both the Council of Aachen in 860 and the Council of Aachen in 862.
89 Augustine, *Adulterous Marriages*, bk. 2, ch. 6, trans. Kearney, 169. Note that the author of the treatise somewhat tendentiously cuts the quotation short; Augustine goes on to state that in the Old Testament there was no question of taking back a wife after adultery.

We see therefore that the corruption of the previous life is cleansed by conjugal purity, and what has been removed through baptism or penance, that is the declaration of continence, which testimony is confirmed by the conjugal promises, should not be brought up as a sin again. Nor should someone who casts aside the filth of pollution, and carefully preserves the cleanliness of chastity in the conjugal union, be considered unclean, so that we do not seem to go against the apostolic doctrine and the faith of the church.

In the Council of Agde:[90]

> We reserve no mercy for incestuous unions, unless they heal the adultery with separation. Incests are not to be considered with the name of marriage, and even to label them as such is deadly.

You can recognize this passage was placed in the chapter copied in the letters you brought to our attention.[91] Those who put it there wanted to prove that the marriage this is about should be called an incest rather than a marriage. But let us see how this passage continues:

> These we consider to be incests: if anyone pollutes himself in carnal union with the widow of his brother, who was previously like a sister to him. If anyone takes his brother's sister as a wife. If anyone marries his stepmother. If anyone associates himself to his cousin. If anyone mixes with the widow or with the daughter of his paternal uncle, or pollutes himself through sex with or takes as a wife the daughter of his maternal uncle or his stepdaughter, or anyone from his own kindred, or anyone whom a kinsman has married. All these we consider to be incestuous people, formerly and under this law.[92]

---

90 The Council of Agde of 506, ch. 61.
91 In other words, the author is here citing the conciliar documentation that has been presented to him (*quas meministis*). This quotation was used in both the Aachen councils of 860 and 862. The second (Gunthar) version of 862 muddles the quotation, which might suggest that the author of this treatise was working from Adventius's version, but this is not certain, since there may have been other corrected copies of Gunthar's version in circulation.
92 The author here is quoting the Agde decree in the version of the Pseudo-Isidorian Decretals.

We therefore see that if someone marries a kinswoman or a woman whom his kinsman has married, this marriage is, or is labeled as, incest, and such weddings should be spurned. But the people this is about are not joined together by any closeness of blood. And even if she is said to have been polluted by her brother [Hubert], she was not taken as his wife. And the crime is either secret or cleansed, since it has not been proven with certain witnesses or acceptable accusers or a manifest conviction, and if it was committed in the frail adolescence of childhood, then a satisfaction has purged [her] through marital confederation with an appropriate emendation.[93] Examples in the decrees of the elders thus teach us how lenient we should be to the slips of youth, since they say that a youth who has sinned with his sister should be cured through the remedy of penance, not separated entirely from his spouse. This matter is clearly proven through the words of the saints.

And the marriage which we are discussing is not covered in the above chapter, since they are distant from any closeness of blood. Even if some carnal pollution occurred through the precariousness of youth, it should be removed by the remedy of penance, and not punished by the separation of the spouse.[94] Nor is the husband polluted through the sinning of his wife, if he was neither involved in the act nor gave consent. If it is accepted that to some extent she fell into pollution, how does it affect the husband, if he lived chastely with her? How can the pollution of a wife pollute a husband, if she has lived chastely with her husband after their marriage? Nor should it be feared that a husband linked to such a woman is cursed, because of what Solomon said: *He that keepeth an adulteress, is foolish* [Prov. 18:22].[95] Since after she married him, she kept her chastity, her old misdeeds should not be counted, if a better conversion has purged them. Just as a faithful person is now no longer unfaithful, and a humble person is no longer proud, and a holy person is no longer unclean: so a chaste person is no longer impure, and so too a marriage clean with the holiness of continence is not bound to the sins of adultery, even if perhaps it happened that either

---

93 The author may be drawing here on Lothar II's language of frailty: if he sinned and can be forgiven, why should she not be?
94 Literally, *lubricum aetatis*: the "slipperiness of his age." Already in classical Rome, youth was perceived as an age prone to be slippery (*lubrica*), in the sense of liable to slip and fall.
95 This passage was quoted in the Aachen 862 council, this document, Text C, p. 65.

of the sexes polluted themselves through some illicit things before they married. And even if she perhaps contracted some corruption before she married, the legitimate marriage cannot be called an adultery, if she kept the faith of chastity to her husband.

If things are so, then how can she be put away for the reason of fornication by her husband, since she has remained chaste with him, whatever corruption either of them committed previously? And it is not licit to dissolve the marriage unless the stain of fornication intrudes. Nor should this marriage be treated as incest, since even if she was perhaps incestuous before, now she is not what she was, since she entered the bond of a legitimate marriage bed, and by living chastely with her legitimate spouse, she condemned whatever she might have done in her adolescence.

For if we wish to consider all illicit sex as incest,[96] then there would be no doubt. But when the canons talk about incestuous people, they talk about spouses, not about all those who unite together illicitly and indiscriminately, who it is clear should be called committers of *luxuria* or adulterers.[97] They are adulterers, if they are placed in a marriage and either of them does not keep the faith owed to the other, by having illicit sex with another man or woman. But those who are not yet married, or who are separated from their spouse by death, if they sleep with some other man or woman, are marked by the crime of *luxuria*, not of adultery. And therefore when the canons speak of these people, they do not call them incestuous, as if every illicit sex was incest, but rather as polluted with the lust of corruption.

As a result, the man this is about [Lothar II] will not be called incestuous if he keeps her who is said to have been polluted by her brother, nor is it as if he is keeping an adulteress. For she was not an adulteress, because she did not have a husband, even if she was polluted by not preserving her chastity. And having rejected her sin, she kept the chastity

---

96 Cf. Jonas of Orléans, *De laicali institutione*, ed. and trans. Dubreucq, bk. 2, ch. 13, 422, which indeed states that "all illicit sex is incest," as noted by Ubl, *Inzestverbot und Gesetzgebung*, 350n300. Jonas wrote in the 820s. A manuscript of Jonas's work (Vatican, Biblioteca Apostolica Vaticana, Vat. Lat. 990) was available at the monastery of Corbie, where this commentary was written; intriguingly, this chapter and those relating to marital morality have been excised from it.

97 *Luxuria* was the vice of lust and other forms of bodily excess (quite different from the modern connotations of luxury).

of her marriage and preserved her faith to her husband: thus she can be called neither an adulteress nor an incestuous person. Whatever she did before she married reflects on her, not on her husband, and if she purged herself of it, and remained chaste after she married, she is no longer what she was. As the blessed Augustine says in his book *On the Good of Marriage*,[98]

> In the same way, if a woman, having broken her marriage faith, keeps faith with her adulterer, she is certainly wicked: but, if she is not even faithful with her adulterer, she is worse. If she then repents of her sin, and returns to marital chastity, renouncing all adulterous agreements and resolutions, I would be surprised if even the adulterer himself will think she is unfaithful.

There is no doubt that a woman is polluted in a union with an adulterer. But if she returns to her own marriage bed, repudiates the adulterer, and lives chastely, then according to the authority of St Augustine, she should no longer be called an adulteress, and nor will he who is joined to her be judged as a fool, nor does he fall under the curse as keeping an adulteress, since she is no longer an adulteress, because she has rejected the crime of adultery and has chosen henceforth to live with her husband. Otherwise, if whatever was committed before a marriage was retained as a crime after the marriage, no small license would be given to husband and wife for dissolving a marriage.

And leaving women aside, there is rarely or never a man who comes to his wife as a virgin. And if the stains of prior life allowed a dispute to be brought against a husband, he would be judged as an adulterer, whether he had a concubine or perhaps committed fornication before he married. But there is no law that says this, nor any author that tries to assert this. Rather, it seems unjust and supported by no authority that he should undergo judgment for something which he has now repented of and has condemned.

So, it seems just to maintain the marriage this treatise concerns, nor can the husband be judged as though he is keeping an incestuous person or an adulteress, since she was neither incestuous after they

---

98 Augustine, *On the Good of Marriage*, bk. 4, ch. 4, trans. Kearney, 36.

married, nor can she be called an adulteress, since even if she had sex with someone else, she did this before and not after she married. Such sex is *luxuria*, it is not adultery.

We have written these words of the fathers as we were asked. Whether they were rightly spoken, you will judge.

6. THE SUMMIT AT SAVONNIÈRES, NOVEMBER 862

In April 862, a third council held at Aachen had enabled Lothar II to take Waldrada as his queen, but Lothar II's uncle, King Charles the Bald, remained reluctant to acknowledge the new situation. One way of resolving this sort of problem was for the Carolingian kings to meet face to face, as happened regularly following the Treaty of Verdun in 843, which had divided the Carolingian empire into separate kingdoms.[1] At one such summit in Koblenz in June 860, Lothar II had acted as a mediator between his uncles Louis and Charles, to draw a line under Louis's invasion of Charles's kingdom in 858 and restore family harmony. Since then, Lothar II's own marriage had become the key political issue. At a summit held at the royal estate of Savonnières in Lothar II's kingdom in November 862, it was Louis the German's turn to act as a mediator, to try to engineer a reconciliation between Lothar II and Charles.[2]

The Savonnières summit started awkwardly, however, since Charles the Bald refused to give Lothar II the kiss of friendship, or even to talk with him, and sent a note to Louis explaining why.[3] The main issue was Lothar II's treatment of Theutberga. Charles's affected dismay shows how Lothar II's handling of his marriage had become toxic, as his attempt to manipulate the language and ideology of queenship turned

---

[1] Costambeys, Innes, and MacLean, *Carolingian World*, 388, estimate that around seventy such meetings were held between 843 and 887.

[2] A council had been held there previously in 859; the site was convenient for West Francia and Lotharingia. For the arrangements leading up to this council, see Airlie, "Unreal Kingdom," 345–6.

[3] Though Charles's text was included in the important nineteenth-century edition of Carolingian capitularies or royal edicts, it is not a piece of legislation, since its main aim was to summarize Charles's complaints against Lothar II.

against him.[4] A problem within the king's household could be represented as a problem with the king, for, as the Irish scholar Sedulius Scottus pointed out in a contemporary treatise informed by Lothar II's controversy, how could a king rule others if he could not rule at home, or even rule himself?[5] If a successful marriage had not been a major benchmark for Carolingian kingship before, Lothar II's maneuvering had ensured it certainly was now.

Lothar II's treatment of Theutberga was not the only issue that Charles raised with his nephew. He also brought up the question of Engeltrude (or Ingiltrude), the wife of an Italian count named Boso. Engeltrude had fled from her husband – in fact eloping with another man – and had received sanctuary at the court of Lothar II, who refused to send her back. Engeltrude was a relative of Lothar II, while Boso was probably Theutberga's brother, so Engeltrude's marriage case was closely linked to Lothar's, and like Lothar's, it attracted much contemporary scrutiny and criticism.[6] Charles was also angry that Lothar II had offered refuge to his daughter Judith, who had eloped with one of Charles's followers, a count named Baldwin.

Only when Lothar II had agreed to the conditions Charles had laid down did the meeting between the kings go ahead. Having first blocked the meeting, Charles now tried to shape how it proceeded. A common feature of summits between the Carolingian kings was that each of the kings would make a public declaration, promising to uphold whatever had been agreed, and expressing his love and respect for the other kings.[7] At Savonnières, Charles provided drafts of written statements not only for himself, but also for his brother and his nephew. These declarations were modeled on a common pattern. Each king promised to uphold the general commitments he had entered

---

4 On this ideology, and the accusations against queens that arose from it, see Dohmen, *Ursache allen Übels*; and MacLean, "Queenship, Nunneries and Royal Widowhood."
5 Sedulius Scottus, *On Christian Rulers*, ed. and trans. Dyson. The precise dating of the treatise is uncertain.
6 Some of this criticism came from Hincmar of Reims, who wrote a treatise about Boso and Engeltrude's marriage, the *De Uxore Bosonis*, which survives in the same manuscript as his treatise on Lothar and Theutberga's marriage. Boso also appealed to the pope: Nicholas, *Reg.*, 517. On this case, see Stone, "'Bound from Either Side.'"
7 Such declarations (*adnuntiationes*) are preserved from ten summits: for instance, at St-Quentin in 857 (see Charles, *Reg.*, 883). On this language of fraternal love, see Costambeys, Innes, and MacLean, *Carolingian World*, 389.

into at the previous royal meeting at Koblenz in 860, and further noted that Charles had demanded action from Lothar II on certain unspecified issues, to which Lothar II had agreed.

Charles had these draft statements read out before the inner circle of the Carolingian aristocracy gathered in a hall, a group of some two hundred key advisers. However, this group refused to allow these texts to be read out before the whole assembly, the *populus*. In the *Annals of St-Bertin*, Archbishop Hincmar of Reims, who was present at Savonnières (and who was probably involved in composing Charles's documents) shed a little more light on the counselors' objections. He blamed one of the most powerful aristocratic advisers, a man named Conrad (a cousin of King Charles the Bald, from a family known to historians as the Welfs), who was trying "to prevent the people from finding out what accusation Charles was making against Lothar."[8] None of the speeches explicitly mentioned what the accusation was; but they did mention that there was an accusation, and that alone would have been enough to provoke further interest.

Who were "the people" whose opinion evidently mattered enough for Charles's speeches to be kept from them? It was not the two hundred counselors, who had already heard the draft speeches in the hall. But of course these elite aristocrats would hardly have traveled to Savonnières alone. On the basis that they would each have brought a group of retainers and followers, Michael McCormick reckoned the total number of people gathered at Savonnières to be around five thousand.[9] What Charles had in mind was surely for the kings to deliver the speeches he had written for them to a crowd of these people (presumably outside, since the hall at Savonnières would have been too small to house so many people). This text suggests that there were two "publics" in Carolingian Francia: on the one hand, an elite core, made up of the wealthiest and most powerful magnates (sometimes labeled using a German term as the *Reichsaristokratie*), and on the other, the wider Frankish aristocracy.[10]

---

8 *Annals of St-Bertin*, trans. Nelson, 103. On Conrad, see Heidecker, *The Divorce of Lothar II*, 146–7.
9 McCormick, *Origins of the European Economy*, 665.
10 Cf. Hincmar, *On the Governance of the Palace*, ch. 30, trans. Dutton, *Carolingian Civilization*, 528–9. For commentary on the possibility of public debates in this period, see Melve, "'Even the Very Laymen Are Chattering about It'"; and in a slightly different context, Pezé, "Doctrinal Debate and Social Control."

The former might have been the decision-making group, but the opinion of the latter carried weight too. Assemblies mattered in Carolingian Francia.[11]

Louis the German and Lothar II's position was clearly that the issue of Lothar II's marriage was now resolved, and everyone could move on; they were presumably hoping for the warm public words of affection and support that these summits usually produced. Charles, however, had no intention of letting Lothar II get away with it so easily, and he had planned to use his speeches to ensure that Lothar's marriage remained publicly recognized as a live issue. Was this in the hope of making gains at Lothar's expense, or simply to distance himself from the scandal? Either way, when his proposed speeches were blocked for fear of their effect on the *populus*, Charles gave his own short address that same evening, to a group of counselors inside the hall.

In the end, the Savonnières summit was a mixed success for everyone. Charles aired his grievances to the top Frankish elite, and he made sure his version of events was written down, which emphasized the conditionality of his friendship; but Lothar II got the kiss of peace from Charles that he wanted, and he avoided having the entire assembled transalpine Frankish aristocracy publicly reminded of his sins.[12] King Charles was a tough and sly negotiator, but thanks to Uncle Louis's support, Lothar II was making some headway. As Lothar II would soon discover, however, the pope was going to prove a rather stiffer challenge.

The Savonnières summit documentation is preserved in full only in early modern transcriptions and editions, notably in a sixteenth-century manuscript, Vatican, Biblioteca Vaticana, Vat. Lat. 4982, based on a now lost medieval manuscript from Beauvais. The documentation probably represents a dossier about the summit made by Archbishop Hincmar of Reims, who was present and involved in drawing up the draft speeches.

---

11 See Wickham, "Consensus and Assemblies"; and from a different angle, Bobrycki, "Flailing Women." Cf. Staubach, *Herrscherbild*, 144.
12 Cf. an entry from 862 in *Annals of St-Bertin*, trans. Nelson, 103: "But Charles, against their wishes, made it fully known to everyone that he had refused to communicate with Lothar before he gave the undertaking mentioned above, for two reasons: first, because Lothar had abandoned his wife and taken another woman, contrary to the authority of the Gospel and of the apostles, and second, because Lothar and his mistress had had communication with excommunicated persons, namely the wife of Boso, and Baldwin …"

Translation[13]

In the year of the Lord 862, when Louis advised Charles that with him he should accept Lothar [II] for a kiss and for discussion,[14] Charles sent back to him through the bishops Altfrid[15] and Salomon,[16] and Adventius[17] and Hatto,[18] the chapters that follow, saying that for these reasons he did not dare to communicate with him [Lothar],[19] unless what was written there was carried out. On Lothar's behalf, Louis and the already mentioned bishops reported to Charles and to the bishops Hincmar,[20] Hincmar,[21] Odo,[22] and Christian,[23] that Lothar had declared that he wished to do so and would do so. With these conditions, Charles and the bishops who were with him received him [Lothar] for a kiss.

[Charles's letter to Louis]

1. After we were recently reconciled to each other with mutual forgiveness at Koblenz,[24] with God's approval and on the advice of our faithful followers, and we confirmed it with an oath about maintaining the peace between us, and about offering help to each other, and we promised to observe the capitularies written by our shared faithful followers,[25] and read out by us, and we publicly announced it to our shared faithful followers: after all this, I do not wish, my only and dearest brother [Louis], to accuse you of not having observed toward me those things that we promised one another. Nor do I hope that you or anyone

---

13 Edition: *Capitularia regum Francorum*, ed. Boretius and Krause, 2:159–65 (http://www.mgh.de/dmgh/resolving/MGH_Capit._2_S._159).
14 Exchanging a kiss was a common way of demonstrating trust and friendship; to refuse to do so was a public display of hostility.
15 Bishop of Hildesheim in East Francia.
16 Bishop of Konstanz in East Francia.
17 Bishop of Metz in Lotharingia.
18 Bishop of Verdun in Lotharingia.
19 That is, interact with (the opposite of excommunication).
20 Archbishop of Reims in West Francia.
21 Bishop of Laon in West Francia.
22 Bishop of Beauvais in West Francia.
23 Bishop of Auxerre in West Francia.
24 This meeting between the kings at Koblenz took place in June 860, drawing a line under Louis the German's failed invasion of West Francia in 858.
25 Note the emphasis on the involvement of the kings' followers (*communes fideles nostri*) in drafting the Koblenz statement.

else is able or wishes to accuse me of not having similarly observed these things toward you. And if anyone has done so, I am ready to give certain account to you about it and to make a worthy satisfaction. And if someone wishes to accuse me of not having observed as far as I can those things which I owe to our nephew Lothar, I am similarly ready to give certain account and to carry out an appropriate satisfaction. How far, however, he [Lothar] has observed toward me those things which he promised to me, not only I but many others know.

2. And it suited us then [at Koblenz] that we should meet again at a fixed time at the same place with the magnates of our kingdoms, so that we might discuss there whatever was worthy and necessary to be amended, both in the holy church of God and in the salvation of ourselves and the people, and that we should amend ourselves toward our faithful followers, and they should amend themselves toward us, and should decree what else should be observed. This I have been ready to follow time and time again, and even now I have come again,[26] as you often relayed to me through our shared faithful followers.

3. But there are various reasons why I did not want to talk with our already mentioned nephew before I took counsel with you. Some of these reasons I wish to note here, some I shall let you know later at a suitable place and in a suitable fashion.

4. When I came on a previous occasion to Tusey to discuss these things,[27] Boso brought to me and to my bishops letters from the lord pope, some to be sent to our nephew and the bishops of his kingdom, which we sent to them according to the lord pope's request, and some letters to be read and observed by us, and we have the text of them here. In these letters, we found that we were criticized for allowing fornicators to stay in our kingdom, and that not just this woman [Engeltrude] but all those who consenting to her crime have been excommunicated from the body and blood of the Lord, until this woman should return to her husband.[28] We know, as St Gregory said, that if someone does not correct what should be cut down when he can, he himself commits

---

26 In other words, this text seems to have been written when Charles was already present at the summit.
27 This refers to a church council that Charles attended at the palace of Tusey in October 860.
28 Engeltrude had fled her husband Boso and sought refuge with Lothar II; Boso appealed to the pope to make Lothar II return her.

those actions.[29] And we have heard that this woman is staying in the kingdom of our nephew, and we have not heard that this [papal] decision has been changed. And we who are weighed down by our own sins are afraid to communicate with someone else's sins by communicating with the excommunicated.[30]

5. Baldwin stole for himself our daughter Judith, a widow, placed under the protection of the church and royal authority according to secular and divine laws.[31] The bishops of our kingdom excommunicated him following a legal judgment, according to the sacred canons and the decision of St Gregory the pope, who said, "If anyone steals a widow for his wife, let him and those who consented be anathema."[32] We ourselves and the bishops of our kingdom informed our nephew Lothar verbally and in writing. And, as you know, we confirmed jointly with the counsel and advice of our faithful followers that none of us [i.e., the kings] should receive this kind of man in our kingdoms or permit him to stay, but should rather force him to return, to give account for himself and to do penance, as is decreed.[33] But what our nephew Lothar did toward us and our relative, and in truth against God and holy authority and the Christian communion, I hope is not hidden from you, since it is known to very many.[34] And St Paul, through whom Christ speaks, said, *Not only those who do such things, but those who consent to those doing them, are worthy of death* [Rom. 1:32].

6. The case of the wife [Theutberga] of our nephew Lothar is known to you, about which he asked for and heard advice from us and the bishops of our kingdom, and from the other bishops present: but he did not afterward follow that advice.[35] And we know too that he wrote

---

29 The same Roman synod of 721 quoted here is also quoted in *Annals of St-Bertin*, trans. Nelson, 97–8.
30 In other words, Charles was refusing to talk with Lothar II until he expelled Engeltrude, in line with the pope's instructions.
31 On this case, see Joye, "Le rapt de Judith par Baudoin (862)" and "Carolingian Rulers and Marriage," 112–14, as well as Stone, "'Bound from Either Side.'"
32 Not Pope Gregory I, but Pope Gregory II, in 721.
33 A reference to the Council of Koblenz in 860, where the three kings had agreed not to shelter troublemakers.
34 In other words, Lothar II had offered Judith and Baldwin assistance.
35 This could be a reference to Hincmar's *On the Divorce*, though there Hincmar does not name the people who had requested his advice.

to the lord pope about this, and afterward received letters from him.[36] We do not wish to deny that we know what the lord pope instructed him and some bishops to do about it. And we know, since we cannot and do not wish to deny it, and nor should we, that the command of the lord pope diverged in no way from evangelical truth and from apostolic and canonical authority: and we have not heard or seen that the instruction about this matter has been carried out.

For that holy see, first in the whole globe of the world, proclaims to us and to all Christians in all the world through the holy Paul, the celestial trumpet, who learned it from the Lord himself when he was taken up to the third heaven and to paradise, *Do not break bread with people of this kind* [1 Cor. 5:11]. And through the holy apostle John, who drew from the eternal and living fountain of Christ's breast, resting on it during the supper when the sacraments of our redemption were celebrated and handed down, and which he pledged for all the redeemed, the apostolic see very clearly forbids anyone to shelter a man of this kind in his home or even to greet him, *since who greets him communicates with his wicked works* [2 John 1:10–11]. And through the blessed pope Gregory, who says in his homily on Ezekiel that, "Just as he who withdraws from faith in God is an apostate, so without doubt he who withdraws from God in his works is an apostate,"[37] for, as the Apostle says, *faith without works is dead* [James 2:14]. And the Lord himself says about the person who is legally warned once, twice, and thrice and is not corrected, that he should be to us as a gentile and someone involved in public crimes, with whom apostolic and canonical authority instructs us not to break bread, as already mentioned.

7. Therefore, my only and dearest brother, take counsel from you yourself, and give counsel to me, and give counsel to our nephew for his salvation and honor, and offer help, as I am also ready to do with you, as much as God will grant me to know and to act, if he [Lothar] wishes to accept it.

8. The counsel that I recently received with my bishops and my other faithful followers, concerned both for our shared salvation and

---

36 This letter from Lothar II to Pope Nicholas I, informing him of the decision of the Council of Aachen in 862, does not survive, nor does Nicholas's reply, though it probably requested that a new church council be held: see Nicholas, *Reg.*, 574.
37 Gregory the Great, *Homilies on the Prophet Ezekiel*, bk. 1, homily 9, trans. Tomkinson, 161.

honor – that is, yours and mine, and for our nephew – and for the shared protection and salvation of all our faithful followers, both in a synod and in a council, I shall tell you, if you wish, you to whom I am prepared to deny no good thing and with whom I am prepared to share all my good things. And if it seems good counsel to you, let us take it together. And if you can show better advice to us, through reason and through divine and human authority, fitting to our salvation and to Christianity, I am ready to take it with all devotion, and very willingly to follow you, with God's help and with the assistance of the counsel and aid of our shared faithful followers.

9. Since it is written that the good king [David], who sinned like a man but acknowledged what he had done like a saint, said, *I shall confess to him from my own will* [Ps. 27:7], let our nephew declare before you and the bishops who are with you, and let him inform us through you and through those bishops, that he wishes to come before a general council, according to the apostolic lord's and episcopal, or rather divine, counsel, with his and our bishops and faithful followers and friends of God, since this is a general matter for all Christians.[38]

And let him show there that he carried out this action about his wife either according to a divine and human law suited to Christians, or according to the counsel of God and a law appropriate to a Christian king, and that he wishes and is obliged to amend those two things we mentioned above. And if he acts in this way, I am prepared to receive him with love and honor, just as a Christian king should receive a Christian king, and as a loving uncle should receive a beloved nephew, and to remain in his friendship for his salvation and honor. And let a suitable time and opportune place be decided upon, when we can peacefully come together and settle this matter for our joint salvation and honor, and that of our faithful followers, since it concerns ourselves, for as scripture says it is our flesh and blood. For we who ought to set a good example to our faithful followers and all Christians in goodness

---

38 That is, Lothar II should follow the advice of the pope and the bishops and arrange a general council to discuss his marriage. Hincmar of Reims had also demanded this path of action in the 858 Quierzy Letter (Document 3, p. 42) and in his treatise *On the Divorce*, trans. Stone and West, 114 and 284. See Heidecker, *The Divorce of Lothar II*, 90–1.

should not give an example for perdition, and we who ought to correct the wicked should not be the head of evil.

And we shall discuss and decide upon those matters which, as we mentioned, we promised at Koblenz we would discuss and maintain, so that we, who are attacked on all sides on account of our sins and the evil of discord which remains in our kingdoms, may deserve to receive the solace of God's mercy, once we have placated him. And let it not be hard for our nephew's mind to do this, for it is written, *Who is hard in mind, falls into wickedness* [Prov. 14]. But let him fear God, and restrain this scandal, which without any need has grown and spread so greatly in this Christendom [*christianitas*].[39] For to many people it seems to have been carried out without full reason or required authority, when it could have been brought to a proper conclusion through reason and authority. And since it is written, *Blessed is the man who is always fearful* [Prov. 28:14], and the Lord says, *I love those that love me* [Prov. 8:15], let him honor himself, his Christianity, and his royal name for the love and fear of God. And let him divest himself and all of us from that calamity which pursues him, and that through him and on his account pursues us, his relatives. And let him honor God, knowing that God says, *I will honor those that honor me; and those who despise me will be ignored* [1 Kings 2:30].

10. And if he prefers not to do this, let him do what he thinks should be done. I wish to remain in your friendship and due fraternity, and to promote it with all due service, and I seek not what is his, but he himself. But if I am not able to have him safely [as a friend], I am not willing to remove myself from God for his friendship, nor do I wish to offer help to anyone for ill.[40] For we read in scripture that God said to a king, *You offered help to the ungodly, and joined in friendship with those who hate me: therefore you have deserved the wrath of the Lord* [2 Chron. 19:2], and the rest that is written there. And again we read that an impious man who turns from some impiety, and says from his heart that he wishes to be converted, is no longer counted among the impious, but should and

---

39 That is, Lothar II's attempt to divorce Theutberga, which Charles significantly describes as a scandal (*scandalum*): on this concept, see de Jong, *The Penitential State*, 232–3. *Christianitas* seems here to have a territorial sense.

40 In other words, Charles insists that Christian obligations take priority over the ties of kinship.

safely can be piously welcomed by the pious. As the scripture says, *Turn around the impious, and they will cease to be* [Prov. 12:7], not that they will no longer exist in essence, but that they will not exist in the blame of impiety. We say all this, not because we wish our nephew to be counted among the number of the impious, but rather hoping that, numbered with the pious, he may be associated with God.

[Royal declarations drafted by Charles][41]

DECLARATION OF THE LORD LOUIS [THE GERMAN]

1. As those of you who were there know, when we recently met together with God's help at Koblenz, and decreed capitularies to be observed by ourselves and our faithful followers, we agreed that at a suitable time and opportune place we would meet again, and with the help of God and the counsel of our faithful followers, we would amend what needed to be amended in ourselves and our kingdoms and our faithful followers, and that we would decree what other emendations would be followed. We fixed a time and place on three occasions, but events occurred to myself, my brother, and our nephew, on account of which we were not able to carry out what we had arranged.

2. In the meantime, I heard that my brother and our nephew were not getting on as they had been when we met together. So I came to the decision that I should be a private mediator between them, so that they would get on as they should by right. Hence my brother informed my nephew, through me and our bishops, and through the bishops of our nephew, both in writing and orally, of the matters because of which he was no longer intimate with him as he had been before. And that if he wished to amend them as he had been advised, he [Charles] would be well disposed toward him, as a loving uncle ought to be to his beloved nephew, and as a Christian king ought to be to a Christian king. About these matters, we and the bishops who were with us from our nephew gave this response: that concerning those matters of which he was accused, he was ready either to amend or to give certain account of them

---

41 Note that these declarations were rejected at a preliminary meeting at Savonnières (this document, p. 87), so they were never formally read out to the whole assembly.

and to carry out a worthy satisfaction. Our brother and the bishops gratefully received this response, and thanks be to God, our brother and our nephew are now as they rightfully ought to be.

3. And we wish that, as we agreed before, faithful envoys should run between us, and that what should be amended in each of our kingdoms and what one of us indicates to another, should be amended, and the houses of God and the priests and servants of God will have the law and honor that is due. And that every faithful follower of ours will have law and justice in our kingdoms, no matter whose man he is, as was the case in the time of our predecessors, and as we now agree and as was decreed in those capitularies which our predecessor kings decreed, and which we confirmed at Meerssen,[42] and now recently decreed at Koblenz. This should happen until with God's help we shall meet again at a suitable time and opportune place, and with the counsel of our faithful followers discuss peacefully what has not been carried out, and then carry it out. And thus we may help each other, so that with God's help we can save ourselves and our faithful followers and resist the oppressors of the holy church. And with shared consent, we had this declaration[43] written down, so that each of us may have it, and may know what he must henceforth maintain, and how. For it is not fitting that a king should deviate from his declaration, just as it is not fitting that a bishop should diverge from his rightful preaching.

DECLARATION OF CHARLES

1. Those things which my beloved brother said that we decreed recently at Koblenz, I have up till now observed as far as I can, and I wish to continue observing, if they are also observed toward me. And I do not wish to accuse him of not having similarly observed them toward me. I believe too that he does not wish, and that no one is able, to accuse me of not having observed them toward him. And if someone does, I am prepared either to amend those things that need to be amended, or to give certain account for those things of which I have been accused.

---

42 A reference to a meeting of the Carolingian kings at Meerssen in 851.
43 The word I have translated as "declaration" is *adcognitatio*, a term that does not appear in classical Latin.

2. And if our nephew does what our brother and the bishops, who with him were mediators between us, announced on his behalf to us and the bishops who were with us, and as our brother now says, then he [Lothar II] will be a close friend and aid according to reasonable possibility, as a nephew ought to be to an uncle, and as a Christian king ought to be to a Christian king. And I wish to be an intimate friend and aid to him, according to reasonable possibility, as a loving uncle should be to a beloved nephew, and as a Christian king ought rightfully to be to a Christian king.

3. What our brother has just said about envoys running between us, and about amending what needs to be amended in our kingdoms, and about the state and honor of the churches and priests and servants of God, and about keeping law and justice to each of our followers in our kingdoms, whosoever's man he may be, both regarding he himself and his property, and about observing the capitularies: so I too wish to observe these things in all ways.

DECLARATION OF LOTHAR II

1. Since my uncle Louis accepted me in his bounty like a son, he has always acted toward me in his mercy as was fitting for him and as was needed by me. So I am ready to show him the service that is owed, as I should rightfully do.[44]

2. And about those matters which my uncle Charles recently sent me when we met together: I wish to observe them, as my uncle Louis and the bishops who along with him were mediators between me and my uncle Charles announced on my behalf to him and the bishops who were with him. And if he will be a private friend and aid to me, according to reasonable possibility, as an uncle should be to a nephew, and as a Christian king ought rightfully to be to a Christian king, so I wish to be a close friend and aid to him, according to reasonable possibility, as a loving nephew should be to a beloved uncle, and as a Christian king ought rightfully to be to a Christian king.

---

44 Louis had offered important support to Lothar II in 855 at a meeting in Frankfurt. However, the promise written here of Lothar II to show his uncle Louis the service "that is owed" (*debitum obsequium*) is perhaps designed to portray Lothar II as very much a junior member of the Carolingian family of kings.

3. What my uncles have just said about envoys running between us, and about amending what needs to be amended in our kingdoms, and about the state and honor of the churches and priests and servants of God, and about keeping law and justice to each of our followers in our kingdoms, whosoever's man he may be, both regarding he himself and his property, and about observing the capitularies: so I too wish to observe these things in all ways.

* * *

After these preceding declarations had been read out in front of all the almost two hundred counselors of the three kings who were present, including bishops and abbots and laymen, Louis and Lothar and their followers entirely rejected them, in order that they should not be read to the people [*populus*], so that the case of Lothar should be entirely unmentioned.[45]

So the lord Charles read out the declaration which follows in these very words at Savonnières in the evening, in the year 862, on the eleventh indiction, on the third day before the nones of November [November 3], in the same house where the previous declarations had been read out, in which a few others came in who had not been there before, since it had been almost full with them.

DECLARATION OF CHARLES

As I have advised to my nephew in writing and orally, through my brother and through the bishops of my nephew, and as they reported back to me on his behalf, so I wish to be a friend to him and to protect him, as an uncle should rightly protect his nephew, if he will protect me and my followers, as a nephew should rightly protect his uncle.[46]

---

45 This is a well-known passage for its evidence concerning the size of royal assemblies. In the *Annals of St-Bertin*, trans. Nelson, 103, Hincmar blames this decision specifically on a prominent aristocrat named Conrad.
46 In this heavily condensed version of Charles's originally planned speech, no reference is made to Lothar II as a "Christian king." Charles promises to *salvare* his nephew, translated here as "protect," though its basic meaning is to save.

7. BISHOP ADVENTIUS OF METZ WRITES TO ARCHBISHOP THEUTGAUD OF TRIER, EARLY 863

Most of our documentation for Lothar II's divorce is material that was designed to influence public opinion in one way or another. Underpinning the formal "policy" and ceremonies, however, were behind-the-scenes deliberations, briefings, and counter-briefings, as Gerd Althoff has suggested was typical for the Middle Ages.[1] Some of these informal or secret discussions were conducted through personal conversations, others through writing intended only for restricted circulation within the court's inner circle. Most of these ephemeral writings have been lost, but occasionally some do survive, such as the letter translated below. The letter was clearly thought to be compromising in some way, since it urged its reader to burn it after reading, but luckily for us a copy was nevertheless preserved.

The letter is from Adventius, bishop of Metz, to Theutgaud, archbishop of Trier, both bishops in Lothar II's kingdom. Technically, as archbishop of Trier, Theutgaud was Adventius's direct superior in the church hierarchy, since Metz lay in the ecclesiastical province of Trier (a province that also included the bishoprics of Verdun and Toul, as well as Trier itself). The precise powers a Frankish archbishop wielded over bishops in his province were contested in the period, but they were for the most part ceremonial. It is nevertheless striking that the tone of Adventius's letter is relatively curt and commanding. As we have seen, Adventius was one of Lothar II's key advisers; his position at court seems to have given him an informal authority that to some extent supervened over the formal church hierarchies.

In a letter tinged with anxiety, Bishop Adventius of Metz informs Theutgaud that he has met with Walter, who had come from the palace (probably Aachen, but potentially any of the network of royal palaces under Lothar II's control), bringing with him information about the king's mood and state of mind. According to Adventius, Walter had requested that he contact Archbishop Theutgaud of Trier with a message: that Theutgaud was not to give any advice to King Lothar before

---

1 See Althoff, *Rules and Rituals in Medieval Power Games*, esp. 61–73.

a council had taken place in Metz, the decision of which the king had agreed to follow in full. The letter reminds us that laymen were important royal counselors, even though the nature of our sources tends to play down their role; as we have seen already, Walter in particular seems to have been very close to Lothar II.[2]

Much about this letter is obscure, precisely because it was a "private" letter that assumed a great deal of shared knowledge. It is not dated, but we know it must have been written before late 863.[3] Most likely the planned council that the letter mentions was scheduled for February 863, to enable Lothar II to confess his sins in private and thus ward off a prospective papal excommunication.[4] If this dating is correct, it shows that the Council of Aachen in 862 had not resolved Lothar's marital difficulties; indeed there is evidence that some of Lothar II's opponents inside the kingdom had "leaked" its documentation to Pope Nicholas I and had asked him to arrange for a further council (which eventually took place in Metz in June 863).[5]

Whatever its precise date, Adventius's letter suggests that some of Lothar II's advisers, both secular and clerical, were growing worried about the gravity of the situation. In another missive written around the same time, Adventius mentions the possibility of a "reduction of the kingdom."[6] The letter also suggests, however, that some of Lothar II's advisers were capable of devising a coherent strategy, and of persuading the young king to follow it. Nevertheless, they were concerned that other groups at court saw things differently and might undermine this strategy, and they were concerned too that the king was wavering, hence the need to ensure that Theutgaud stayed "on message." The theatrical burn-after-reading instruction might have been intended to impress on Theutgaud the seriousness of the matter (it is rather undermined by the fact that Adventius kept his own copy of the letter).

---

2 On Walter, see Document 1, p. 13.
3 The letter is addressed to Archbishop Theutgaud, but in 863 Theutgaud was deposed by Pope Nicholas I, and Adventius accepted this judgment (see Document 11, p. 125).
4 Heidecker, *The Divorce of Lothar II*, 132–4; cf. Staubach, *Herrscherbild*, 189–92. Pope Nicholas I first explicitly threatened the excommunication of Lothar II in early 863, probably too soon for Adventius to have heard, but he might have anticipated this turn of events.
5 Nicholas, *Reg.*, 580.
6 *Regni minoratione*: Adventius, *Letters*, no. 15 (to Bishop Hatto of Verdun), 233 (cf. Staubach, *Herrscherbild*, 189).

The letter thus gives us a snapshot of "policy making" at Lothar II's court, as factions battled for the king's ear, offering alternative solutions to his predicament. Whether Theutgaud paid any attention to Adventius's secret letter, we cannot say, but the fact that the proposed Metz council in February does not seem to have taken place suggests that Lothar II was swayed by other, more optimistic readings of his options.

The letter is preserved along with several others relating to Lothar II's marriage in a collection apparently put together by Bishop Adventius of Metz himself, which survives only in an early modern transcription.[7]

Translation[8]

To the most reverend and holy father Theutgaud, cherished by us in all ways, Adventius, your devoted son and zealous supporter, wishes the peace of happiness and glory.

We humbly request through God and for God that no other mortal man should see this letter, but let hungry Vulcan consume it, once read.[9] Let your aged dignity fix this mature advice to the firmament of wisdom, as a safe anchor of prudence in faith: that you should not say anything to our lord [Lothar II] to the left or to the right at this moment, until all our brothers have met in Metz on the Purification of the Holy Mary [February 2], as they have all been certainly summoned.[10] For you should know for certain that our lord is decided in every way that he will promise to obey their collective advice in all things, whatever may seem best to them, according to God, and that, obeying their warnings and advice, he will do nothing else henceforth.

It is therefore fitting for you, dearest father, to act cautiously, lest (may it not happen) he may through vain hope wander from the path of God and apostolic texts, and incur the noose of Avernus.[11] For you

---

7 See Document 5, p. 55.
8 Edition: Adventius, *Letters*, no. 4, 214–15 (http://www.mgh.de/dmgh/resolving/MGH_Epp._6_S._214).
9 Vulcan was the classical god of fire; the convoluted phrase simply means burn after reading.
10 No records survive from this meeting of bishops in February 863, if it took place. It is possible that it was postponed to June that year, perhaps to accommodate the papal legates.
11 Avernus is a deep lake in Italy, reputed in classical times to be an entry point to the underworld.

may be certain that if he err through our fault or by some vain trust, that prophecy will be fulfilled, *I will demand his blood from your hands* [Ezek. 3:18].

We write these things because we today met Walter, the faithful follower [*fidelis*] of our lord, returning from the palace.[12] He told us this deliberation in confidence from the part of our lord, as we said, and many times requested that for the love of God we should tell these things to you, and that we should consider it in all ways, so that he [Lothar II] should not hear from you or in person anything that should make him waver from his salvation. It seems better to me to pretend to be ill, than that the sick stomach should reject the medicine prepared by God.[13]

8. KING LOTHAR II GRANTS A CHURCH TO THE CONVENT OF ST-PIERRE IN LYON, MAY 18, 863

Though his marital problems were a priority for Lothar II, they were not the only issue he had to deal with. In May 863, the king was in Lyon to arrange the partition of the kingdom of his younger brother Charles "of Provence," who had died earlier that year on January 24, leaving no children.[1] Charles was still young when he died, and he had been ill for a while; a contemporary stated that he had "long suffered from epilepsy." Throughout his short reign he had relied heavily on his aristocratic supporters, notably Count Gerard of Vienne. Already in 858, Charles had agreed that Lothar II would inherit his kingdom, which was based around Lyon, Vienne, and Arles, should he die without heirs.[2] Emperor Louis II of Italy, as Charles and Lothar II's older brother, took a different view; in the end the two surviving brothers divided the kingdom between them.[3] Lothar II's kingdom was thus

---

12 Probably Aachen. For Walter, see this document, p. 100.
13 In other words, it is better to do too much penance than too little.

***

1 Zielinksi, *Die burgundischen Regna 855–1032*, offers the best overview of Charles's short reign (855–63), a topic that is not well served in English.
2 *Annals of St-Bertin*, trans. Nelson, 87.
3 Offergeld, *Reges pueri*, 330–7.

considerably enlarged by the acquisition of the territories around Lyon and Vienne, while Louis II picked up Arles.

To mark his succession in Provence, Lothar II took the opportunity publicly to honor his deceased brother's memory by making a donation to the convent in which he was buried, St-Pierre of Lyons.[4] The donation was not insubstantial, consisting of a church together with thirty-five farms, but its true importance was symbolic. These farms were to pay for the lighting of the church, to represent Lothar's bond with the brother buried there.[5] Prayers were also requested for Lothar's brother Louis II, symbolizing the renewed friendliness between them.

This charter is also Lothar II's first to mention Waldrada, described here as his wife (*coniunx*), as well as their son Hugh. In other words, they were publicly acknowledged as part of Lothar II's household. As has often been noted, Hugh's name – which is conspicuously not one of the names Carolingian kings tended to give to their designated heirs, such as Charles, Louis, and Lothar – suggests that he had not been intended as a successor when he was born.[6] It may be that Lothar II and Waldrada had been hoping for another son after Waldrada's coronation as queen in the autumn of 862.[7] However, the couple's children after Hugh all turned out to be daughters (Gisela, Berta, and Ermengard, all royal names). Plans change, and this charter suggests that Hugh was now being primed as Lothar II's heir.[8] That Waldrada is described as wife and not queen is probably insignificant, since this title was not always used in royal charters. The appearance of his wife and son in a charter devoted to dynastic commemoration demonstrates Lothar II's (misplaced) confidence that his marital problems were now resolved, or shortly would be at the Council of Metz, which took place a month later. As such, the charter arguably marks the high point of Lothar II's reign, when things seemed to be finally going his way.

The charter survives in its original form, a sheet of parchment, and is now stored in the Bibliothèque Nationale de France in Paris (Collection de Bourgogne, vol. 75, n. 21).

---

4 Koziol, *Politics of Memory*, 106–8. Cf. the later donations for Lothar II's soul, Document 19, p. 172.
5 Fouracre, "Lights, Power and the Moral Economy," at 375–6.
6 Airlie, "Private Bodies and the Body Politic," 17.
7 See Document 5, p. 52.
8 For a different view, see McDougall, *Royal Bastards*, 85.

Translation[9]

In the name of Almighty God and our Savior Jesus Christ, Lothar, king by divine clemency.

If we grant something to the places dedicated to God on account of reverence for divine consideration, we have no doubt that this will assist us in acquiring the perpetual life to come.

Therefore let the entirety of the faithful followers of the holy church of God and of ourselves, present and future, know that when we came to the monastery established in honor of St Peter the prince of the apostles[10] in the town of Lyon between the Saône and the Rhône, we thought it appropriate – for the love of God and for the benefit of the souls of our father and mother and of our beloved brother Emperor Louis and of our brother Charles [of Provence] the former king, whose body is buried there, and so that divine mercy might more easily overlook our sins – that we should enrich this monastery with a gift of some of our property.

Therefore we ordered these documents of Our Excellence to be put together, by which we grant to this monastery of St Peter (or the church of St Mary) certain properties lying in the county of Maurienne: that is, the cell of St Maximin with the buildings around it, to which are known to belong thirty-five free and servile farms with all the properties and dependents rightly and legally pertaining to them.[11] Henceforth, let these properties serve in perpetuity for the lighting of candles and for supplementing the provision of the nuns who are constantly in the Lord's service there, for the reward of the abovementioned most pious princes and the salvation of our dearest wife [*amantissima coniunx*] Waldrada and our son Hugh.

And let none of our successors or any bishop dare to transfer the cell of that place with its properties and dependents to other uses, except

---

9 Edition: King Lothar II, *Charters*, no. 19, 414–16 (http://www.mgh.de/dmgh /resolving/MGH_DD_Lo_I._/_DD_Lo_II._S._414).

10 This is the convent of St-Pierre des Terreaux in Lyon, which was probably established in the seventh century. In the ninth century it housed around forty nuns and seems to have been under direct royal control. Very little is known of its history in this period. See Reynaud, *À la recherche d'un Lyon disparu*, 107.

11 The Latin term for these farms is a *mansus* (pl: *mansi*), meaning an agricultural holding.

solely, as we have said, for the daily provisioning and for the preparation of lighting. And so that this proof [*auctoritas*] of our grant may have an unbreakable confirmation, we have confirmed it with our own hand below, and ordered it to be sealed with our seal ring.

Signum of the glorious king Lothar.

Ercambald the archchancellor of the royal dignity authorized.

[in Tironian notes: *"Ercambald the archchancellor of the royal dignity authorized and subscribed: the lord himself ordered this to be made"*][12]

Dated in the fifteenth kalends of June [May 18] in the eighth year of the rule with Christ's support of our lord Lothar the glorious king, in the twelfth indiction; enacted at the city of Lyon. In the name of God, Amen.

9. BISHOP ADVENTIUS REFORMS THE MONASTERY OF GORZE, JUNE 863

In June 863, Lothar II hosted yet another church council, this time at Metz. Here he promoted a new argument that in truth he had been formally married to Waldrada before 855. That meant his marriage to Theutberga was a second marriage and therefore invalid.[1] This council was attended by Lothar II's bishops, but it was led by two Italian bishops, Radoald of Porto and John of Cervia, who were there as envoys or legates of Pope Nicholas I. The presence of these legates undoubtedly presented a challenge to the king, since Pope Nicholas seems to have intended that they would preside over a council to judge him; surprisingly, however, Lothar II won their consent to his marriage with Waldrada.[2]

The acts of the Metz council sadly do not survive, except for one or two snippets quoted in later texts, but a crucial insight into what

---

12 Tironian notes were a kind of shorthand used in Carolingian royal chanceries.

***

1 The most developed expression of this argument is in Adventius, *Letters*, trans. Dutton, *Carolingian Civilization*, no. 5, 387–9.
2 Nicholas, *Letters*, no. 10 (Nicholas, *Reg.*, 604), written in early 863, summoning the Frankish bishops to the Metz council, and *Letters*, no. 11, with instructions to the legates, make clear the pope's intentions.

happened there is offered by the charter translated below.[3] It is a formal record of measures taken by Bishop Adventius of Metz to improve the condition of the monastery of Gorze, which lay in his diocese. As such it may seem quite distant from the question of Lothar II's divorce, but closer inspection reveals it is very closely connected indeed.

The monastery of Gorze had been founded in the eighth century by a previous bishop of Metz, Chrodegang (†766).[4] It soon became a rich and powerful institution. In the ninth century, like all Frankish monasteries, its monks were supposed to live a communal life of holy prayer guided by the Rule of St Benedict.[5] According to Adventius, however, Gorze was in a terrible state because, at King Lothar II's command, it had been granted to a layman named Bivin. Bivin had acted as a titular or lay abbot, profiting from the monastery's revenues. Giving out monasteries in this way was a practice that was reasonably common in ninth-century Francia as a means to reward a king's important political supporters (indeed, Theutberga's brother Hubert had been a non-monastic abbot of St-Maurice in the Alps and was later granted St-Martin of Tours), but it often led to complaints that it resulted in a decline in monastic discipline, as expressed for instance by the West Frankish bishops in 858.[6]

In the charter, Bishop Adventius announced that Bivin had now been stripped of his control of Gorze, and a monastic abbot named Betto had been appointed to lead the community. Moreover, Adventius initiated the return of the monastery's long-alienated properties to enable its monks to carry out their spiritual duties properly.

All this might seem perfectly straightforward: a morally upstanding bishop rectifying a long-standing financial and spiritual problem affecting a monastery within his diocese and putting this important monastery back onto an even keel. However, there was more going on here than might be apparent at first glance.

---

[3] For some snippets from the lost council, see Nicholas, *Letters*, no. 53 (Nicholas, *Reg.*, 863), trans. d'Avray, *Dissolving Royal Marriages*, 35.

[4] On the foundation of Gorze, see Rosenwein, *Negotiating Space*, 99–114.

[5] See Kramer, "Monasticism, Reform, and Authority."

[6] See Document 3, p. 33. When Hubert (or Hucbert) fled to West Francia, Charles the Bald gave him other monasteries, notably St-Martin of Tours and Lobbes. Hubert was in minor clerical orders but was not a monk. For a broadly contemporary case study of Count Vivien of Tours, a lay abbot of similar status and a contemporary of Bivin, see Kessler, "A Lay Abbot as Patron."

Perhaps the first point is that Adventius did not commit to the instant restoration of the monastery's properties but undertook to oversee this as a gradual process over the coming years. That the Gorze monks complained about their poverty after his death suggests he may not have followed through. It is also apparent that although the blame for Gorze's impoverishment is put on Count Bivin, Adventius's own lay followers held some of Gorze's land too; in other words, the bishop had been complicit in the diversion of Gorze's revenues away from its monks. Nor had Bivin's tenure been quite as detrimental for the monastery as the charter implies. John Nightingale has shown how, under Bivin's control, the monastery continued to develop relations with local patrons and donors, and indeed Bivin's family retained strong connections with the monastery in later generations.[7]

More intriguing still is what had motivated Adventius to take action at this precise moment, several years after he had become bishop. The charter explains that the decision had been taken at the command of none other than the legates of Pope Nicholas I, Radoald of Porto and John of Cervia, at the Council of Metz.[8] The wording of the charter suggests their instruction to restore church property was general, rather than being targeted at Gorze; after all, how could Italian legates have known about the particular circumstances of specific monasteries in Lothar II's kingdom?

For this reason, we may suppose that the restoration of church, and perhaps specifically monastic, lands in Lothar II's kingdom was a condition imposed by the papal legates at the Council of Metz, in exchange for their confirming Lothar II's marriage with Waldrada (and perhaps as a way of winning over any doubting bishops). This was presumably what Pope Nicholas I was driving at when he later complained that his two legates had been corrupted. Yet Radoald and John may have believed they had achieved a good result, forcing the king to preside over a round of quite far-reaching "church reform" in exchange for their consent to his marriage.

Nevertheless, Lothar II's court had reason to be pleased too. Not only had the council been steered into approving Lothar II's marriage

---

[7] Nightingale, *Monasteries and Patrons*, esp. 39–50.
[8] On these legates, see Rennie, *The Foundations of Medieval Papal Legation*, 144–50.

with Waldrada, but it had also provided a convenient political opportunity. For the Count Bivin who was ceremonially stripped of Gorze's revenues was none other than Queen Theutberga's brother-in-law. Adventius had deftly used the legates' direct instructions at the council to legitimize further weakening the position of Queen Theutberga and her supporters, while at the same time burnishing his own reputation as a guardian of monastic discipline and cementing his control over a key asset in his diocese. It was a neat move, and one perhaps repeated elsewhere in the kingdom to strip Theutberga's allies of their wealth. No wonder that the papal legates were accorded the reward of entry into the Remiremont *Liber Memorialis* that was discussed above.[9]

The original charter of Adventius no longer survives, but it was copied into Gorze's twelfth-century cartulary (that is, a book collecting the monastery's charters together). This cartulary was unfortunately destroyed in the Second World War, but luckily not before the text had been edited. The Latin, written perhaps by one of Gorze's monks, is complex and sometimes hard to construe precisely; it is not impossible that the text was altered when it was copied into the cartulary in the twelfth century, to align it more closely to notions of monastic reform present at that time, but this can be no more than a suspicion.[10]

Translation[11]

The resourcefulness of pastoral office, while keeping watchful guard over the flock entrusted to it, does not fear to restrain the harshness of those who attack, disguised in sheep's clothing. Whoever therefore takes up the office on behalf of God, the eternal king, so that through the power of his name there should be no discrimination,[12] and the inviolate judgment of equity should be strengthened, should absolutely not dissimulate the freedom of truth. For as the Lord says, *You shall have distress in the world. But have confidence, because I have overcome the world*

---

9 Gaillard, *D'une réforme*, 44.
10 Cf. here Nightingale, *Monasteries and Patrons*; Gaillard, *D'une réforme*, 171n90, is, however, unconvinced by the suggestion of interpolation.
11 Edition: d'Herbomez, *Cartulaire de l'Abbaye de Gorze*, no. 60, 106–10.
12 Literally the "accepting of persons," that is to say, bending rules to favor particular individuals.

[John 16:33]. It is no small crime to share in another's sins. It is right that those who preside over the holy sees of churches for the appropriate exaltation of reason should keep watch with enormous care and great concern, so that the spiritual sheep may be able to carry out their holy warfare without any occasion of disruption.[13]

Therefore I, Adventius, by the grace of divine consideration bishop of the holy and venerable see of the city of Metz, exerting myself in guarding the people committed to me with diligent sagacity of mind, have restored to their proper state the monasteries and properties belonging to the magnificent altar of Stephen,[14] the most precious martyr of Christ, which had previously been seized from it after the death of my predecessor Drogo, archbishop of worthy memory.[15] This we have done not only through the confirmation of a royal edict issued by the most outstanding king Lothar,[16] but also by the authority of a synodal decision which was canonically held in our see, at the command of the great and universal pope Nicholas.[17] There we also accepted instructions from the legates of the Roman see, that we should restore the properties of our churches, as contained in the privilege which was enacted in that holy synod,[18] at the command of the legates of the blessed pope Nicholas, and with the consent of the bishops of many provinces.

It is clear to everyone how many losses our church has suffered, when monasteries have become the residences of secular men, and the inheritance of God has been stripped of almost all its due respect, at the behest of a wicked arrangement.[19] Among the losses caused by this plundering, one of the noblest of the monasteries in our diocese, which was established on the River Gorze in honor of the blessed apostles Peter and Paul and the blessed protomartyr Stephen, and where

---

13 The representation of monastic life as a kind of spiritual warfare was a common theme in the early Middle Ages.
14 That is, the altar of the cathedral of Metz, dedicated to St Stephen.
15 Archbishop Drogo of Metz died in 855. After his death, Metz had reverted to the status of bishopric (rather than archbishopric): see Document 1, note 16.
16 If Lothar II issued a charter on this topic, it has been lost, but it could have been merely a spoken command.
17 That is, the 863 Council of Metz.
18 This document is also lost, presumably as a consequence of Pope Nicholas I's decision to quash the council.
19 That is, the practice of appointing "lay abbots," vigorously condemned by Frankish bishops (see Document 3, p. 33).

the outstanding body of the blessed martyr Gorgon is kept buried,[20] suffered losses of its properties all around in the times of our predecessor [Drogo]. When the abbot of this monastery, Haldin,[21] was taken from this world's light, the situation was so bad that there was scarcely enough food for the troop of holy monks, which we cannot speak of without grieving. And when the abovementioned king Lothar decreed that this place should obey the command of laymen, committing it to a certain count Bivin, the supplies of food and clothing ran short, and so the observance of the Rule [of St Benedict] gradually declined, monastic religion weakened, the church buildings were deprived of any ornamental grace, and the altars were dishonored by the rain and their nakedness.[22]

I was wounded by the cries of lamentation, as the prophet lamented, saying, *Who will give water to my head, and a fountain of tears to my eyes? and I will weep day and night for my people* [Jer. 9:1]. For since my care for this monastery pressed upon me each day, a monastery which my predecessors had founded with a new and generous endowment, I went to the most glorious king Lothar and showed him the privileges and charters with which the holy place was adorned. I hastened to rescue it from the power of an illicit domination, and I established there an abbot of regular observance named Betto,[23] so that the monks, mindful of their profession, should not neglect to take up the collar of Christ's most gentle yoke.

For after my predecessor of blessed memory Archbishop Chrodegang had set up this monastery with its new endowment, and until the time of the terrible oppressions of the calamity already discussed, Gorze was governed by regular abbots,[24] who controlled and commanded the entirety of its associated assets.

Therefore, since with God's cooperation we have freed the monastery with all that pertains to it from this wicked and wrongful subjection, we decree that the monastery of Gorze, in honor of St Peter the apostle

---

20 The relics of the martyr Gorgon, brought from Rome by Bishop Chrodegang in 765, were Gorze's most important holy possession.
21 Abbot Haldin is last attested in 835: see Gaillard, *D'une réforme*, 168.
22 This is a classic, and somewhat clichéd, description of a monastery in need of "reform." Bivin is first attested as a lay abbot of Gorze in 856.
23 Betto was a close confident of Adventius: Document 11, p. 123.
24 Regular in the sense of abiding by the Rule of St Benedict.

and St Stephen the martyr, and where the famous martyr Gorgon glitters with wonderful praise of his virtues, will be governed according to the Rule.[25] And we have decided that it and all its property, restored to pristine conditions, will be in the hands of Abbot Betto and his successors forever. So, whenever one of our vassals or any person who holds benefices from its properties goes the way of all flesh, we absolutely prohibit that their sons and heirs will obtain these lands, but rather without delay, without any contradiction, they will be returned to Abbot Betto and to his successors and to the monks who fight on God's behalf there. If in the meantime it happens that we can conveniently make an exchange from the land we hold directly, or some of those lands which many still hold through our benefice, then we shall transfer our own land so that the complete restitution of the properties of St Peter may proceed.[26] The aforementioned abbot with the monks committed to him will inspect the loans and exchanges, and do what he judges to be useful. We reform the chapels of the villages and their endowments to their ancient condition, so that they may serve the necessities of the brethren as they did in the time of Theomar, abbot of that place.[27] The servants [*familia*] of this monastery will remain in the same condition of servitude to the monastery as they did in ancient times.[28] Finally, we humbly pray that this place, with all its appurtenances, may continue in the privilege of honor that is contained in the decrees of my predecessors. The estates of villages that have been bought, or which have been or will be given by noble men, will be perpetually at the use and disposition of the abbot and the monks, so that they may have a sufficiency in spiritual and temporal matters, and may be pleasing to God in perpetuity.

If I myself or any of my successors goes against or weakens what I have arranged to be maintained in the divine gaze, in reverence of God and the patronage of the saints located there, then let them know that they will have to give a terrible account on the day of trembling Judgment

---

25 That is, the monastic Rule of St Benedict.
26 The point of this convoluted sentence is that Adventius might give the monks some of his own lands in the place of those lands they had historically owned.
27 A somewhat cryptic instruction. Theomar is attested as abbot of Gorze between 762 and 776 (Gaillard, *D'une réforme*, 208).
28 A reminder that improving the conditions for monks did not mean improving the conditions for those who worked their lands.

for such sacrilegious daring, when the Lord, the most just Judge, will come to judge and to give due reward to each deed. And so that this decree of our decision should be kept for eternity and changed by no one, we have confirmed with the subscription of our own hand.

Adventius, bishop of the holy church of Metz, have confirmed with my own hand this privilege of restitution of church properties, and implore and humbly demand that it be strengthened by the hands of all my successors through Christ.

In the year 863, eleventh indiction, twenty-eighth epact, eighth year of the younger Lothar, at Metz, the monastery of St Peter and St Gorgon the martyr obtained this present completed deed for full restitution, as the authority of the most excellent pope Nicholas confirmed through his legates in that city, and as is contained in the privilege of St Stephen [of Metz].[29]

10. EBERHARD AND GISELA MAKE A WILL, c. 863

As will by now be clear, Carolingian kings such as Lothar II had by no means a free hand in their actions and decisions. Besides taking the interests of their royal relatives into account, and of course the views of their clerical advisers too, they had to build a working relationship with their lay aristocrats, that is to say the elite and wealthy families who underpinned their rule, for these kings had no salaried civil service as an alternative source of support.

If a king turned against an individual aristocrat, or simply failed to reward them adequately, the aristocrat always had the option of seeking better rewards in a rival king's realm, often with the help of relatives already there.[1] A well-connected aristocrat named Hugh, for instance, left Louis the German's kingdom for Charles the Bald's in the 850s,

---

29 This final clause implies that the charter was issued during the Council of Metz itself in June 863.

***

1 For analysis of some of the forty-six Frankish aristocrats present at the Council of Koblenz in 860, see Heidecker, *The Divorce of King Lothar II*, 135–7 (for a comprehensive survey, see Heidecker, *Kerk*, 215–19).

and then between 861 and 866 joined the court of Lothar II.[2] Kings could turn against entire families too, as we have seen in the case of Lothar II and the "Bosonid" family, but this was risky.[3] We have already seen what could happen when a sufficient number of magnates grew disenchanted with their king, since this situation is what lay behind the invasion of Charles the Bald's kingdom by Louis the German in 858 (see Document 3, pp. 19 and 46).

For the most part, the aristocratic calculations that were so important for kings are hidden from us, but one text that throws a spotlight upon them is the will translated below.[4] It was drawn up around 863 by a husband and wife named Eberhard (or Evrard) and Gisela, who were based at the court of Lothar II's brother, Emperor Louis II of Italy. This couple were not merely aristocratic but at the very top of the Frankish elite, and the will reveals their staggering wealth. In large part it reads like a treasure list, as it itemizes immense quantities of golden, silver, and ivory objects, from bejeweled swords to golden liturgical combs.[5] Some of these objects were probably of recent manufacture, while others may have been valued antiques. Eberhard and Gisela were literate and had built up a considerable library of sixty-two books, including multiple copies of key works, which were individually divided up among the couple's children, including their daughters.[6]

Nevertheless, the bulk of their wealth lay in landed estates, including the labor of the people who worked on them. The will does not give

---

2 Historians have identified this Hugh as belonging to an aristocratic group known as the Welfs; he was a cousin of both Charles the Bald and Lothar II. On Hugh, see Nelson, *Charles the Bald*, 177–80; and Heidecker, *The Divorce of Lothar II*, 136n155. Lothar II rewarded him with control of the archbishopric of Cologne; his defection back to West Francia may suggest that he had lost confidence in the future of Lotharingia, though it may also reflect Archbishop Gunthar's unwillingness to relinquish his see.
3 On Lothar II's relations with his aristocrats, see Heidecker, *The Divorce of Lothar II*, 52–62.
4 For a detailed study, see La Rocca and Provero, "The Dead and Their Gifts," whose dating of the will to 863/4 I follow here.
5 For discussion and identification of the "treasures" in this will, see Riché, "Trésors et collections d'aristocrates"; for a wider discussion of treasure in early medieval wills, see Reuter, "You Can't Take It with You."
6 Kershaw, "Eberhard of Friuli," provides a study of the intellectual currents that can be discerned from Eberhard and Gisela's library. The couple owned two copies of the life of St Martin of Tours, four Psalters, and three copies of Isidore of Seville's *Synonyms*.

a precise value or acreage, but it is obvious that Eberhard and Gisela were vastly rich, with property in what is now Germany, Italy, Belgium, and France; in contemporary terms, their portfolio was scattered across the realms of four Carolingian kings.[7] This spread of estates reflects the time before these separate kingdoms were formed in 843. For Gisela was a daughter of Emperor Louis the Pious, and she had married Count Eberhard, himself a member of a powerful family known to modern historians as the Unruochings, in around 836. Her and her husband's holdings had therefore been established when Louis the Pious ruled a united Frankish kingdom, though they had probably acquired even more lands afterward. It is Gisela's royal status that explains why the will was issued in both their names, rather than, as was more conventional, in the name of a single individual. All the property is described as joint, except a Psalter that Gisela had for her personal use.

Eberhard and Gisela were part of a powerful trans-Frankish elite, with contacts and connections, and indeed cousins, across the Frankish world. The existence of aristocrats of such standing posed a challenge for kings. Eberhard and Gisela doubtless had their own ideas about what made a good king and could even compare the rulers of their day with the great Frankish kings of the past recorded in a history book they owned. These were exactly the magnates who might most readily turn to another king if their own proved unsatisfactory in some regard. Eberhard would have known all the Frankish kings of his day personally, including Lothar II. He had been present with other aristocrats at the meeting between Lothar II, Louis the German, and Charles the Bald in Koblenz in 860; his wife Gisela, meanwhile, was respectively these kings' aunt (Lothar II), sister (Charles), and half-sister (Louis the German).

Yet such connections could also represent an opportunity for kings, for it meant that they had access to elite networks in neighboring kingdoms. Conversely, the plurality of kings posed a potential problem for aristocrats of this rank, because they depended on good relations with kings to maintain their status, and political fragmentation meant they might have to pick sides. Eberhard was chiefly loyal first to Emperor Lothar I, and then to Emperor Louis II of Italy, on whose behalf he

---

7 An indicative map of these estates is provided in Costambeys, Innes, and MacLean, *Carolingian World*, 304.

sometimes acted as an envoy. But what if this loyalty provoked one of the other Carolingian kings to confiscate whatever of Eberhard and Gisela's lands were within his kingdom, whether in retaliation or out of suspicion? This is indeed an eventuality that the will anticipates; should this happen, then the couple's younger sons were supposed to compensate their unlucky sibling.

The will can also be read as showing how families at the highest levels of the Frankish aristocracy were adapting to new political realities. To keep things simple, Eberhard and Gisela ensured that the three younger sons (two of whom were clerics) were each allocated coherent blocs of property, while the oldest son Unruoch (or Unroch) was granted the lion's share; the daughters were given only smaller portions of land.[8] The great spread of land that marked Eberhard and Gisela's holdings was becoming more difficult to sustain; as a result, the political divisions of the Carolingian empire were gradually being reflected in the strategies of elite families, as they planned ahead for an uncertain future.

The will survives only in a fifteenth-century copy made at the monastery of Cysoing, which Eberhard and Gisela founded; it is possible that the copyist omitted elements of the original, such as a prologue.

Translation[9]

I, Count Eberhard, with my wife Gisela, have decided to establish how our children ought to share our property among themselves in ownership after our death, without any impediment or quarrelsome animosity, divided by us reasonably and in detail, along with the slaves [*mancipia*][10] and other items [*mobilia*] which belong to us.

We wish our firstborn son Unruoch to have whatever property we have in Lombardy and Alemannia, with all that pertains to that property, that is in Lombardy and Alemannia, except Balingen and what

---

8 On the gendering of these bequests, and the role of the daughters in family commemoration, see Garver, *Women and Aristocratic Culture*, 94–8 and 145–6.
9 Edition: *Cartulaire de l'abbaye de Cysoing*, ed. de Coussemaker, no. 1, 1–5. I have drawn on the French translation by Lebecq, "Le testament d'Evrard et Gisèle de Cysoing," which also provides valuable commentary.
10 *Mancipia* here refers to the peasants working the land, with the implication that they were unfree.

belongs to it. The second, Berengar, we wish to have our estate at Annappes with all that pertains to it there, except Gruson, and our estate *Hildeina*[11] in Hesbaye with all which adjoins to it, and whatever we have in the county of Condroz. The third, Adalard, we wish to have our estate at Cysoing, and Camphin with all that pertains to it, and Gruson, and all that I have decided to give to the church at Cysoing, on condition that he will maintain that church in that condition in which I have established it, and not allow anything to be taken from those properties I gave to it, by himself or by anyone else.[12] And also our estate Somain. Our fourth son, Rodolph, we wish to have Vitry and Maistang, with all that pertains to those places, except the church at Vitry, which I decided to give to our church at Cysoing with all that pertains to it. And we wish that he will have whatever we have in *Scelleburd* that Matfrid[13] previously had, and all our properties that lie in the county of Texandria.

We wish to establish this partition so that if Adalard and Rodolph have fewer holdings [*mansi*] than Berengar, they can equalize among themselves with Annapes, including the slaves [*mancipia*] who belong there. We wish this division to be permanent among them, unless some king of the Lombards or the Franks or even of the Alemans – may it not happen, and we think it will not – takes the property divided up by us from one of the brothers, by violence or without cause.[14] Then we wish that they will share out the remainder among themselves equally.

About our daughters:[15] we wish that Engeltrude will have *Ermen* and *Maresham*. We wish Judith to have Balingen, and our estate in the district of *Moila* which is called Heelsum. We wish Heilwich to have Otegem and Luinge and Vendegies, and one holding [*mansus*] in Angreau.

We decree such a law about these properties that if one of the heirs rises up against another in some contention against what we have

---

11 Some of the lands mentioned in the will have not yet been identified, including *Hildeina*; in these cases, I have provided their names as they are written in the original Latin text, in italics.
12 In other words, Adalard is put in charge of the church at Cysoing.
13 Perhaps the count Matfrid who was the father of Engeltrude, wife of Boso.
14 Note that confiscation by kings is a possibility that Eberhard and Gisela take care to address. The geographical terminology they use to talk of the kings is intriguing.
15 Note that one of the daughters, Gisela, is not mentioned here, perhaps because she had already received her share of the inheritance when she became a nun in San Salvatore in Brescia, in northern Italy. She is, however, mentioned in this document, on p. 120.

decreed, or summons him to a public court, then the instigator who has dared go against our will shall pay whomever he has calumniated a thousand pounds of gold.

Of our movables, we wish our firstborn, Unruoch, to have the sword with the golden hilt and golden pommel, a dagger of gold and gems,[16] a belt with gold and gems, two spurs with gold and gems, a tunic embroidered with gold, a cloak embroidered with gold with a golden brooch; and we want him to have another sword, a water basin, a silver conch, a golden drinking vessel, two golden cups, a coat of mail, a helmet and a gauntlet to go with it, two leg guards, and a silver mortar with a pestle. Of the movables from our chapel, a pyx with a golden cross and a golden case,[17] a silver chalice with a paten, a golden crown with the Lord's wood,[18] a golden cross with a crystal on a canopy, two chasubles, one prepared with gold, the other with silk, a dalmatic prepared with gold,[19] three altar cloths prepared with gold, two phylacteries hanging from a cross,[20] a Gospel prepared with gold, golden funnels, two armbands prepared with gold, a missal prepared with silver and gold, a similar lectionary, a water basin, a silver conch, a silver thurible, a gold pipette, ivory tablets prepared with gold, a golden liturgical comb, a silver fan, an ivory casket, two silver candelabras:[21] all this we wish that our firstborn son shall have.

Our second son, Berengar, we wish to have two swords, one with a silver and golden hilt, a dagger of silver and gold, two belts with gold and gems, two golden spurs, a tunic prepared of gold, another golden dagger with gems, two vessels of horn and silver with gold, two silver shields, two silver spoons, a coat of mail, a helmet, and a gauntlet. From the movables of our chapel, a silver altar, an ivory chalice with a golden

---

16 A *facilus*, a term not found in classical Latin.
17 A pyx is a vessel for holding the consecrated bread.
18 That is, a fragment of the holy cross.
19 A dalmatic was a liturgical vestment worn by clerics. On the importance of these gorgeously decorated ecclesiastical vestments, see Miller, *Clothing the Clergy*.
20 In the will, a "phylactery" probably means a small portable container for relics (below, one is listed as containing relics of St Remigius). The so-called "Talisman of Charlemagne," a sumptuous example of ninth-century jewelry now stored in Reims, gives an indication of what they might have looked like. See Panczer et al., "The Talisman of Charlemagne." Another similar reliquary, now in Monza, Italy, is associated with Berengar, one of Eberhard and Gisela's sons.
21 These objects all had liturgical functions.

paten, an ivory casket prepared with gold, a phylactery of silver with gold, a Gospel decorated with ivory, a similar lectionary, a similar missal, a similar commentary,[22] a similar antiphonary, a similar Smaragdus,[23] a silver thurible, two chasubles, one with fur, the other with silk, a fur dalmatic, a similar one of silk, a cloth for the altar, two tablets for singing,[24] prepared in silver and gold. We wish Berengar to have all this.

Our third son, Adalard, we wish to have two swords, one with an ivory and silver hilt, a similar dagger, an ivory and gold belt, another golden dagger, and two golden belts with gems, a drinking cup of marble prepared with silver and gold, a silver goblet,[25] a silver cup, two palliums,[26] silver cups with two drinking vessels, a coat of mail and a helmet with a hauberk, a gauntlet and two leg guards. From the movables of our chapel, an altar of crystal and silver, a casket of gold and silver, a glass chalice prepared with gold, a silver chalice with a paten, a gospel prepared with silver, a doubled chasuble, another chasuble with silk, a dalmatic, a piece of silk, an altar cloth, a phylactery with the relics of St Remigius: all this we want Adalard to have.

Our fourth son, Rodolph, we wish to have three swords, one hundred mancuses,[27] a belt, two silver drinking vessels, three spoons, a coat of mail, two gauntlets. Of the movables from our chapel, a crystal box with relics, a phylactery made of crystal and almandine garnet, a silver phylactery, a wooden chalice with gold and silver, a silver chalice with a paten, two chasubles, one altar cloth: all this we want Rodolph to have.

Our daughter Engeltrude we wish to have a silver plate and one pallium. Judith we want to have a silver plate, and one pallium. Heilwich we want to have a silver vessel, and a pallium. To all of these, so they do

---

22 Probably an exegetical commentary on a book of the Bible; for the purposes of the will, its ivory decoration – presumably in the form of a carved cover – was more important than the details of its authorship or subject.
23 That is, a work by the Carolingian author Smaragdus of St-Mihiel, perhaps his liturgical work the *Liber Comitis*.
24 *Tabulae ad canendum*: presumably wax tablets intended for liturgical chant.
25 *Garale*: a term not found in classical Latin (cf. "grail").
26 A *pallium* is a length of fabric, which could be used to decorate an altar or as an ecclesiastical vestment, but could be a term for fabrics used for secular purposes, as probably here.
27 A *mancosus* or *mancus* was a term often used to refer to gold coins. The Carolingian rulers minted gold coins only very rarely (see Document 2, pp. 16–19), but such coins were widely made in the Islamicate world, as well as in the Byzantine Empire.

not seem to lack the blessing of our chapel, we give individual phylacteries made of gold.

We also wish to divide the books of our chapel among them. First of all we wish Unruoch to have our double Psalter,[28] and our Bible,[29] and the book of St Augustine *On the Words of the Lord*, and the book *On the Laws of the Franks, Ripuarians, Lombards, Alemans and Bavarians*,[30] and the book *On Military Matters*,[31] and the book *On Various Sermons* which begins "About Elias and Achab,"[32] and the book *On the Use of Penance*, and the book *On the Constitutions of Rulers and Edicts of Emperors*, and the *Synonyms* of Isidore, and the book *On the Four Virtues*,[33] and the Gospel, and the *Book of the Bestiary*[34] and the *Cosmography* of Aethicus Ister.

Berengar we wish to have the other Psalter, written in gold, and the book of St Augustine *On the City of God*, and his *On the Words of the Lord*, and the *Deeds of the Roman Pontiffs*,[35] and the *Deeds of the Franks*, and the books of Bishops Isidore, Fulgentius, Martin, and the book of Ephrem and the *Synonyms* of Isidore, and the book of glosses, explanations, and days.[36]

Adalard we want to have the third Psalter which we have for our use, and the *Commentary on the Letters of Paul*, and the book of St Augustine *On the Words of the Lord*, and *On the Prophet Ezechiel*,[37] and the lectionary on the Epistles and Gospels written in gold, and the *Life of Martin*,[38]

---

28 This book possibly survives in the Vatican Library (Biblioteca Apostolica Vaticana), shelved as Reg. Lat. 11, with an ex libris of *Euuardus*, i.e., Eberhard (see Kershaw, "Eberhard of Friuli," 82).
29 Complete Bibles were relatively rare in the ninth century.
30 This legal compilation was edited by Lupus (of Ferrières?) in the 830s and presented to Eberhard; it survives in two slightly later copies.
31 By the Roman author Vegetius: perhaps to be identified with the manuscript Biblioteca Apostolica Vaticana, Vat. Lat. 4493. King Lothar II was presented with some extracts from Vegetius around the time of his accession: see Document 1, note 4.
32 Probably by Ambrose of Milan.
33 Probably a work by Martin of Braga.
34 See on this Dorofeeva, "Miscellanies, Christian Reform and Early Medieval Encyclopaedism."
35 That is, the *Liber Pontificalis*.
36 Precisely what work lies behind this title is not clear. Lebecq, "Le testament d'Evrard et Gisèle de Cysoing," suggests it could be a book by the Venerable Bede, but Grondeux, "Le rôle de Reichenau," suggests it refers to a book of glossaries (something like a modern dictionary or encyclopedia) and an exegetical commentary on the book of Genesis, known as the *Explanatio sex dierum*.
37 Presumably the homilies of Gregory the Great, cited in Document 3, p. 26, and Document 5, p. 92.
38 Probably the *Life of Saint Martin of Tours* by Sulpicius Severus. Another copy was given to Rodolph.

and the book of Anianus,[39] and the volume of *Seven Books* of the great Paul Orosius, and the book of Augustine to Jerome the Priest, on what James said: "Whoever keeps the whole law, and offends in one item, he is guilty of everything."

Rodolph we wish to have the Psalter with its exposition which Gisela has for her use,[40] and Smaragdus, and the *Collectaneum*, and Fulgentius, and the everyday missal which we always have in our chapel, and the *Life of St Martin*, and the *Physionomia* of Loxus the doctor,[41] and the list of the earlier rulers.[42]

Our firstborn daughter, Engeltrude, we wish to have the book called *The Lives of the Fathers*, and the book which is called the *Book of the Doctrine of St Basil*, and the Apollonius, and the *Synonyms* of Isidore. Judith we want to have one missal, and the book which begins from the sermon of St Augustine *On Drunkenness*, and the Lombard law, and the book of Alcuin to Count Wido.[43] Heilwich we want to have one missal, and a passionary[44] and a book of prayers with psalms, and a little book of prayers. Gisela we want to have a book *On the Four Virtues*, and the *Enchiridion* of St Augustine.[45]

All this we wish to remain divided among them in this way after our death, whenever it happens. From this day on, whatever we acquire in movable or immovable property, if the Almighty grants us life and health, and if we have not made arrangements before our death, whether in agricultural land or in livestock in our property which we have divided or in our benefices, we wish that Unruoch and the rest of our faithful followers, who are present when we decided this, will distribute half of it for the salvation of our soul, both

---

39 A Roman law collection better known as the Breviary of Alaric.
40 In other words, as a kind of private prayer book.
41 Physiognomy focused on how a person's character and emotions could be discerned from their physical appearance: an intriguing book for Eberhard and Gisela to own. For more details on what this book might have been, see Bricout, "Note sur deux laïcs," 460–1.
42 *Ordo priorum principum*: presumably a history book about the Frankish rulers.
43 A "mirror for princes," giving advice on moral conduct for secular officeholders.
44 A book detailing the martyrdom (or "passions") of the saints.
45 The daughter Gisela, who was already by this date a nun at Brescia, is mentioned only here. Although she had probably already received her share of the lands when she entered the convent, her parents reserved two books for her.

in Francia and in Lombardy and Alemannia, whether in ownership or in benefice, as we mentioned.[46] Our slaves [*servi*] whom we were pleased to free in these places from our holdings, whether in Francia or Lombardy or Alemannia, we wish that they will be free, and those we wished to give to someone, we shall keep in our power while we are alive. And similarly for our dependents [*familia*] who are not on our holdings, but whom we have acquired from elsewhere, we wish that whichever of our children we give them to, they shall be given without the others disputing it. We wish that all these things shall remain thus.

I, in the name of God Count Eberhard, with my wife Gisela, have made this testament of division between our children, whose names are these: Unruoch, Berengar,[47] Adalard, Rodolph, Engeltrude, Judith, and Heilwich, in the presence of our faithful followers who were present, whose names are these: Adalroch our nephew, Wellebert the priest, Werimbert, Lanfrid, Drumar, Uto, Diso, Engelhad, Heribert, Otpert, Fredeco. Made in the county of Treviso, in our estate at Musestre, in the reign of the august Louis [II], in the twenty-fourth year of his reign, Christ willing.

11. BISHOP ADVENTIUS OF METZ WRITES TO POPE NICHOLAS I, EARLY 864

If Lothar II thought that the Council of Metz in June 863 would square things with Pope Nicholas I in Rome, he had made a catastrophic miscalculation. Even though Nicholas's own legates had been involved in the council's confirmation of the king's marriage to Waldrada, the pope's reaction when presented with the acts of the synod was volcanic. At a council held in Rome on October 30, 863, Nicholas quashed the synod and deposed both of Lothar II's key archbishops, Theutgaud of Trier and Gunthar of Cologne. He then sent letters announcing this

---

46 Note how this clause cements Unruoch's position as leader of the next generation of the family.
47 Berengar would become king of Italy in 887, and later emperor.

decision north of the Alps, including to Lothar II himself, blasting him for having failed to control his own body.[1]

The pope's annulment of a church council and deposition of two archbishops was unprecedented in a Frankish context and evidently had not been anticipated by King Lothar II and his advisers. The outraged Archbishop Gunthar, who refused to accept the sentence, complained that the pope wanted to become "emperor of the whole world."[2] Exactly why Nicholas took this dramatic and unprecedented course of action is difficult to say, in part because the acts of the Metz synod that so angered him have not survived. However, the pope had been following Lothar II's case for some time (Theutberga may have first appealed to him as early as 859, as well as in 860, and again in 862),[3] and as already noted he had sent two legates to participate in the 863 Metz council, which he had assumed would force the king to recall Theutberga.

It is likely that perceived slights to his authority as pope were as important to his thinking as technical legal questions about remarriage. Nicholas had a high opinion of his office, as demonstrated by his deposition, on a quite different matter, of the archbishop of Ravenna in 861, as well as by his turbulent relations with the emperors and patriarchs in Constantinople, which consumed a good deal of his energy.[4] He even attempted to summon representatives of the whole Frankish church to Rome in 865 (though in the event the bishops did not attend).[5] It is no wonder that the nature of

---

[1] Council: Nicholas, *Reg.*, 670. For the letter to Lothar II, see Nicholas, *Letters*, no. 22 (Nicholas, *Reg.*, 677): "Thus you decided to yield to the agitations of your body, and loosening the reins of pleasure, you threw yourself into a lake of misery and a filthy and forbidden mud, so that you, who were put in place to lead peoples, have become a ruin for many ..." Only a fragment of the letter's content survives: perhaps it was too damaging for Adventius to copy. The text of Nicholas I's letter to Archbishop Hincmar of Reims was copied into the *Annals of St-Bertin*, trans. Nelson, 107–10, while part of his letter to Archbishop Ado of Vienne is translated in d'Avray, *Dissolving Royal Marriages*, 20–2.

[2] Gunthar's letter was copied into the *Annals of St-Bertin*, trans. Nelson, 113–16.

[3] See Nicholas, *Reg.*, 496, 508, and 575.

[4] On the deposition of Archbishop John of Ravenna, see Belletzkie, "Pope Nicholas I and John of Ravenna." On Nicholas I's stance toward Patriarch Photios of Constantinople, see the still classic Dvornik, *Photian Schism*, esp. 91–131.

[5] Nicholas, *Letters*, no. 32 (Nicholas, *Reg.*, 724); the summons has been described as a novelty in the history of synodal law.

Nicholas's pontificate is debated, with some historians seeing him as a prefiguration of later medieval popes.[6]

Whatever its motivation, the decision of Pope Nicholas to annul the Council of Metz in 863 threw Lothar II into a new and perilous position. The extent of this transformation is expressed in the letter translated below, which is Bishop Adventius of Metz's response to a circular letter sent by the pope in October 863, announcing the decisions he had taken.[7] As we have seen, Adventius had been one of Lothar II's close advisers, albeit not a constant member of the king's innermost circle. Yet his letter to Nicholas comes across as a groveling capitulation. Rather than defending the decisions taken at the Metz council, or offering support to his deposed colleagues, Bishop Adventius extols the papacy's authority, promises that he will studiously avoid contact with Gunthar of Cologne, and explains that he himself had hardly been involved with the Metz council (even though it had been held in his own episcopal city, as he had proudly noted at the time), and that he had simply followed the lead of the archbishops, as canon law required. Moreover, he declared that he knew very little about Lothar II's marriage with Theutberga since at that time (855) he was not yet a bishop.

The lack of resistance to Nicholas's intervention that this letter exemplifies is striking. However, it does not mean that Bishop Adventius had switched sides; he would continue to offer valuable support to King Lothar II (see Document 17, pp. 163–7). Rather, he seems to have recognized that it was futile or dangerous to resist the pope's decision directly, and that the situation called for different tactics from those that Lothar II had employed hitherto. Better, the letter implies, to try to win over the pope through emollient flattery. Adventius did not shrink from seeking support elsewhere too. He sent a legate (Betto, whom he had recently put in charge of the monastery of Gorze: see Document 9) to ask King Charles the Bald to write to Nicholas on his behalf, which Charles duly did, describing Adventius as a "faithful follower and friend" – another

---

6 Noble, "Pope Nicholas I and the Franks." The *Regesten* of Pope Nicholas I's activities published by Klaus Herbers in 2012 includes a valuable introduction in German on the sources for Nicholas's pontificate.

7 The version addressed to Adventius does not survive, but a version addressed to Hincmar of Reims was copied into the *Annals of St-Bertin*; a version addressed to the bishops of Louis the German's kingdom was copied into the *Annals of Fulda*; and Archbishop Ado of Vienne kept his own copy (Nicholas, *Letters*, no. 18; Nicholas, *Reg.*, no. 671).

reminder of the personal relationships that crisscrossed the Frankish kingdoms.[8] In September 864, Nicholas replied, forgiving Adventius for his involvement in Metz, so the bishop's efforts paid off.[9]

Adventius's letter is undated, but was probably written in the spring of 864. It is preserved, like most of Adventius's other letters, in a single early modern manuscript now in Rome (see Document 5, p. 55), based on a now lost medieval manuscript.

Translation[10]

To the most glorious shepherd of the Lord's flock, the blessed lord Nicholas, highest and universal pope: Adventius the humble bishop of the see of Metz, greetings now and in eternity.

Christ, the Lord God, looking after the flock he acquired with his own blood with his own accustomed piety, gave to you the dignity of the highest priesthood. Among the many ornaments of spiritual virtues with which you adorn the holy mother church in inimitable sanctity, let the holy dogma of ancient authority shine forth, through which the Christian people, happily endowed with the effective example of such a father, may avoid the traps of sin and, with God's help, seize the eternal prize; and may the discipline of the ecclesiastical order remain inviolate in your times. For this My Smallness and all those entrusted to me by divine grace, rejoicing with me, give thanks to Almighty God. And we plead with devoted prayer that Almighty God may deign to keep Your pontifical Highness long unharmed, to the consolation of your holy church and of all faithful souls.[11]

The decrees[12] of Your most excellent Apostolicity were sent to us while we were occupied with the most savage attacks of the pagans[13] and the most intense disputes of perverse Christians, and were hoping to manage the care of the Lord's flock according to Our Humility's

---

8 Adventius, *Letters*, no. 9: *nobis fidelis et amicus*.
9 Nicholas, *Letters*, no. 31 (Nicholas, *Reg.*, 721).
10 Edition: Adventius, *Letters*, no. 8, 219–22 (http://www.mgh.de/dmgh/resolving/MGH_Epp._6_S._219).
11 The letter begins with a flattering introduction.
12 That is, the letter sent by Nicholas I in October 863 to the Frankish bishops (Nicholas, *Reg.*, 672, and in *Annals of St-Bertin*, trans. Nelson, 107–10).
13 Presumably the Northmen.

capacity. I would have wanted immediately to rush to give a response to them to the dignity of Your Majesty in person, were not great old age weighing me down, and were not persistent ill-health pressing me often and unexpectedly to breathe out the spirit.[14] For I would have had a great and almost complete joy, if the weakness of my health had permitted me to go to the threshold of the apostles and into your most desired and preeminent presence.

But because the pain of gout and my aged limbs deny what I seek, I commit the measure of My Smallness to the omnipotent God and to holy Peter and to your incomparable mercy, you who hold the delegation of God, and you who sit as the true apostle on the most revered throne of the great prince, so that I may be succored by your solace. For if I have been deceitfully defamed in the sight of Your Gentleness as if a supporter of vice, I humbly beg that you will not disdain to accept in the paternal mood of piety the explanation of my excuses, not overshadowed by the fog of any lies.[15] These explanations I have taken care to set out to Your Mercy one by one.

Chapter 1. In no way do I accept into the catalogue of bishops the former archbishop Theutgaud, who up to now has patiently borne the sentence of his deposition carried out by you according to preceding custom, and has not at all dared to touch anything of the sacred ministry.[16] But as a very meek man, he declares that he has foolishly fallen by his own speech, deceived by the most pertinacious obstinacy of someone else, and setting out on the path of humility and obedience, he awaits an opportunity of satisfaction from your pious generosity.[17]

Chapter 2. I do not count Gunthar, former archchaplain of the sacred palace, in the list of bishops, nor do I dare to enter into communion with him or his supporters, since he has made use of the

---

14 In other words, Adventius claims to be at death's door and thus unable to travel to Rome in person. He lived for at least a decade longer, which suggests a certain level of hyperbole.

15 Adventius appears to have been worried about what other people had been telling the pope about him.

16 That is, Theutgaud has not carried out any liturgical ceremonies. Nicholas I's October letter had expressly requested the exclusion of Theutgaud and Gunthar from the "catalogues."

17 Archbishop Theutgaud accepted his deposition by Pope Nicholas I. According to Adventius, Theutgaud blamed "someone else" for deceiving him, who in this context can only be Gunthar.

forbidden office and has not feared to treat as nothing the apostolic excommunication.[18]

Chapter 3. These former primates of the church, with other archbishops and their co-bishops, discussed the case of the most pious king Lothar concerning his two wives in the presence of your legates in our city, and took the leadership of our teaching [*magistratus*].[19] It is not hidden to Your Holiness what they decreed about the complaint of our ruler. By the witness of God with his angels and archangels, I thought that these things, which were spoken with the agreement of many consuls, were pure and true. Alone amidst the decisions of the already mentioned archbishops and bishops at the time, and least in merit and in ordination, who was I to resist the authorities and judgments of the teachers? I feared that I might in some respect go against the decretal of Pope Leo, who at Title 32 wrote thus: "Therefore according to canons of the holy fathers established by the Spirit of God, and consecrated by the reverence of the whole world, we decree that metropolitan bishops should keep intact the rights of their ancient dignity over their provinces handed down to them."[20] If they strayed from the rules set down either by license or by presumption, I was entirely unaware of it. And so it is written in Chapter 9 of the Council of Antioch, "It behooves bishops through all the regions to know that the metropolitan bishop bears the responsibility for the whole province. Because of that, let all those who have issues in all respects come to the metropolitan," and so on.

I know of what happened at the origins of that already mentioned complaint only by the account of many, by ear and not by sight, since I was not then a bishop but was busy keeping watch in the temple of the blessed Stephen the protomartyr,[21] and had only very recently been sought out from the clergy in the kingdom of my lord [*senior*] Lothar and elected by the people; God knows that I took on the care of the

---

18 Unlike Theutgaud, Archbishop Gunthar continued to contest the papal deposition. See Document 16, p. 155, note 4.
19 That is, the Council of Metz in 863.
20 Pope Leo I, *Letters*, letter 14 to Bishop Anastasius of Thessalonica (JK 411), trans. Feltoe, 56. On Pope Leo (†461), see now d'Avray, *Papal Jurisprudence*, 106–19.
21 That is, Metz cathedral. Adventius claims that because he had not yet been appointed as bishop at the time Lothar II married Theutberga, he knew little about what had happened. Adventius, who had been a canon at Metz, was ordained bishop of Metz on August 7, 858, after the see had been vacant for three years.

pastoral office not for ambition, but because I was canonically invited. It may be that I was much more trusting in the words of the archchaplain [Gunthar] and the other fathers who were present than they were to me: and if I perhaps acted naïvely in some regard, then it remains for me to hasten back to the teacher of truth. Let your unique wisdom determine the rule in this matter, and behold, I am ready to obey the edicts of your authority as if obeying God, on whose behalf you make determinations. I rely on your holy and healthy advice, and I humbly submit myself to the yoke of obedience.

For although I am aware of the commotion of criticism raised against me by some people's foolishness, no one can accuse me in this matter of anything except naïvety [*simplicitas*]. For I faithfully say, *Behold my witness is in heaven, and he who knows my conscience is on high* [Job 16:20]. And the vessel of election says, *Our glory, that is the testimony of our conscience* [2 Cor. 1:12]. And blessed Pope Gregory writes thus in the letter to the patrician Theoctista: "in all things," he says, "that are said about us externally, we should hasten back to the inner secrets of the mind. And if someone's conscience does not accuse him, then he is free even if everyone else blames him."[22]

Chapter 4. If the decree of Your Authority, by the judgment of the Holy Spirit, determined that the already mentioned metropolitans have been deprived of all power of the pastoral office for their excessive ordinances and for their absolution of the anathema issued by the apostolic see upon Engeltrude the wife of Boso: then know most truthfully that I was not at all involved in that absolution.[23] After I heard by truthful account that she was wounded by an inauspicious kind of adultery, I have always abominated her like a lethal poison. I advise everyone to in no way have communion with the excommunicated, if they dare to use sacred things, as the fourth chapter of Antioch shows, which orders all those communicating with them to be thrown out of the church.

Chapter 5. I absolutely deny that I am a supporter of the condemned or that I am seditious, or that I am guilty of plotting or conspiracy.[24] I declare that I in no way agree with those supporting such things.

---

22 Gregory the Great, *Letters*, bk. 11, letter 27, trans. Martyn, 3:764. Theoctista was the sister of the emperor Maurice, described here with the honorific title *patricia*.
23 On Engeltrude, see Document 6, pp. 90–1.
24 This is a direct reference to Nicholas I's October letter (Ch. 3).

Rather, I state that in all things and canonically I support the head, that is the holy and venerable seat of blessed Peter, to whom he gave the keys of the kingdom of heaven, on which stone Christ the eternal king built his holy church, against whom the gates of hell will not prevail.

But the sanctity of Your Paternity has inviolably decreed that in no way should the loss of honors be feared on account of presumptuous acts or subscriptions,[25] and that pardon will not be denied, if we agree with you and take care to send our assent in writing, whether in person or through our legates. Let the most generous Sanctity of your preeminence know that our legate, who now has shown you the already mentioned profession and has clarified it with many words, was delayed because I called our other co-brothers from various places together, encouraging them to perceive and think like you.[26] Once I had ascertained the unanimity of them all, then placed at the edges of this present life, I sent to Your holy Paternity this legate as a herald, the present bearer of these letters. I allow nothing uncertain or condemnable to remain in me, to whom the dissolution of my own body promises to set out on the path of all flesh. But I trust greatly in the mercy of the omnipotent God, that he may concede to me as a sinner the space of this calamitous life, until, purged by a worthy satisfaction, I shall know that the grace of your paternal piety has been restored to me who seeks it, and I may be congratulated as accepted back into your fellowship which is worthy to God.

For we believe that with the support of God and of the prince of all the apostles, you, spiritually occupied in almsgiving and fasting and secret prayers, ought to take care with all your strength and by divine disposition that the limbs living in the body of Christ should not perish because of a false deception. Therefore if Your Mercy is in any way swayed by my tearful prayers, I humbly beg through the holy and

---

25 A reference to the acts of the Council of Metz to which Adventius would have given his signature. Adventius here is alluding to a section of Pope Nicholas I's letter of October 863: see this document, note 12.

26 Note that Adventius here says that he has taken on a leadership role among Lothar II's bishops. A letter similar to his was sent to Nicholas I by Rathold, the bishop of Strasbourg, and it seems likely that Bishop Franco of Liège wrote along the same lines, possibly both as a result of Adventius's coordination. The legate Adventius mentions was the monk Betto, who had recently been appointed abbot of the monastery of Gorze (see Document 9, p. 106).

individual Trinity that through the bearer of these letters, I, placed in the shipwreck of life, may deserve to receive from your holy hand, if nothing more is possible, what your gentle master Christ said to some of the disciples hesitating before the closed doors, when he appeared to them and prayed, *Peace be with you* [John 20:26].

We humbly beg with assiduous hopes and prayers that the Excellence of your holiness will long thrive unharmed.

12. THE BISHOPS OF LOTHARINGIA WRITE TO THE BISHOPS OF WEST FRANCIA, c. 865

The royal battle for the moral high ground that formed the backdrop to Lothar II's divorce case was not a purely abstract or theoretical contest. It had potentially serious consequences for the distribution of power, and by 865 Lothar II's bishops were extremely worried. It was probably around this time that Lothar II's remaining bishops – that is, apart from the deposed Theutgaud and Gunthar – made a desperate appeal to their episcopal colleagues in the kingdom of West Francia. They lamented the situation their kingdom found itself in, where the entire state (*res publica*) had "fallen almost into ruin," as a consequence of the crisis, though they suggested a corner had been turned. We see here a rhetoric of social and political collapse that would recur later in the Carolingian period, and that has often been associated with the disorders of the tenth century.[1]

What lay beneath this rhetoric was the bishops' alarm in the face of a dangerous escalation. For they had heard that King Charles the Bald, in view of Lothar II's plight, was now considering an invasion to dispossess and depose the young king, "as if he is despised and abandoned by his people." In other words, just as Louis the German had tried to drive Charles out of his kingdom in 858, now Charles was considering deploying the same strategy against Lothar II: to invade, and

---

[1] For different evaluations of these kinds of lamentations, see Howe, *Before the Gregorian Reform*, 13–49, who reads them as reflections of real social disruption; and Diesenberger, "Making the Past in Late and Post-Carolingian Historiography," who argues that they reveal a sense of living in a different period of time.

to attract enough support from disaffected internal elites to remove the ruling king. Lothar II's long-standing failure to replace Theutberga with Waldrada had brought heavy political costs to his standing and legitimacy. Carolingian kings could dominate their aristocracy, but a Carolingian king whose aristocrats chose en masse to throw their support behind a rival would not be king for long. It was not just Lothar II's succession but his immediate political and perhaps even personal survival that was now at stake.

It was to counter this development that Lothar II's bishops copied the tactics of the West Frankish bishops and wrote a collective letter in the style of the 858 Quierzy Letter; unlike the Quierzy Letter, however, this letter was addressed to Charles's bishops, not the king himself. The bishops insisted that Lothar II's kingdom, despite the strain it was under, was hanging together. They emphasized their loyalty to a king who had indeed made mistakes but was now back on the right track. And they asserted the duty of the West Frankish bishops to help sustain Lothar II's kingdom: "Are all the statutes, agreements, and oaths between the rulers which have been confirmed so many times to be treated as nothing?" They pointed to Charles's success in meeting the challenge he had faced when Louis the German had invaded in 858, implying that Lothar II would mount a similarly effective defense. And they suggested that Lothar II's deposition would threaten the entire Carolingian political order: that "evils would grow far and wide, indeed everywhere."

Unfortunately, the letter is undated. It has been interpreted as a response to an alliance between Lothar II's uncles made in February 865, which led Lothar II to suspect them "of wanting to take away his kingdom from him."[2] The absence of any reference to Theutberga might suggest it was written before she returned to Lothar II's court in the summer of that year. However, some historians have preferred a slightly later date, seeing the letter as a response to another meeting between Louis and Charles that took place in 867 (see Document 18, p. 169). Since the letter does not refer to Louis at all, only Charles, neither of these datings is definitive, and it may be safest simply to place the letter in the latter part of Lothar II's reign.

---

2 *Annals of St-Bertin*, trans. Nelson, 121–2. Cf. *Die Konzilien der karolingischen Teilreiche 860–874*, ed. Hartmann, 198, drawing on Staubach, *Herrscherbild*, 201ff.

The letter survives only in the dossier of Bishop Adventius of Metz that we have encountered already;[3] there is no way of knowing which of Lothar II's bishops signed on to it, or how far its claim to represent them all was borne out in reality. We cannot even be certain that it was actually sent, rather than simply drafted for discussion, and though Charles did not in the end invade Lothar II's kingdom at this time, we do not know what role, if any, this letter played in his calculations. It is nevertheless a valuable illustration both of the depth of the crisis that Lothar II's botched attempt to separate from Theutberga had generated and of the tactics the bishops had at their disposal in responding.

Translation[4]

To the most holy and venerable brothers in Christ, the fellow bishops residing in the kingdom of the most outstanding ruler Charles, the unanimous council of bishops residing in the kingdom of the glorious king Lothar sends greetings and plentiful blessings in the grace of our Savior.[5]

Your venerable Fraternity knows how in recent years, commotions of both inward and external discord have grown in this kingdom, and the whole state of our commonwealth,[6] and all peace and safety have fallen almost into ruin. Everywhere there is an increase in grieving and calamity, destruction and ravaging, murder and arson and innumerable kinds of wickedness, on account of dissension and most unjust ambition, and on account of certain whisperers and inventors of wickednesses, burning with the flames of greed and the pricks of jealousy.[7]

But the Lord has taken pity on the urgent prayers of pious devotion addressed to him, and on the groaning prayers of those who are

---

3 Rome, Biblioteca Vallicelliana, MS I 76, fols. 25v–27v (see Document 5, p. 55).
4 Edition: *Die Konzilien der karolingischen Teilreiche 860–874*, ed. Hartmann, 198–200 (http://www.mgh.de/dmgh/resolving/MGH_Conc._4_S._198). (It is also edited as Adventius, *Letters*, no. 13.)
5 Note the letter's claim to represent the unanimity of Lothar II's episcopate. The absence of any names could suggest that the unanimity might have been exaggerated.
6 "*Status nostrae rei publicae.*" See Document 1, p. 13, for the question of the Carolingian "state."
7 Note how the parlous situation of Lothar's kingdom is blamed on ambitious "whisperers."

suffering. And he has converted the shadows of affliction into the light, as it were, of an adopted serenity. What should we repay to the Lord for such a beneficence of mercy if not worthy thanks, beseeching his inestimable clemency that he will not permit the peace and concord he has allowed to flower a little in his people to dry up, so that he may lead his chosen people through this transitory peace to the joys of eternal peace? We should pray that the enemies of peace and those who attack Christian concord and security may turn back from the traps of the devil, recognize the path of peace, and hold firmly to it.

We have heard that there are some in your regions who are trying to persuade your ruler that he should in some way acquire the kingdom of our king, and should expel our ruler from his inherited kingdom, as if he is despised and abandoned by his people.[8] In the same way, perfidious and malign people wanted to pretend about your king Charles that even his bishops wished to desert him and to expel him from the kingdom. But *the vain voice lied to itself* [Ps. 26:12]. For the outstanding ruler was aided by the Omnipotent and helped by faithful followers, and not only did he not lose his kingdom, but he repelled his enemies by the judgment of God, and made them flee, full of confusion.[9]

We declare that we are and wish to remain loyal to our king, to whom we promised constant loyalty when he was raised to kingship by his father's hand. He has indeed erred because of weakness and youth, which often happens to men of his age, and he desires to improve all this with the best advice, as we trust. And we would prefer to keep and have him as our ruler, once he is corrected and guided, than to lose or desert him. And if there are some people who are deceived by fraud or disloyalty or greed, and who are thinking about or planning harm to their lord, it is not fitting for you to *be yoked with the unfaithful* [2 Cor. 6:14].[10] Are all the statutes, agreements, and oaths between the rulers which have been confirmed so many times to be treated as nothing? May it not be, may it not be that we should give such great offense before God and his saints and before the whole Catholic Church, or that we should give such joy to the angels of Satan.

---

8 In other words, Charles was considering (though had not decided upon) an invasion of Lothar II's kingdom (*patrium regnum*).
9 This is a reference to 858, when the kingdom of Charles had been invaded by Louis the German: see Document 3, pp. 19–46.
10 Here the bishops allude to opposition to Lothar II from within his own kingdom.

We cannot therefore break the oaths of faith and of the Christian sacrament taken to our lord and king, lest we shall pay an eternal penalty with the world. Especially since this king, seduced for a while by the instability of adolescence and the cunning of men, is now turned to better things, and hurries with the Lord's aid to mold himself wholly according to episcopal decrees and healthy advice, and the counsel of good men. So, having hope in divine mercy because of the auspices of such devotion, and knowing very well what it can implement in this young man who is now working to want what is good, we unanimously admonish the reverence of Your Sanctity, and beseech in concord that you should with all your authority notify and correct those who are trying to sow scandals and the seeds of discord in the people of God. Remember, lord brothers, how we were once ready to go forth with you against all evils, and swiftly to carry out whatever you wished to begin.[11]

We do not wish it to be hidden from Your Presence that whoever is an inciter of wickednesses, whoever is a sower of discord, whoever is a disrupter of ecclesiastical concord, whoever, finally, tries to perturb the little peace preserved by the Lord's piety in these parts of the kingdom: he will be subjected to the terrible shame of anathema and will be *wrapped in the robes of confusion* [Ps. 108:29], and *his days will be shortened* [Ps. 88:46], and he will not escape eternal woe, unless he very quickly amends himself with worthy satisfaction.

It seems good to us, most loved brothers, that we should in no way hide all of this nor be silent. Rather, relying on the inseparable and ineluctable sacerdotal authority through which we received the power of binding and releasing from the greatest priest the Lord Christ, we should anticipate the wicked intentions of certain people, and should resist their wicked wishes and evil efforts with all our power, so that they should find nothing at all in us other than one heart and one mind. Thus the wicked men will realize that they are less able to carry out the evils which they are preparing, because they recognize that we are not favoring them in any illicit business. Alas! Why does the wretched boldness of men, since it is not punished immediately, raise up against itself the dispositions and orders of the Almighty, nor realize that all power in heaven and on earth comes from him and through him and in him,

---

11 It is not clear what previous joint action this is referring to, though cf. Document 3, note 3.

whose preknowledge and predestination allow no mortal nor even the whole world to change?[12]

And now, dearest ones, we all unanimously and most devotedly beseech the clemency of the Most High, for the peace of the church and for the inviolate concord of our kings, that the most noble rulers should not be deceived by the advice of evil-wishers. May it not happen that they should stray from the mutual association and love and from the bond of kinship, as a result of which evils would grow far and wide, indeed everywhere. But with God's mercy, let there be a peaceful concord between them, and let what is harmful vanish, and all good things follow. May he deign to bestow this, who lives and reigns in the Trinity as the almighty God, for ever and ever, Amen.

13. KING LOTHAR II GRANTS QUEEN THEUTBERGA LANDS, JANUARY 17, 866

In the winter of 864, Pope Nicholas I had turned the screws on Lothar II by declaring that he was treating the king as if excommunicated, though the pope did not go so far as to carry out a formal excommunication.[1] In early 865, he sent a new legate, Arsenius, bishop of Orte, armed with a sheaf of letters, including a blistering remonstration aimed specifically at Lothar II's bishops.[2] Meanwhile, the king's uncles deepened their alliance.

Faced with these threats, in the late summer of 865 Lothar II buckled. On August 3, 865, at Douzy, Queen Theutberga was restored to her position as queen at Lothar II's court, in the presence of the legate Arsenius and numerous bishops, and oaths were publicly sworn by twelve lay aristocrats on Lothar II's behalf that she would now be treated properly.[3] On August 15, King Lothar II and Queen Theutberga

---

12 A reference to the predestination debates associated with the theological teaching of Gottshalk of Orbais? On this controversy see Gillis, *Heresy and Dissent*.

***

1 Nicholas, *Letters*, no. 32 (Nicholas, *Reg.*, 724).
2 Nicholas, *Letters*, no. 35 (Nicholas, *Reg.*, 742; cf. Nicholas, *Reg.*, 761 for traces of a now lost letter sent specifically to Bishop Hatto of Verdun).
3 *Annals of St-Bertin*, trans. Nelson, 124–6.

ceremonially wore their crowns together at the royal palace of Gondreville. It has been suggested by some historians that this was the moment at which Lothar II gave her the Susanna Crystal, a beautifully engraved rock crystal gem depicting a woman freed from legal persecution, though others are skeptical.[4] After this, the legate Arsenius departed with Waldrada, whom he was tasked with escorting to Rome.

Yet despite this setback, Lothar II continued to maneuver for a definitive separation from Theutberga. As we shall see, he and his supporters exerted as much pressure as they could upon the queen. The *Annals of St-Bertin* report that Lothar II held a meeting at Trier in late 866 in a bid to persuade her to take the veil. Theutberga, who must have had immense strength of character, refused.[5] Lothar II, however, also offered (or maybe she demanded) incentives for her cooperation. This remarkable charter, issued at the great palace of Aachen on January 17, 866, is key evidence for this combination of carrot and stick, suggesting not only Lothar II's determination, but also that Theutberga may have had more capacity for action than we might suppose.

The charter is a large and impressive sheet of parchment, about sixty centimeters wide and tall, which still bears its original wax seal in the bottom right corner. Through this document, Lothar II conferred upon Theutberga a set of named estates, located in various regions (known in Latin as *pagi*).[6] This was a substantial amount of land that would have provided Theutberga with considerable wealth. Behind the names of each of the twenty villages that this charter transferred stood a community of farming families, whose consent to the transaction was neither sought nor needed. It is not clear what difference the change in ownership of the land on which they lived would have made to these hundreds of people, who would have continued paying their dues to their estate managers as usual.[7]

---

4 *Annals of St-Bertin*, trans. Nelson, 126n14. For a recent interpretation that places the Susanna Crystal in a different (tenth-century) context, see MacLean, "Royal Adultery."

5 See the 866 entry in *Annals of St-Bertin*, trans. Nelson, 136: "but he could not make her do so." That said, Theutberga does seem to have written to Pope Nicholas I not long afterward to ask to be released from the marriage: see Document 16, p. 159.

6 An approximate map of the properties concerned is provided by Ducourthial, "Géographie du pouvoir," at 213.

7 On these managers, see the 858 Quierzy Letter, Document 3, pp. 39–40.

The estates, which are listed as if in order of an itinerary, were located mostly around the Alps, rather than scattered throughout Lothar II's kingdom.[8] This was the region in which Theutberga's brother, Hubert, had been based for many years. So why was Lothar granting Theutberga lands here? In an important article, Régine le Jan suggested that Lothar was expanding Theutberga's "bridewealth," lands he had given her at their initial marriage, after he had been compelled to take her back in August.[9] Perhaps this charter represented the totality of that initial grant. Another possibility, however, is that these lands were family property that Theutberga had brought with her into her marriage in 855 as a dowry, and that Lothar II was now returning. Admittedly, the charter does not explicitly state this; indeed, the charter's explanation for the grant, the sentiment that loyal service should be rewarded, is pure Carolingian boilerplate that can be found in countless other charters. To mention a dowry of any kind would have been to concede that Lothar II and Theutberga had been legally married, which was precisely what the king was now trying to avoid.

The awkwardness of the grant is revealed by another peculiarity. In the text, Theutberga is not at any point given any label, such as wife or spouse, as was common in royal charters (see Document 8, p. 104, for Waldrada's description as "dearest wife"). Lothar II was determined not to acknowledge any legal connection, even in passing. Moreover, after Theutberga's name, the scribe – whom we can identify as the veteran notary Rodmund, who had written the rather less solemn charter for Winebert in 856, and who had now been working at the royal court for over twenty years – left a blank space fractionally larger than the normal separation between words. It is almost as if Rodmund had hesitated, unsure of what to say about Theutberga, before moving on; or perhaps it was intended to draw the eye to the absence of any marital label.

There is yet another twist to this charter. Though it was in every way formally completed, and stands as a fully ratified document, Rodmund wrote another version of the grant just a couple of years later in 868, this time including some additional lands (marked in the translation

---

8 As pointed out by Ducourthial, "Géographie du pouvoir."
9 Le Jan, "Douaires et pouvoirs des reines," 465.

below).[10] These lands had belonged to Theutberga's brother Hubert, who had died in rebellion in 864; Lothar II had declared them to be confiscated and here transferred them to Theutberga.

Does this second charter, identical except in these particular additions, mean that the first charter had not come into effect? What points toward this interpretation is the location of both charters today, in the archive of the northern Italian city of Parma. This was not a city or region that had any direct connections to Theutberga, or indeed Lothar II, so how could they have ended up there? François Bougard has suggested that Lothar II took both these charters to Rome with him in 869. On his return north, Lothar II died, as it happened on lands owned by Empress Angilberga, the wife of Louis II: in other words, Lothar II's sister-in-law. It seems that these documents at this point passed to Angilberga, whose archives in turn ended up in the monastery she founded in 874, San Sisto of Piacenza, whose records eventually found their way in the modern period to Parma.[11]

In short, Lothar II seems to have kept both the documents and taken them to Rome with him in 869 as tokens of his goodwill, to "seal the agreement made with Theutberga";[12] the very fact that they were still in his possession implies that the grant had not really been enacted in 866, and perhaps not even in 868. Had Theutberga refused the offer? And why did Empress Angilberga keep the records even after Lothar II's death? The charter still holds on to some of its secrets.

Translation[13]

> In the name of Almighty God and our Savior Jesus Christ, Lothar, king by divine clemency.

---

10 The second charter is ostensibly dated to November 24, 867, but this is probably an error for November 24, 868, not least since it is likely one of the scribes involved, Grimbland, was in or on his way to Rome in late November 867. Lothar had sent him as an envoy, and he returned with letters from Pope Hadrian II dated to February 868; given traveling speeds, this makes it unlikely (if not impossible) that he was involved in redacting charters in November 867. See *Chartae Latinae Antiquiores*, 93:64–7.
11 Bougard, "En marge du divorce de Lothaire II," 50. On Angilberga, see La Rocca, "Angelberga, Louis's II Wife, and her Will (877)"; and MacLean, "Queenship, Nunneries and Royal Widowhood," 26–32.
12 Bougard, "En marge du divorce de Lothaire II," 50.
13 Edition: King Lothar II, *Charters*, no. 27, 428–9 (http://www.mgh.de/dmgh/resolving/MGH_DD_Lo_I_/_DD_Lo_II_S._429). A facsimile edition with a detailed technical analysis is available in *Chartae Latinae Antiquiores*, 93:64–7.

It is the custom of Royal Highness to enrich and honor those faithfully serving us with many gifts and enormous honors.[14] Therefore, let it be brought to the attention of all the faithful of God's church and of ourselves, both present and in the future, that it pleased the generosity of Our Highness to confer certain properties in our ownership upon our beloved Theutberga,[15] in the *pagi*[16] of Grenoble, Belley, Maurienne, Geneva, Lausanne, Amous, and Escuens, and also the *pagus* of Lyons,[17] the villages whose names are as follows:[18]

Chavord, Lémenc, Novalaise, Meyrieux, Aix-les-Bains, Héry-sur-Alby, Seynod, Pringy and Mont-St-Martin, Annecy, Balmont, Talloires, Doussard, Marlens, Vergloz, *Durelium*, Thusy, Colonne, Oltingen, Montigny-les-Cherlieu,[19] and whatever properties are located by the Grozonne,[20] so that she may keep them in ownership permanently.

And so that this generous donation might remain ratified and intact, we ordered this charter of Our Excellence to be drawn up, through which these villages located in these aforementioned *pagi*, in full integrity, that is with their churches, halls, and other buildings, cultivated and uncultivated lands, vineyards, woods, fields, meadows, pasture, standing and flowing waters, mills, entrances and exits – all of them in their entirety, whatever is known to pertain to these lands, we give to the abovementioned dearest Theutberga.[21] And we transfer them from our ownership to her, so that whatever from this day and henceforth she wishes to do with this property, she has the free and practical power to do in all ways, whatever she chooses. And so that this authority of our gift shall have a fuller power in the name of God, we have confirmed it below with our hand, and have ordered it to be given the impression of our seal.

SIGNUM the glorious King Lothar.

I, Rodmund the notary, confirmed this charter on behalf of Grimbland.

---

14 For *honores*, see Document 3, note 22.
15 There is a noticeable gap here in the charter, though not quite large enough for a word such as wife (*uxor*).
16 *Pagi* (singular: *pagus*) is a label for regions, similar in size to the English county or shire.
17 Addition in the November 24, 868 charter: "and also in the *pagus* of Ripuaria."
18 For identification of the place-names I have consulted Dupraz, "Deux preceptes de Lothaire II." The estate of *Durelium* has not yet been identified, and so it is presented here in its Latin form.
19 Addition after Montigny in the November 24, 868, charter: "Ubach." This is a village in the north of Francia, near Aachen.
20 Addition in the November 24, 868, charter: "and all the property of her late brother Abbot Hubert, which Our royal Dignity acquired on account of his disloyalty."
21 There is another slight gap here in the charter.

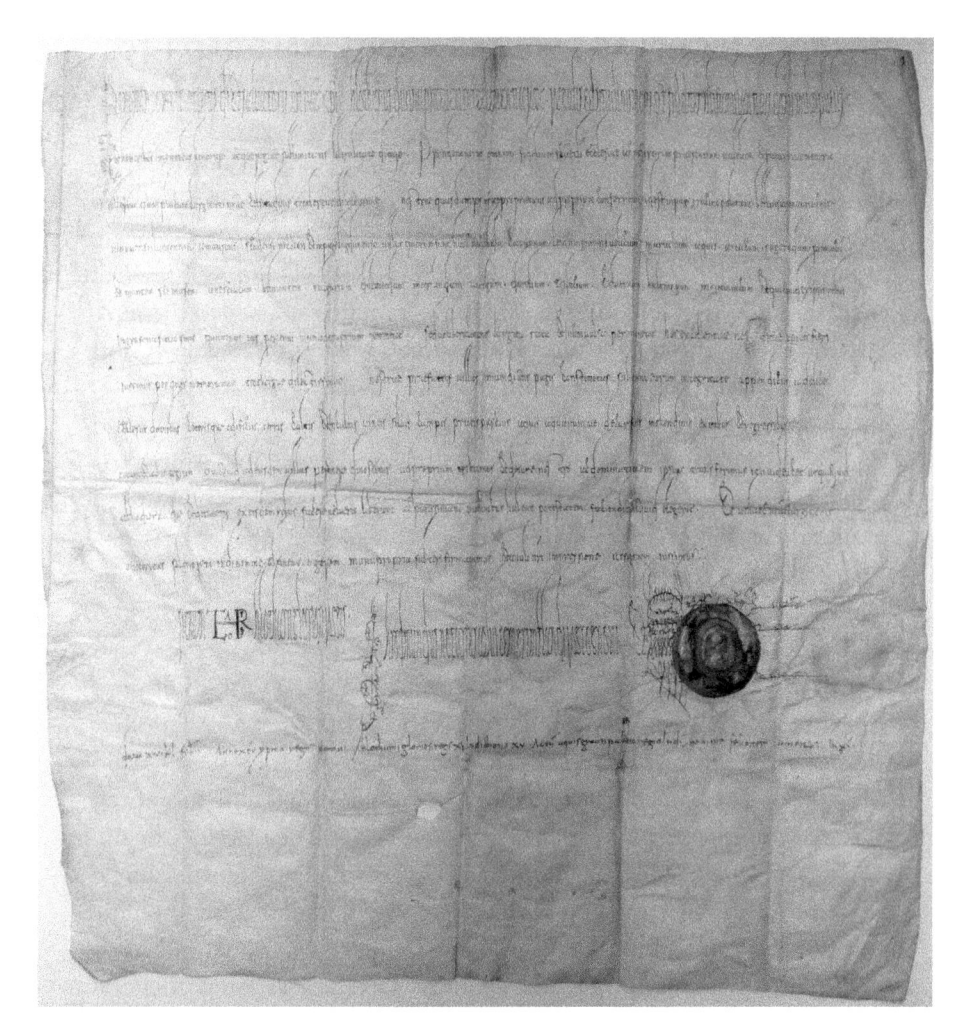

Figure 6. Lothar II's charter for Theutberga (Parma, Archivio di stato, Diplomatico, diplomi imperiali, cass. 1, n. 10)

Dated sixteenth kalends of February [January 17], in the eleventh year of the reign with Christ's assistance of the glorious king Lothar, fifteenth indiction.[22] Issued at the palace of Aachen, in the name of God, Amen.

---

22 The "indiction" date (the year reckoned in a fifteen-year cycle) does not quite match the rest of the dating clause, which has led to some doubt about this charter's precise date; the most likely solution is that there was a small calculation error.

14. POPE NICHOLAS I WRITES ABOUT WALDRADA TO THE BISHOPS OF GAUL, GERMANY, AND ITALY, JUNE 13, 866

When Pope Nicholas I sent his legate Arsenius to Lothar II in 865 to restore Theutberga as queen, Arsenius was under instructions to bring Waldrada back to Rome with him on his return, so the pope could deal with her in person. The *Annals of St-Bertin* state that she began the journey south with the legate after Theutberga's restitution as queen. But then Waldrada escaped or ran off, together with a Frankish aristocrat in a parallel position: Engeltrude, the estranged wife of Boso, who had been similarly summoned to Rome and who likewise absconded.[1] As a consequence, on February 2, 866, Pope Nicholas excommunicated Waldrada at a church council in Rome. This meant that she was separated from the mystical body of the church and was supposed to be shunned by all Christians.

Yet Waldrada remained steadfast. According to Pope Nicholas in a letter translated below, written in June 866 to all the Frankish bishops north of the Alps, she continued to dominate the *res publica*, in other words the state or commonwealth, and had found ways for her and Lothar II to keep meeting discreetly at various locations: and, moreover, she was continually plotting how to bring about Theutberga's death. Nicholas's letter frames Waldrada as an anti-queen: over-influential even in her absence, leading Lothar II into sin and damaging the public order. From another perspective, it is an image of a woman who was determinedly pursuing her own agenda.[2] Over a year later, Nicholas was still worried by Waldrada's influence and wrote directly to Lothar II to prevent Waldrada from having any sway over the choice of new archbishops of Trier and Cologne.[3]

What gave Waldrada this extraordinary sticking power? We might imagine she was given support by her family, but we know very little of them. In the tenth century, we hear of a bishop's illegitimate daughter who was approached to become a king's mistress, and perhaps Waldrada

---

1 As noted by Regino of Prüm, *Chronicle*, trans. MacLean, 144. On Engeltrude, see Document 6, pp. 90–1.
2 Cf. Karras, *Unmarriages*, 38–42, for an analysis of the situation from Waldrada's point of view.
3 Nicholas, *Letters*, no. 50 (Nicholas, *Reg.*, 855, from October 867).

came from a similar social context.[4] In any case, Nicholas's letter points the finger chiefly at Waldrada herself, not her allies and supporters, who are mentioned only in passing. Was this concentration on Waldrada as an individual a way of attacking Lothar II indirectly, keeping the focus on the marital pair, or does it reflect how things had been represented to Nicholas by his unnamed sources, keen to portray Lothar II as still under the thumb of a wicked concubine? Or does it simply reflect the genuine importance of Waldrada's personal role? The fact that in October 867, Nicholas was still convinced that Waldrada was the de facto queen, deciding remotely who received royal favor and who did not, suggests that she did indeed wield great personal influence.[5] Clearly, she was not merely the passive object of Lothar II's affections.

It is significant that Nicholas complains of how Waldrada had been entrusted with control of (unidentified) religious communities. These might have been provided as a source of income, but perhaps they were also intended to maintain her social standing and position. After all, as Simon MacLean has argued, Carolingian queens were often established as patrons of female monasteries, and we know for instance that Theutberga had acted as an intercessor for a female monastery in Metz, though the relevant charters are now lost.[6] Association with established female religious communities, such as Remiremont, might have helped shield Waldrada from the hail of attacks raining down on her reputation and personal morality.

---

4 Ekkehard of St Gall, *Fortune and Misfortune at Saint Gall*, trans. Albu and Lozovsky, 85. Waldrada is sometimes said to have been the niece of Archbishop Theutgaud, but this is based on a misreading of Regino of Prüm's *Chronicle* entry for 864, trans. MacLean, 139–41, which clearly differentiates between the niece and Waldrada. Goldberg, "*Regina nitens sanctissima Hemma*," 86, identifies Waldrada with a woman of the same name who owned properties in Louis the German's kingdom, but this could well be a different individual. As Dohmen, *Ursache allen Übels*, 186, points out the name was not especially uncommon in the ninth century: it occurs for instance twenty-seven times in the Remiremont *Liber Memorialis* (on which see Document 4).

5 Cf. Nicholas, *Letters*, no. 51 (Nicholas, *Reg.*, 861), partially translated in d'Avray, *Dissolving Royal Marriages*, at 24–7, and Letter 53 (Nicholas, *Reg.*, 863), partially translated in d'Avray, *Dissolving Royal Marriages*, 27–43, esp. 38 and 42 (where Nicholas I writes that she "dominates Lothar," *dominatur Hlotharii*).

6 MacLean, "Queenship, Nunneries and Royal Widowhood." The tenth-century *Translationes sanctae Glodesindis* talks of Lothar II making a grant to the monastery of St-Glossinde "through the persuasion of his wife Queen Theutberga, by the intervention of Bishop Adventius" ("suasu conjugis suae Teutbergae reginae, interveniente eodem Adventio episcopo"), col. 232. See Vanderputten, *Dark Age Nunneries*, 61.

This letter was by no means the first that Pope Nicholas had sent regarding Lothar II's divorce. Some contemporaries treated the pope's letters with the same respect they paid to those of his ancient predecessors, carefully copying them into papal letter collections (for instance in a ninth-century manuscript now in Rome, Biblioteca Vallicelliana, MS D 38).[7] Lothar II's bishops, however, were more reticent. In his letter, Nicholas expresses his concern that these bishops were deliberately ignoring him and were dragging their feet in implementing the excommunication of Waldrada he had pronounced in February. The apparent volte-face represented by Adventius's 864 letter seems, in other words, to have had its limits, and at this point there was little the pope could do other than send more, increasingly angry letters over the Alps.

This particular letter of Nicholas was copied in the letter collection of Adventius of Metz. As such, it was available to the monk Regino of Prüm, who quoted it in abbreviated form in his chronicle that he finished in 908. Regino did not substantially distort the letter's meaning, but he did conspicuously leave out the passage about Waldrada's ongoing influence, perhaps to avoid implying that the commands of Pope Nicholas, whom Regino greatly admired, failed to have instant effect.[8]

Translation[9]

Bishop Nicholas, servant of the servants of God, to our most reverend brothers the archbishops and bishops established throughout Italy, Germany, Neustria, and the Gauls.[10]

We had decided to temper the manner of punishment for the adulteress Waldrada with mercy more than with rigidity, though she

---

7 For a study of how the popes' letters were copied in this period, see Jasper and Fuhrmann, *Papal Letters*, esp. 110–25 on Pope Nicholas I; for ninth-century papal letter writing more generally, see Unger, *Päpstliche Schriftlichkeit im 9. Jahrhundert*.
8 Regino of Prüm, *Chronicle*, trans. MacLean, 147–9. Regino mistakenly dates this letter to after Nicholas I's letter to Charles in January 867 (see Document 16, pp. 153–63).
9 Edition: Nicholas, *Letters*, no. 42, 315–16 (http://www.mgh.de/dmgh/resolving/MGH_Epp._6_S._315) (Nicholas, *Reg.*, 800).
10 Following established conventions, Nicholas I arranges the recipients not according to political borders – the kingdoms of the various Frankish rulers – but according to older spatial categories. The awkward exception is Neustria, which here indicates the kingdom of Charles the Bald.

remained stubbornly unrepentant, and to pronounce a just punishment, but not according to what she deserved for such an evil crime. But with an obstinate spirit, she has determined to remain constantly in the filth of adultery and has paid no heed to sacred advice, nor to our nor your frequent exhortations. Although it would have been against his wish, it remains very clear to God, who sees into the heart, and to those faithful to him in all things, that by her own will she would have remained in this terrible crime up till now, indeed forever if she could, had not Our unceasing Diligence worked with the strength of the great Creator to abolish it, and had not her companion [*socius*: Lothar II] showed somewhat greater obedience concerning the wickedness carried on with her.[11]

That things stand as we say is made plain, since she has neither acknowledged her sin nor confessed it, according to the scriptures: *tell thy iniquities so that you may be justified* [Isa. 43],[12] nor has she sent a sorrowful embassy to demand mercy from us, since we began to prosecute her case. Nor has she deserved a fitting indulgence through a preceding remedy of penance, as Solomon says, *He that hideth his sins, shall not prosper: but he that shall confess, and forsake them, shall obtain mercy* [Prov. 28:13]. Finally, the moment came for her to travel directly to us and to seek the aid of the see of St Peter, so that we might settle her case with a decision pleasing to God, according to what had been ordered.[13] But she turned back to Satan and journeyed back to the province, so that she might rule over it.[14]

Although she has been summoned back to Italy a second time by the industry of our legate,[15] she pursues the glory of the world, as if she had done nothing to generate a great scandal in the church of Christ, and she dominates the state [*res publica*].[16] And, what is worse, she is known to be in charge of holy places and religious

---

11 Pope Nicholas I here suggests that Waldrada was more obdurate than Lothar II.
12 The quotation comes from a version of the Bible quoted by the early church fathers, not the Vulgate.
13 Waldrada was summoned to Rome in the late summer of 865 but broke off the journey before arriving.
14 *Ut principaretur in ea*: Heidecker, *The Divorce of Lothar II*, 169, takes this to mean "so that he [Satan] might rule over her," but I think Nicholas I is emphasizing Waldrada's power.
15 Arsenius, bishop of Orte and papal legate.
16 *Reique publicae dominatur*: a very strongly phrased statement of Waldrada's power.

people,[17] and according to many has by no means ceased plotting the destruction of Queen Theutberga. Meanwhile, she aims to keep returning to those places where she has easier access to King Lothar, and he to her. And, to summarize, each and every day she explores with various ideas how she may return to her previous pleasures.[18]

Truly, to declare with the distinguished Apostle what must often be repeated against her and her like, she is *treasuring up wrath through hardness and impenitent heart for the day of wrath* [Rom. 2:5, adapted]. So, until she has given satisfaction for her actions to the church of Christ and particularly to us, who chiefly take responsibility for her and who have begun to follow and investigate her case, and until by taking our counsel she removes from herself every inauspicious suspicion, we have deprived her from receiving the precious body and blood of the Lord, and from every association with the holy church, along with all her supporters and associates and allies.[19] This we have done by the judgment of the Holy Spirit and the blessed apostles Peter and Paul and by the authority of our humble selves.

We recall that we promulgated this judgment on February 2,[20] and we sent it to you in writing.[21] But since we do not know whether it came to your attention, we have taken care to publicize it to Your Reverence a second time. For while the matter is still in the balance, and what has begun well has not yet been completed, and while it is indicated by various signs that the wicked are still panting after their earlier crimes, it is necessary to take very great care, so that a brand-new and worse error does not succeed the previous one, due to our sluggishness. We would

---

17 In other words, Waldrada had been placed in charge of monasteries. Her later association with Remiremont is clear, and she may also have been linked to the convent of St-Felix in Zürich, possibly residing there between 856 and 863 (see Butz, "Das Königtum Lothars II.," 25–6); she appears in a charter for the convent in 869 (King Lothar II, *Charters*, no. 34). Gaillard, *D'une réforme*, 77n120, hints at a link between the queen and the otherwise unknown Merovingian-period "St Waldrada," who suddenly appears in the ninth-century hagiography of another convent, St-Pierre-aux-Nonnains in Metz.

18 Regino in his abbreviation omits this whole paragraph, except for Waldrada's plots against Theutberga.

19 Excommunication was "infectious," in that it also applied to anyone who knowingly remained in contact with the excommunicated.

20 The feast day of the Purification of the Virgin Mary, as Regino of Prüm noted in his *Chronicle*, a date that Nicholas I may have chosen deliberately: see Airlie, "Private Bodies and the Body Politic," 34.

21 This letter does not survive. Regino's *Chronicle* omits the rest of this paragraph.

in vain be called watchmen, if we did not see the wolf coming from a distance.[22] We would in vain be called bishops, that is inspectors, if we did not at all contemplate the death to come through its preceding signs, especially since we have experienced what we see, and the display of previous matters brings forth certainty about those of the future.

So let Your Charity at least grieve for the daily attacks against Queen Theutberga, and sympathize in all your thoughts with this limb of the Lord's body.[23] And so that our effort may not have been in vain, let Your Fraternity join us in taking up spiritual arms against the aforementioned adulteress, and all those in touch with her,[24] and in each diocese where you govern the Lord's people, and where she might be present, publicly and bravely announce in person that this excommunicated woman and her supporters are prohibited from remaining there, until she has submitted herself to a fitting penance by our own judgment.[25]

And if someone should perhaps cleverly and contrivedly say that not just this woman but also King Lothar committed wrong in this regard, and thus he should be bound with a similar penance? Although it is not necessary for us to reply to someone arrogantly saying such things, whether he says them to promote himself or to criticize us, it is appropriate that whoever he is, he should seek the resolution of this matter in the ample prerogative from whose authority this sanction flows. The apostolic authority, to which pertains the care of all the churches, has a suitable rudder by which it gives advice to all, and through which the discipline of salvation instructs the unlearned, and imposes the form of worthy discretion upon those who reproach it.[26]

---

22 A reference to the description of watchmen in Ezekiel 33, often considered to be prefiguring the role of the bishop.
23 Theutberga is a limb of the Lord's body, which Waldrada is not, because she has been excommunicated.
24 *Communicantes*, i.e., those who were ignoring her excommunication.
25 The Latin here does not make complete sense. This translation draws on a marginal note in the Vallicelliana manuscript that suggests a word has been omitted. Regino, who had access to the now lost original manuscript, rather than the later transcription that survives today, offers a clearer but different reading, but this could reflect his editorial input. His chronicle omits the rest of the letter.
26 The wording here is somewhat cryptic, but the point is clear enough: it is up to the pope alone whom he chooses to excommunicate, and whom he does not, so he is within his rights to distinguish between Waldrada and Lothar II if he wishes. This passage is evidence that Nicholas I had not gone so far as to excommunicate Lothar II, despite some equivocation in certain other letters (see Document 13, p. 134).

Meanwhile, whichever of you receives this letter of sanction, let him take great care to send it to the other metropolitan bishops, and disseminate examples of it through the neighboring regions, and so show himself to be such in all these things, that in the zeal of another Phineas,[27] he may demonstrate that he is fervent in avenging shame in all things to mitigate God's wrath, and not in defending a prostitute.

We wish Your Fraternity to fare well in Christ now and always.

Dated the ides of June [June 13], fourteenth indiction.

15. QUEEN ERMENTRUDE'S CORONATION, AUGUST 25, 866

In the summer of 866, a large church council was held at the monastery of St-Medard outside Soissons in the kingdom of West Francia, organized by Archbishop Hincmar of Reims on the request of Pope Nicholas I. Its chief purpose was to settle a long-running dispute relating to the deposition of Archbishop Ebbo of Reims over two decades earlier; for this purpose, thirty-five bishops assembled, mostly from West Francia but with some attendees from the kingdoms of Lothar II and Louis the German.[1] However, the *Annals of St-Bertin* inform us that before the council closed, some new business arose. King Charles the Bald took the opportunity of such a large gathering to request that the bishops anoint and crown his wife, Queen Ermentrude. The liturgical ceremony, which was staged on Sunday, August 25, 866, blessed both Ermentrude and Charles. We should imagine a grand and highly choreographed affair, with a large audience watching the royal couple arrayed in all their finery.

The ceremony placed especial emphasis on Ermentrude's prospects for childbearing, with frequent references to women in the Old Testament who had successfully conceived after prayer. We know this because

---

27 Phineas is a figure in the biblical book of Numbers, ch. 25. He takes direct action against a prostitute and her client, named Cozbi and Zambri, respectively, entering the brothel to stab them both; as a consequence of his zeal, God stops punishing the Israelites.

***

1 Archbishop Remigius of Lyon and Bishop John of Cambrai from Lothar II's kingdom, and Archbishop Liutbert of Mainz from Louis the German's kingdom. On the case of Ebbo of Reims, see van Doren, "*De Divortio* and *de Resignatione*."

the script for this public ceremony, a kind of text known as an *ordo*, survives. It is one of the oldest coronation rites for queens to be preserved from early medieval Europe.[2] Because of this, historians have sometimes used it to make arguments about the nature of early medieval queenship in general. Yet we should remember that this ritual was designed, written, and performed at a particular moment for particular reasons and was not intended as a timeless monument to queenship in abstract terms.

Indeed, at first sight Ermentrude's 866 coronation might strike the modern observer as somewhat strange; the text suggests that the onlookers might have been surprised, too. Ermentrude had been married to King Charles the Bald for over twenty years and had played an active role as queen.[3] Her political influence is demonstrated through surviving letters and by her involvement in various royal charters, in which she had acted as a sponsor on behalf of those wishing to receive the king's favor. She may have played a role in brokering meetings between her husband and Lothar II (and had presumably met Theutberga during the queen's long stay in Charles's kingdom). Moreover, the couple had had by this point in their relationship at least eleven children: five daughters and six sons. Why, then, was it decided that Ermentrude should undergo this particular ceremony at this stage in her life?

There are, broadly, two possible lines of interpretation. One is that Charles and Ermentrude were sincerely set on having more children, and perhaps sons in particular, and wanted to use the holy power of the bishops concentrated at Soissons as spiritual aid for this goal. Here we should consider how the prospects for the inheritance of Charles's kingdom stood in 866. Though Ermentrude and Charles had already had six sons, three had died young, and one had been sent into the church (and was the abbot of the monastery in Soissons where his mother's coronation was staged). Another, Charles, had suffered an accident in 864, when an altercation with a member of his retinue got out of hand.[4] He never recovered, and his death in September 866 may well have been anticipated. That left Charles the Bald with just one son, Louis the Stammerer, of whom it seems clear that Charles

---

2 For wider discussion, see Smith, "The Earliest Queen-Making Rites"; and Nelson, "Early Medieval Rites of Queen-Making."
3 Hyam, "Ermentrude and Richildis."
4 *Annals of St-Bertin*, trans. Nelson, 112. For a revised interpretation of this event, see Goldberg, "'A Man of Notable Good Looks.'"

was not terribly fond. Moreover, when Ermentrude died in 869 after twenty-seven years of marriage, Charles struck up a new relationship, with extraordinary speed (within three days of hearing the news), with a young aristocratic woman named Richildis and seems again to have been eager for more children.[5] In this reading, the 866 coronation of Ermentrude may appear as simply a fertility ritual intended to facilitate further offspring. We should note that the text clearly implies that the ceremony was the queen's idea, not the king's.

However, there is a further context to consider, as Zubin Mistry has recently emphasized.[6] Almost exactly a year earlier, as we have seen, Lothar II had been compelled to accept Theutberga back as his queen. He had done so with reluctance, and not long afterward Theutberga wrote to Pope Nicholas to ask to be released from the marriage on grounds of sterility. What better way, then, for Lothar II's uncle to advertise his own marriage's virtues than by publicly praying alongside his wife for yet more children, before an audience of bishops assembled from across the Frankish world north of the Alps? More broadly, the 866 ceremony would have served to highlight the harmony of the West Frankish royal couple, throwing into starker relief the ongoing crisis at Lothar II's court and household. The conclusion of the liturgy, requesting God to keep Ermentrude and Charles safe from "the stain of any adultery" and secure in mutual love, made a point that contemporaries could not have failed to appreciate.

So the coronation at Soissons in 866 might have been an expression of the West Frankish rulers' wish for more children, but it might also, as Jane Hyam suggested, have been "a lesson in hope to Lothar II." More cynically, it was designed to pile on pressure, deliberately representing Charles and Ermentrude as fulfilling the role of royal couple in ways in which Lothar II and Theutberga were conspicuously incapable. As we shall see, this did not mean that Charles was not open to negotiations with his unfortunate nephew; but he would be entering these negotiations from a position of unassailable moral superiority. Lothar II's efforts to divorce Theutberga had inadvertently created an ideological competition around royal conjugality, and Ermentrude's 866 coronation signaled her and Charles's untouchably high standing in this field.

---

5 Hyam, "Ermentrude and Richildis."
6 Mistry, "Ermentrude's Consecration."

The complete coronation *ordo* survives today only in an early modern edition and a transcription, both based on a now lost medieval manuscript from Liège.[7] As far as we can tell, this lost manuscript was made up mostly of writings by Archbishop Hincmar, and it is all but certain that he was the author of this text as well. The *ordo* may have been written in some haste; Hincmar drew in part from a liturgical ceremony he had composed a decade previously in 856 for the marriage of one of Ermentrude's daughters, Judith. The prayers of the ceremony are packed full of references to the Old Testament, not all of which are marked up in the translation.

Translation[8]

The address of two bishops[9] in the church of St-Medard when Ermentrude was consecrated as queen:

We wish you to know, brothers,[10] that our lord and *senior*, the glorious king Charles, besought the devotion of Our Humility that, by the authority of the ministry conferred upon us by God, just as he was anointed and consecrated as king by episcopal authority with sacred unction and blessing, as we read in the scriptures that God commanded kings should be anointed and consecrated into royal power; so too we should bless his wife [*uxor*], our lady, in the name of queen, just as we understand was done before for other queens by the apostolic see and by our predecessors.

---

7 On the lost Liège manuscript, see Pokorny, "Sirmonds verlorener Lütticher Codex"; and West, "Between the Flood and the Last Judgment."
8 Edition: *Die Konzilien der karolingischen Teilreiche 860–874*, ed. Hartmann, 223–4 (http://www.mgh.de/dmgh/resolving/MGH_Conc._4_S._223). Pokorny, "Sirmonds verlorener Lütticher Codex," draws attention to an independent transcription of Ermentrude's coronation *ordo* made by André Duchesne. I have consulted this unpublished transcription and found the text there is mostly very close to Sirmond's edition but omits a central section, leaving open the possibility that this segment was an afterthought. A new edition would clarify the problem.
9 One of these bishops was probably Archbishop Herard of Tours, since part of the script appears in a different manuscript attributed to him. The other may have been Archbishop Hincmar of Reims. It is unfortunately not clear which parts of the ceremony were presented by which bishop.
10 That is, the other bishops present at the council. Thirty-five are known to have been in attendance. Most of these were from the kingdom of Charles (see this document, note 1, for representation from Lothar II's and Louis the German's kingdoms).

And we shall hasten to explain to Your Fraternity the reason, so that it should not be a surprise to you that he [Charles] is asking. So, as is known to many people, the omnipotent God by his grace wonderfully brought this kingdom together in the hands of his predecessors, which kingdom those predecessors nobly governed, and through succession their offspring have ruled up to these times.[11] And God gave sons to our lord, as is known to you. His faithful followers rejoiced in great hope in the nobility of these, for the holy church and kingdom which God has given to him [Charles] to rule. From these Charles gave some to God, that he might offer an oblation to God from the fruit of his loins.[12] Some God by his Grace took from this world while they were still at a young age, *lest*, as is written, *wickedness change their hearts* [Prov. 4:11]. Some, as is not hidden to you, he allowed to incur the suffering of his judgment, as his faithful followers grieve.[13] Therefore Charles seeks the episcopal blessing of his wife, so that God may deign to give him a child from her, whence the holy church may have solace, the kingdom its necessary defense, his faithful followers their desired aid, and Christianity its wished-for peace, law, and justice, along with those children he has already, with the agreement and assistance of the Lord.

And about this, we have this authority in the holy scriptures, that as God said to Abraham, *In your seed all peoples will be blessed* [Gen. 22:18], and to this hundred-year-old man, God gave his son Isaac from his ninety-year-old wife. And he made Isaac accept a sterile wife, so that in this, as he is often accustomed to do, he might demonstrate the generosity of his mercy. And as the scriptures say, since *Isaac prayed to the Lord for his wife, because she was sterile* [Gen. 25:21], she conceived.

And let it not be a surprise to you that he did not do this before.[14] For as the holy scripture says, in the first union of male and female, the

---

11 The bishops place strong emphasis here on the dynastic nature of Carolingian rule.
12 A reference to Charles's son Carloman, who was ordained as a deacon (though he later tried to reclaim his royal status as heir).
13 This is probably a reference to the young Charles, who had been seriously injured in a fight with one of his retinue, and never recovered.
14 I interpret this "he" as a reference to Charles, rather than to God (cf. Mistry, "Ermentrude's Consecration," 581, for a different suggested reading). The sense of the passage seems to be suggesting that the ceremony was Ermentrude's idea. Early in the history of marriage, women had obeyed men, but when Abraham and Sara were already accustomed to legitimate union and advanced in age ("moribus in legitima coniunctione maturi et provectae aetatis"), like Charles and Ermentrude, God told Abraham to do what his wife said.

Lord said to Eve, *You will turn to your husband, and he will rule over you* [Gen. 3:16]. And when Abraham and Sara were already accustomed to legitimate union and advanced in age, and when as St Peter says, *Sara obeyed Abraham, calling him lord* [1 Pet. 3:6], God said to Abraham – which previously we read that he had not said to him or anyone else – *All the things which Sara says to you, listen to her words* [Gen. 23:12]. For at this time Abraham was rightly called priest, and womanly things, that is all lasciviousness, were absent from Sara.[15] And they accepted the blessing of the blessed seed from God, in whom all peoples are blessed. Amen.

Supported with these authorities, "in dispensing the gifts of God," we [bishops] who are constituted his ministers by him for this purpose, as [Pope] Leo says, "ought not to be hard."[16] Nor should we neglect the petitions of devout people, especially if we plainly see that those petitions spring from the mercy of God. For to assist human salvation, the mercy of God has many times decreed that this salvation might be obtained especially by the prayers of the priests. In their works, as we read in holy letters, the Savior himself intervened: nor is he ever absent from those things which he committed his ministers to carry out, saying, *Behold, I am with you for ever* [Matt. 28:20]. And as Leo says, "if we accomplish anything in due order and with satisfactory results through our service, let us not doubt that it was vouchsafed to us through the Holy Spirit."[17]

Therefore, brothers, since things are so, and our ministration for you is joined with your devotion to us, let there be a single prayer to the Lord, as we read that priests are appointed to do, that they should first pray for their own sins, then for those of the people. And *there was a prayer without ceasing to God for Peter* [Acts 12:5], that is for the whole chorus of bishops. So while we pray for our common salvation and necessity, indeed for the salvation and necessity of the whole church and people, let this common prayer follow the common will, to him who makes *all in the household* live unanimously [Ps. 67:7], and lives and reigns, world without end, Amen.

---

15 In other words, Sara was past childbearing age.
16 Pope Leo I, *Letters*, letter 108 to Bishop Theodore of Fréjus (JK 485), trans. Feltoe, 198.
17 Pope Leo I, *Letters*, letter 108 to Bishop Theodore of Fréjus (JK 485), trans. Feltoe, 197, slightly adjusted.

Prayer. Holy Lord, almighty Father, eternal God, who made all things from nothing by your power, and having ordered the beginnings of the universe, established the inseparable help of woman for the man made in your image, and gave fleshly origin to the female body from the man, teaching that since it pleased you to institute them from one flesh, so it should not be licit for mankind to separate them.[18] Look kindly upon this your woman servant, joined in marital union [*maritali consortio*], who seeks to be fortified by your protection. May there be in her the yoke of love and peace, may she marry in Christ faithfully and chastely, and may she remain the imitator of holy women. May she be as lovable as Rachel was to her husband, as wise as Rebecca, as long-lived and faithful as Sara. May the author of prevarication [i.e., the devil] usurp nothing in her by his actions, may she remain bound up in the commands of faith, may she flee from illicit contact, joined to a single marriage bed. May she fortify her weakness with the strength of discipline. May she be weighty in modesty, venerable in decency, educated in heavenly doctrines. May she be fertile in offspring pleasing to you, may she be tested and found innocent. Through this holy unction of merciful, joyful, and exultant oil, may she receive health of mind, integrity of body, safety of salvation, security of hope, corroboration of the faith, and the fullness of love.

Crown her, Lord, with a crown of justice. Crown her with holy fruits and with blessed works. May she be a queen by merit and in name and virtue, cleaving to the right faith in this world with good works, and crowned in future honor and glory by the right hand of the King, dressed in good works, and girded with the variety of virtues. Make her to bring forth offspring who belong to the inheritance of your paradise. Bestow, Lord, upon this woman servant such an intention of love, zeal for mercy, and growth of religion, that she may constantly be worthy of your help. Repel from her the venom of the cunning serpent, and defend her, protected by the breastplate of faith, with the shield of salvation; correct her actions, improve her life, order her habits, and deign to bring her in at a ripe old age to the celestial kingdoms. Through our Lord [Amen].

---

18 A reminder to all present that divorce was not possible in the dominant Carolingian understanding of marriage.

May the Lord crown you in glory and honor, and with eternal protection. Who lives and reigns [Amen].[19]

May Almighty God, who blessed Adam and Eve, saying, *Go forth and multiply* [Gen. 1:28], and blessed the marriages of the patriarchs, and who sent Raphael his angel with Tobias, by whose ministry he repelled the demon from Sara his wife, bless you and this your future wife.[20] So that according to the precept of God, *two may be made one flesh. What God has joined, let no one separate* [Gen. 2:24], and may he give to you the blessing *of the heavenly dew and the fatness of the land* [Mark 10:9].

And we bless you both in the name of the Lord, who sends his good angels that they may always look after you, and drive all fantasy and wickedness and trickery of all wicked spirits and of men away from you.[21] And may they protect, fortify, and defend you from the stain of any adultery, and from all the traps of men and demons, by the grace of our Lord Jesus Christ.[22] May he pour his love and fear constantly into your hearts, that you may both grow old together in a good old age, and see the children of your children flourishing in the will of the Lord. And may peace remain with you. And persevering in the right faith, good works, good concord, and a sincere conjugal love, and in the confession of the holy Trinity and communion of the Catholic Church, may you both reach eternal life. May he deign to grant this, whose kingdom and rule lasts without end, world without end, Amen.

16. POPE NICHOLAS I WRITES TO KING CHARLES THE BALD, JANUARY 25, 867

Despite all the adversities and setbacks he encountered, and despite the oaths taken by his followers in 865 that he would treat Theutberga as his queen, Lothar II remained undaunted, and his goal remained

---

19 At this point in the ritual, Ermentrude was formally crowned.
20 This part of the ritual is aimed at Charles; the reference to a "future wife" was probably borrowed from an exemplar.
21 This part of the ceremony is addressed to the couple together ("you" here is in the plural).
22 Here, as elsewhere, the ceremony may have alluded to the very different position of Theutberga in neighboring Lotharingia.

unchanged: to make Waldrada his recognized wife. It was this perseverance that led Pope Nicholas I to send a salvo of four letters concerning Lothar II's marriage, all written on January 25, 867. One was addressed to Theutberga, another to Lothar II, a third to Lothar II's bishops.[1] The fourth, directed to Lothar II's uncle King Charles the Bald, is the one translated here. This letter provides crucial clues about Lothar II's new strategies for bringing his marriage crisis, now nearly a decade old, to a satisfactory conclusion.

As the letter notes, Theutberga had apparently written personally to Pope Nicholas to ask to be released from her marriage (unfortunately her letter does not survive).[2] King Charles had granted her the monastery of Avenay in West Francia in 864, and perhaps she was intending to live there.[3] Nicholas informed Charles that he discerned Lothar II's hand at work, either in directly forcing Theutberga to write or in wearing her down until she had had enough; we might also wonder whether Lothar II's "alimony" settlement (Document 13) had helped smooth Theutberga's change of position. In his reply to Theutberga, the pope sought to counter this new development, bluntly ruling out the possibility of her leaving the marriage unless Lothar II also committed to a life of celibacy and retired to a monastery. This stern message he repeated in very similar terms in his letter to Lothar, alongside renewed exhortations to send Waldrada to Rome.

Yet Nicholas's letter to Charles reveals that Lothar II had other ideas up his sleeve that went beyond enlisting Theutberga to his campaign. Rumors had reached the pope that Lothar had a plan B and a plan C, in the form of two new trials. The first was a retrial to prove that Theutberga was not his wife. If that failed, he would arrange a secular trial by ordeal – this time a trial by battle, unlike the trial by hot water in 858 – to determine whether Theutberga had committed adultery; if

---

[1] Respectively Nicholas, *Letters*, nos. 45, 46, and 47 (Nicholas, *Reg.*, 840–2). A translation of Letter 45 (to Theutberga) is available on the *Epistolae: Medieval Women's Letters* website (https://epistolae.ctl.columbia.edu/), which is devoted to letters to and from women in the Middle Ages; a partial translation of letter 47 (to the bishops) is provided by d'Avray, *Dissolving Royal Marriages*, 24.

[2] Nicholas, *Reg.*, 802, dating the letter to July–November 866.

[3] Flodoard, *Historia*, ed. Stratmann, 349, calendaring a letter from Hincmar of Reims addressed to "Abbess Theutberga" of Avenay; for the grant, see *Annals of St-Bertin*, trans. Nelson, 121.

found guilty, she would be executed on the spot. Perhaps the threat of execution was designed to persuade Theutberga to collaborate in the initial trial; perhaps it was genuinely Lothar II's last throw of the dice.

Moreover, and for Nicholas worst of all, Lothar II seemed to have won Charles the Bald's agreement to this procedure, by bribing him with the gift of a wealthy monastery. A large part of Nicholas's letter is devoted to dissuading Charles from lending his nephew support, by illustrating the logical and legal flaws in Lothar II's ideas. Though Nicholas does not quote any canon law verbatim to make his case, as Frankish bishops were accustomed to do, he does refer to some well-known canonical principles, such as that when parties have jointly chosen a judge for their case, they cannot appeal from the ensuing judgment, and that no appeal is possible from a papal decision.

Yet while the letter to Charles shows Nicholas in full rhetorical flow, it also reveals some of the difficulties that Nicholas was facing in enforcing his will. These difficulties centered above all on communication, a perennial problem in early medieval Europe. Rome was a long way away from Lothar II's kingdom. And Lothar II's bishops were, it seems, simply claiming that they had not received any instructions from Nicholas; indeed, some were actively removing his letters from circulation. This was a form of resistance that was more passive than ex-archbishop Gunthar's thunderous proclamations and overt lobbying against Nicholas, but perhaps more effective.[4] In particular, Nicholas was worried that his excommunication of Waldrada in February 866 was still not being respected, nearly a year on.

To this the pope's response in January 867 was threefold. First, he wrote to Lothar II's bishops again to urge them to stay in touch and to make sure his letters were being circulated. Second, he sought to employ Charles the Bald as effectively his man on the ground. It was to

---

4 In February 865 Gunthar launched an appeal for clemency at a council in Pavia in northern Italy: on his influence on the archbishop of Milan, Tado, see Tessera, "Milano, gli irlandesi e l'impero carolingio"; and Vocino, "A *Peregrinus*'s Vade mecum." As well as appealing to Emperor Louis II, Gunthar may even have contacted Patriarch Photios of Constantinople: see Dvornik, *Photian Schism*, 120. In January 866 Gunthar was still in control of Cologne cathedral's assets, though acting not as archbishop but as its "governor" or *gubernator*: see King Lothar II, *Charters*, no. 25, 423–6; and van Espelo, "Rulers, Popes and Bishops." He was still lobbying for his restitution in 867 (Nicholas, *Reg.*, 862). However, Gunthar never regained his position, and a new archbishop of Cologne, Willibert, was finally appointed in 870.

Charles that Nicholas sent his letters to Lothar II and his bishops and, we may suppose, to Theutberga too; Charles was to distribute these letters on the pope's behalf through a trusted envoy. Moreover, in a kind of "tracked delivery," Charles was to let Nicholas know which of Lothar's bishops had received the letter, so he could be sure that his message had reached them and therefore punish them for disobedience if they failed to comply or denied receipt.

An appendix to his letter, moreover, indicates a third tactic. In this appendix, Nicholas also asked Charles to keep a secret copy of his letter to Lothar II, which he was to disseminate only if Lothar II refused to obey its instructions to treat Theutberga properly and to send Waldrada to Rome. We might wonder: why not just ask Charles to disseminate it at once? After all, the letter's contents were hardly surprising for anyone familiar with Nicholas's approach up to this point. Perhaps Nicholas thought it would have more impact if its contents were revealed only later; perhaps he liked the idea of making Charles his partner in a shared secret, creating trust and cementing the link between them; perhaps Lothar II was intended to know that Charles had a "secret" copy of the letter. Whatever the case, the implication was that Nicholas was determined to keep Lothar II in his marriage with Theutberga and was making strategic use of the written word in order to do so, not just by writing letters but by trying to control the extent and even the timing of their dissemination.

From another perspective, though, what the letter illustrates is how the pope was reacting to an agenda that Lothar II was once again shaping. Lothar II and Waldrada had certainly suffered a setback in October 863 when Pope Nicholas annulled the Council of Metz, and they had struggled to remain on top of things for several years afterward. But the king and his advisers were resourceful and resolute, and capable of coming up with creative new solutions. Employing Theutberga herself as an advocate for ending their marriage, planning a new set of trials, and bringing his uncle on board cumulatively amounted to a new strategy tailored to the changed situation in which Lothar II now found himself, and to which the pope was now forced to respond in a case that he must have hoped would have been settled long ago.

The original copy of Pope Nicholas's letter to King Charles, which would have been written on fragile papyrus, does not survive, but it was copied into various medieval manuscripts. Of these the earliest and most important is a ninth-century manuscript now in the Bibliothèque nationale in Paris, shelved as MS Lat. 1557, where the letter can be found on folios 44–46. The manuscript seems to have been compiled in the 870s by Bishop Hincmar of Laon, the nephew of Hincmar of Reims and at one point a close adviser to King Charles.[5] The manuscript also contains copies of the pope's accompanying letters to Theutberga, Lothar II, and his bishops, in a continuous sequence, suggesting that they were obtained by Hincmar of Laon as a single dossier.

Translation[6]

Bishop Nicholas, servant of the servants of God, to his beloved son the glorious King Charles.

Nothing brings pain as much as frustrated hope does, and nothing harms the mind as much as troublesome news coming unexpectedly. Let me explain what I mean.

We recall that among the other religious guardians of the holy church of God and strenuous defenders of the truth, there was no one more concerned by the suffering of the glorious queen Theutberga than you, and no one who has sympathized more with her difficulties than you. When her brother [Hubert] was alive, you brought his case to the apostolic see, and you maintained her with the generosity of your munificence for no little time, and you often strove to exhort us to come to her aid.[7] So the apostolic see, observing that you held such love for her, and since it was not able to resolve her case quickly because of perverse and stubborn obstruction, committed her to your protection and merciful defense, as God watched on and the holy St Peter, prince of the apostles, assisted.

---

5 For a discussion of this manuscript, see West, "'And How, If You Are a Christian, Can You Hate the Emperor?'" Images of the manuscript can be freely accessed online via the Bibliothèque nationale de France's *Gallica* website, at https://gallica.bnf.fr/ark:/12148/btv1b100324392/f91.item.

6 Edition: Nicholas, *Letters*, no. 48, 329–32 (http://www.mgh.de/dmgh/resolving/MGH_Epp._6_S._329) (Nicholas, *Reg.*, 843).

7 Charles had sheltered Theutberga since 860, and as noted in this document, note 3, had given her the rich convent of Avenay (near Reims) in 864. The association with a convent by no means implied she was considered to be a nun. Carolingian queens were often associated with female religious institutions: see Document 14, p. 141.

But now, according to what we have heard, King Lothar has again taken up arms against this Theutberga, and he is said to have entered into a pact with you, that he might be able to join your assent to his wicked intention. A rumor spreading far and wide claims that you have agreed to his destruction of Theutberga in exchange for a certain monastery in his kingdom.[8] If this is true, as many claim, it is vehemently to be grieved and bitterly to be deplored. That is, that instead of the pious advice of the past, you now give advice of an inverted impiety, and that you who till now favored justice, now give assent to iniquity. O incomparable harm! O ineffable loss of a pious king's compassion!

But may this not be the case with such a pious ruler, may it be far from the hearts of the faithful to believe readily these things of such a devotee of Christ. It should rather be believed that the faithful should rightly reprehend those who imitate Balaam, who gave counsel against the life of those he had previously demanded to resemble even in dying, and when he found an opportunity for avarice, at once forgot whatever innocence he had aspired to.[9] And since we cannot yet bear to believe in full that you offered agreement to wickedness, it remains that we should guide our pen to exhort you to finish the pious and incomplete work toward this queen.

For behold what the Truth says: *Whoever perseveres to the end will be saved* [Matt. 10:22]. Behold what is written about blessed Job, offering a continuing sacrifice: *Thus Job did for all his days* [Job 1:5]. The blessed Gregory expounds on this, saying: "His holy action was shown in sacrifice, his constancy of action in sacrifice was shown in all his days."[10]

---

8 In the entry for 866 in the *Annals of St-Bertin*, trans. Nelson, 132, Hincmar specifies that it was the monastery of St-Vaast, as agreed in a summer meeting between King Charles and Queen Ermentrude and Lothar II. Ermentrude's presence here is interesting, suggesting that she might have brokered the deal, as Heidecker, *The Divorce of Lothar II*, notes at 171.

9 A reference to the prophet Balaam in the book of Numbers. Balaam was asked by the king of the Moabites to curse the Israelites, but he refused to do so, saying, "Let my soul die the death of the just, and my last end be like to them" (Num. 22:10). Later, however, Balaam is said to have given advice against the Israelites (Num. 31:16). Nicholas I's point is that Charles should, unlike Balaam, be consistent in his support for Theutberga.

10 Gregory the Great, *Morals on the Book of Job*, bk. 1, ch. 10, trans. Parker 38. Gregory was an important exemplar for late ninth-century popes: see Bougard, "Composition, diffusion et réception des parties tardives du *Liber pontificalis* romain"; as well as, more generally, Leyser, "Memory of Gregory," 192.

With all these things having been set out, we wish Your Excellency to know that King Lothar has subjected his spouse Theutberga to varied afflictions and innumerable pressures, against the oaths he offered, to such an extent that she is now forced to write to us, to say that she now wishes to be divested of the royal dignity or bond, and desires henceforth to be contented with a private life alone. We have written back to say that that this can only happen if her spouse Lothar chooses the same life.[11]

In truth, as we have heard from many people, Lothar has decided to hold a meeting and is planning to submit Theutberga to an examination and judgment. Then, if he can show through false trickery or riddling argumentation that she is not his legitimate wife, he intends at once to remove her from himself. If not, he intends to accept her as if his legitimate wife, but will then pretend that she has committed adultery, and for this he will force one of her men to a duel [*monomachia*], and if the queen's man falls, then he will kill her without delay.[12]

The greatness of Your Prudence already rightly realizes how far removed these things are from all divine law and the law of the holy fathers. But we wish to illustrate this here in brief, first of all pointing out that Theutberga should not be called up again for another response to the previous controversy. What has been properly decided once and settled with oaths should not be repeated again, except perhaps before a greater authority. Moreover, whoever seeks the refuge of the church and requests an ecclesiastical judgment should not be submitted to the judgment of secular men.[13]

Finally, since we were called upon as the judge by both parties, that is by both Theutberga and Lothar, and we pursued each one's controversy, it is not fitting to seek other judges on this matter, since according to the holy canons it is not permitted to appeal from judges chosen by common consent.[14] And when an appeal is granted, it is only possible

---

11 A reference to Nicholas, *Letters*, no. 45 (Nicholas, *Reg.*, no. 841).
12 Frankish custom permitted the execution of wives who had committed adultery: see Stone, *Morality and Masculinity*, 202–4.
13 For a study of the relationship between ecclesiastical and secular courts in the period, see West, "Pope Leo of Bourges."
14 An implicit reference to the Council of Carthage of 419, which forbade appeals in cases where both parties had agreed on a judge. D'Avray, *Papacy, Monarchy and Marriage*, 52, argues that Nicholas I preferred rhetorical over detailed legal argument, to avoid "trading texts" with the Frankish bishops, but here we see Nicholas's familiarity with the canons of the church.

to appeal to a greater authority. Since there is no greater authority than the authority of the apostolic see, which has pursued the case of each, we do not understand that it is possible to anyone to appeal against its judgment or to retract its decision. Thus as church law and ancient custom carefully declare, we are aware that judgments have been taken to the apostolic see and that it has dissolved the judgments of others, but we are not aware that there has ever been an appeal from the apostolic see, or that its decision has ever been violated.[15]

As for Lothar's allegation of Theutberga's adultery, who cannot see that this is full of deception and iniquity? For if she is not his wife, as he claims, why does it fall to him to draw up the accusation about her adultery, since she cannot commit adultery if she is no one's wife? But if she is accused of adultery by Lothar and punishment is prepared if she is convicted, then it follows that she should be admitted to be his wife. Does he not work in vain, worry over, and seek to prove in whatever ways and with whatever arguments that she is not his wife? It is necessary, I say, that she is admitted to be his wife prior to all debate, if he thinks that she can be attacked for adultery. She wished to clear herself of this accusation in the presence of our envoys, but he did not accept it.[16]

As for the duel, in truth we do not find that it was ever commanded to be accepted into the law. For although we read that some people took part, as the holy history says about David and Goliath, never does divine authority permit that it can be held to be a law, since it and those acting in this way seem only to be tempting God.[17]

These things having been said, we earnestly beseech Your Beloved that the care and solicitude and help and assistance that you have always warmly showed to this woman should not be chilled by any agreement nor cooled by any treaty. But rather, as much as the heavenly forces arrange, let Your double Love[18] permit no harm to her in any fashion,

---

15 A clear expression of Nicholas I's elevated view of papal judicial authority.
16 Presumably a reference to the legate Arsenius's visit to Lothar II's court in the summer of 865, when Theutberga was formally restored to her position as queen. Note the protagonism of the queen, who had already escaped from Lothar II in 860 and refused to take the veil in 866.
17 On this articulation of suspicion toward the trial by ordeal, a suspicion that became part of later canon law, see Bartlett, *Trial by Fire and Water*, 118.
18 A reference to the Augustinian notion that love is twofold, for God and for one's neighbor.

lest if any harm should befall her, you will be compelled to give account for it in the terrible judgment of God, since while God looked on, and on behalf of the prince of the apostles, whose defense she has obtained, we commended her to your protection for safekeeping. At this last moment, when no remedy for her safety and immunity can be found, and a most certain death looms over her, take her on yourself, and until whatever God will reveal about her is arranged, nourish her within your kingdom, and administer to her the accustomed beneficences of Your Piety, and only finally then, if anything is charged against her, let her enemies prosecute her, provided we have given permission. But note that we permit this only because it is known to you and to those who understand with us that there is no hope remaining for Theutberga's safety.[19]

Moreover, whether the judgment is to be about the bond of marriage or the crime of adultery, it is clear that Theutberga cannot reasonably enter into a legal conflict with Lothar nor undergo a legitimate challenge in the dispute unless she has been already returned for some time to her powers, and freely associated with her own kin.[20] A place must be provided in which there should be no fear of the crowd's might,[21] and where it is not difficult to gather witnesses and other people who are required for such disputes by both the holy canons and the venerable Roman laws. We say this not to command that this trial take place, since we have taught above that it cannot take place without our decree or command, but to demonstrate the conflict of laws that Lothar indicates he is engaging in, when he takes the person, whom he wears out and beats down every day in private, to judgment whenever he likes and returns her to the cloister whenever he likes. And when she is brought out, who can tell to how many evils she has been subjected in order that she should say nothing except what he has commanded to her? It is appropriate that she who wishes to show that she is free of the accusations should be returned to her own full liberty, and be freed from all the oppression and power of him with whom there is conflict, and be able to avail herself of her supporters and to be distanced from mistrusted people.

---

19 Nicholas I's point is that he is only permitting the separation of the spouses in these exceptional circumstances.
20 That is, the "Bosonids": in the first instance, presumably her nephew Count Boso.
21 On the role of the crowd (here, the *vis multitudinis*) in early medieval Europe, see Bobrycki, "Flailing Women," as well as his forthcoming book, *The Crowd in the Early Middle Ages*.

But now let us put an end to this letter, my dearest son, advising you always to remember what we noted above about the good works of the blessed Job, and always to have before your eyes the case of this oft-mentioned queen. For anything carried out praiseworthily is in vain if the person does not follow it through in all the days of his life. And he runs into the arena in vain if he falls before he reaches the designated point. For it is written, *Woe to them who have lost patience* [Eccles. 2:16]. *So run that you may obtain [the prize]* [1 Cor. 9:24].

What we have decreed about Waldrada, the excommunicated fornicator, is not hidden from you. What we wrote to the bishops of Lothar's kingdom about her return to live in Gaul without our permission, you can read in the letter we have sent them, the exemplar of which we ask Your Glory to have copied and sent to the venerable bishops governing the church of the Lord in your kingdom.[22]

Moreover, we ask that Your Highness will speed a letter addressed to the oft-mentioned king Lothar, the exemplar of which we here have sent to your beloved self, via some prudent and loyal man.[23] We ask you to do the same with the letter which we have sent to the bishops of his kingdom.[24] It should be known that some of these bishops will disdain to accept our letter for the sake of fear or favor, and others will accept it, but will be afraid to do so openly, or wishing to please Lothar, will even wickedly remove it from the sight of others. So we earnestly beseech that Your Wisdom sends our letter to these bishops through a man who will proceed cautiously and pass over none of the bishops to whom it is clear that it has not been given in some way. Once this has been carefully carried out, we ask to be informed immediately who accepted the letter and who did not, through legates or a letter from Your Love. For although they should all be reprimanded for their too great sloth and laziness, those should be much more severely criticized and punished who, as often as they are roused by us, remain sunk in the sleep of a pestiferous torpor, and flee. But before we truthfully know who these are, justice demands that nothing be done definitively on account of their absence or rather ignorance. We wish Your Glory to fare well in Christ now and always, my dearest son.

---

22 Nicholas, *Letters*, no. 47 (Nicholas, *Reg.*, no. 842). In other words, Nicholas I is asking Charles to circulate a letter he sent to the bishops of Lothar's kingdom.
23 Nicholas, *Letters*, no. 46 (Nicholas, *Reg.*, no. 840).
24 Nicholas, *Letters*, no. 47 (Nicholas, *Reg.*, no. 842).

Given on the eighth kalends of February [January 25], fifteenth indiction.

Additional Note

We encourage Your Excellence to keep hold of a copy of this letter sent to Lothar, without anyone knowing, until you know that he has completely obeyed our instructions. If he does not cease from his obstinacy and puts off carrying out what we have requested of him to do, or if he does not retain Theutberga with the honor that is owed to her, let Your Highness bring to everyone's attention what we decreed to him, and disseminate widely what we sent to Your Glory, according to the degree of our censure.

17. BISHOP ADVENTIUS ORGANIZES PRAYERS AGAINST THE NORTHMEN, MAY/JUNE 867

While King Lothar II remained entangled in efforts to be rid of Queen Theutberga after he had been forced to accept her back in 865, exploring both amicable settlement and judicial trial by ordeal, he also had other immediate problems with which to contend. The letter presented below deals with the king's preparations for a battle against "barbarian peoples," who were most probably vikings or Northmen.

The lack of detailed annals from Lothar II's kingdom means that we do not have a full understanding of Scandinavian raiding there, though archaeology is beginning to provide more information.[1] Though the Northmen were capable of destroying kingdoms in England, they did not pose an existential threat to the more powerful Frankish kings, whose kingdoms were much larger (Lothar II's kingdom, for instance, was perhaps five times the size of King Alfred's realm of Wessex). When it came to pitched battles against the Northmen, the Franks tended to win.

---

1 For a study based on archaeological remains of viking raiding armies in this period in England, see Hadley and Richards, *The Viking Great Army*. For a discussion of the archaeological evidence for viking activity in Frisia, see IJssennagger, "Between Frankish and Viking." For an up-to-date overview of viking raiding in Francia, see Cooijmans, *Monarchs and Hydrarchs*.

Nevertheless, the Northmen were still troublesome for Lothar II. Their raids were persistent enough to compel the bishop of Utrecht, in the north of Lothar II's kingdom, to abandon his exposed see around 857 and to take up temporary residence at Sint-Odilienberg, hundreds of kilometers inland.[2] In 863, Lothar II chased off a group of Northmen from the Rhineland. The *Annals of Xanten* record that he wanted to launch an assault on their fortified island camp, but that his followers refused, presumably because of the risks involved: an indication of the king's courage, though perhaps also of difficulties in imposing his authority.[3] In 864 he resorted, according to the *Annals of St-Bertin*, to raising a tax of four pence from every household (*mansus*) to pay off the Northman Rodulf.[4] There were tens if not hundreds of thousands of households in Lothar II's kingdom, so if exacted efficiently this would have amounted to a very large sum of money, which suggests the severity of the challenge. Carolingian kings did not customarily levy land taxes, but the viking raids presented exceptional circumstances. Buying off the Northmen was not a popular move with contemporary chroniclers but, as Simon Coupland has pointed out, it does seem to have been effective.[5] We also know that around 865, Lothar II took lands from one of his sisters to grant to some Northmen (perhaps to a Northman named Rorik), presumably as a way to win them over.[6]

Yet while the Northmen were undoubtedly a headache for Carolingian kings, they also represented an opportunity to demonstrate martial valor as Christian warriors. The letter translated here, written by Bishop Adventius of Metz, one of Lothar II's key advisers, shows how Lothar II might make the most of such a chance. In the letter, Bishop Adventius declares that Lothar II has commanded a three-day fast to

---

2 The see did not return to Utrecht until the 920s under Bishop Baldric.

3 *Annales Xantenses*, ed. von Simson, 21 (the entry is dated to 864 but the annals are out by a year): "Lothar prepared boats and thought about assaulting them, but his followers did not agree to it." Cf. an 863 entry in *Annals of St-Bertin*, trans. Nelson, 104.

4 *Annals of St-Bertin*, trans. Nelson, 112. Such a means of raising money had already been used by Charles the Bald in 860: see *Annals of St-Bertin*, trans. Nelson, 92, "a tax to be levied on the treasures of the churches and on all *mansi* and on traders."

5 Coupland, "The Frankish Tribute Payments to the Vikings."

6 See Nicholas, *Letters*, no. 44 (Nicholas, *Reg.*, 729), concerning land that Lothar II had taken from his (half?) sister Hiltrude to give to pagan Northmen. On the Northman Rorik, see Cooijmans, *Monarchs and Hydrarchs*, 166, for a summary of Rorik's activities, and 176 for a map of his benefice around Dorestad.

win God's favor ahead of a military confrontation with the "barbarian peoples." Here we see a very different Lothar from the king depicted in most of our other sources: not a penitent king unable to control himself, as presented in the Council of Aachen in 862, or a king plotting against papal decrees, as Pope Nicholas I presented him, but a powerful and capable protector of his people, marshaling his bishops and leading his armies into war with God's blessing. The labeling of the Northmen as "barbarians" is not unprecedented and suggests a heightened ideological framing of the conflict.[7] Of course this was a one-dimensional representation of relations that were in reality more complex and nuanced.[8] After all, as we have seen, Lothar II had not held back from peaceful negotiations with Northmen; twenty years later, after his death, one of his daughters, Gisela, would even briefly marry a Northman leader named Godfrid.[9] Adventius's letter, however, insists on a more starkly oppositional image.

Of particular interest is how this image was being propagated not just to the elites of Lothar's kingdom but, via local priests, to ordinary people in local communities.[10] The kingdom's bishops, and the priests under their jurisdiction, were the most thorough and comprehensive communications network available to Lothar II, and Bishop Adventius's letter shows that Lothar knew how to take advantage of it. These people – apparently ordinary peasant households – were required to participate in an extensive mass ritual of divine propitiation for their king unless they were physically ill. Though the only surviving evidence relates to the diocese of Metz, it seems likely that this was intended to be a kingdom-wide event; we can reasonably imagine there were other similar letters from other of Lothar II's bishops that are now lost. In 860, Hincmar of Reims had alleged that peasant women in weaving sheds were discussing Lothar II's marriage;[11] whatever the reality of that allegation, we see here that measures were taken to involve the general populace in

---

7 In his treatise for the young Lothar II (see Document 1, note 4), Archbishop Hraban had justified including extracts on military matters because of the "very frequent attacks of barbarians."
8 Cf. Nelson, "England and the Continent in the Ninth Century."
9 Regino of Prüm, *Chronicle* (883), trans. MacLean, 187.
10 For the importance of these local priests in Frankish society, see van Rhijn, "Royal Politics in Small Worlds," and now van Rhijn, *Leading the Way to Heaven*.
11 Hincmar, *On the Divorce*, trans. Stone and West, 122.

the kingdom's affairs. We may suppose that Lothar II would have much preferred people to be talking about and praying for his victories than gossiping about his divorce.

Finally, it is worth noting that in orchestrating religious fasting and processions ahead of a battle, Lothar II was hewing closely to established royal and indeed imperial tradition. Charlemagne had done much the same, for instance by organizing a three-day fast before his battles with the Avars in 791.[12] Lothar II's own father had done likewise in 846 before setting off to fight Muslim raiders in Italy.[13] A general penitential procession before a battle was designed therefore not only to help to win God's favor but also to signal to everyone, including people in Lothar II's own kingdom, how competently he was meeting the conventional expectations of Carolingian kings, despite his ongoing marital controversy. This is a reminder that in many ways, and despite the frantic innovations brought on by the divorce case, Lothar II was attempting to act as a thoroughly traditional Carolingian king, just as he had at the beginning of his reign.

Bishop Adventius's letter survives in the manuscript Leiden, University Library, MS Voss. Lat. 0 92. This is a composite manuscript, with varied contents; the letter was copied on a flyleaf, as an afterthought, perhaps in the tenth century.[14] In other words, it is preserved in a quite different context from the rest of Bishop Adventius's letters, which were deliberately collected as a dossier by Adventius himself.[15] At certain points the letter is now illegible, though thankfully not much of the text has been lost; these places are indicated in the translation by ellipses. The letter is unfortunately dated only by month, not by year, but the editor Daniel Misonne has suggested it was written in 867, when the *Annals of St-Bertin* mention that Lothar II raised an army to fight the Northman Rorik, and I have followed this hypothesis.[16] In a letter to Pope Nicholas I written a few months later, Adventius declares that Lothar II had won a battle in July, in which "not a small multitude of

---

12 McCormick, *Eternal Victory*, 342–61.
13 *Capitularia regum Francorum*, ed. Boretius and Krause, 2:67.
14 The manuscript is catalogued in the online *Codices Vossiani Latini* database (https://primarysources.brillonline.com/browse/vossiani-latini/) as VLO 092. I am grateful to Anna Dorofeeva for her advice here.
15 See Document 5, p. 55.
16 *Annals of St-Bertin*, trans. Nelson, 139.

pagans fell to the sword's edge," so perhaps the fasting and processions worked.[17]

Translation[18]

Adventius, bishop of Metz through the mercy of God.

According to the royal order sent to us, please understand that we have ordered a three-day fast to take place throughout our diocese. That is, on June 9, June 12, and June 13, we wish the whole people of both sexes to go to church on the sixth hour of the third day … Let them come together with ash on their heads, dressed in sackcloth, barefoot, and process behind the cross until the ninth hour of the day.

Let everyone abstain from meat and wine, except the ill who should redeem themselves with alms, and let them beseech with prayers the mercy of Almighty God, that Almighty God will submit all the barbarian peoples [*barbarae nationes*] to our lord king, for our perpetual peace. And let him give the king safety and long life, and destroy all his enemies with his victorious right hand … Let him allow his armies to triumph with a celestial victory, and keep us safe and sound under his protection.

Let all priests and other ordained ministers all together beseech the Lord with litanies, psalms, and antiphonies, together with the common people. We order and firmly command that every priest takes care to announce this to his parishioners during these three rogation days …

18. THE METZ OATH, c. 868

For many historians, Lothar II's political failure was purely circumstantial. In the words of Karl Heidecker, "In the end Lothar's marriage strategy failed because of his untimely death."[1] We have seen plenty of evidence for the king's determination and political innovation, and it

---

17 Adventius, *Letters*, no. 16: "multitudo non modica paganorum cecidit in ore gladii," 234.
18 Edition: Adventius, *Mandement*, ed. Misonne.

***

1 Heidecker, *The Divorce of Lothar II*, 176.

is true that Lothar II died unexpectedly early, in his early thirties, from an infectious disease. There is good reason, however, to suspect that this accident may have merely accelerated, rather than changed, the denouement. As we have seen, Lothar II's bishops were anxious about the prospect of a hostile invasion as early as 865.[2]

That invasion did not in fact take place, but that the bishops' anxieties were well founded is suggested by the oath, translated below, which Lothar II's uncles, Kings Charles the Bald and Louis the German, swore to each other at a meeting in Metz. The oath has been memorably described as "probably the most cynical political act of this heinous time."[3] Through it, Charles and Louis agreed that they would divide up the kingdoms of their nephews if God granted the opportunity. The nephews in question were Louis II of Italy and Lothar II. It is true that both faced potential problems in their succession. Yet neither was in ill-health, and they were only around forty and thirty years old, respectively, while their father and grandfather had both lived into their sixties. As Nikolaus Staubach has argued, Lothar II's uncles were not banking on his premature death, which they could not have envisaged; they were preparing for his deposition.[4] A post–Lothar II future was here being sketched out by his older uncles, while the king was still a young and vigorous man.

What is more, the oath was taken in Metz, a city in Lothar II's own kingdom and laden with dynastic symbolism (see Document 1). The Carolingian Frankish kingdoms were not sovereign states in a modern sense, and a general overarching notion of Frankishness remained important; still, for Charles and Louis to arrange a meeting about their nephew, in the heart of his kingdom and in his absence, was a clear indication of how much trouble Lothar II was in. The meeting has often been described as "secret," but if so, it would have been a very open secret.[5] Those present included six of the most important bishops in the two kingdoms, who would hardly have traveled alone or incognito. So it is inconceivable that the meeting was expected to remained unnoticed,

---

2 See Document 12, pp. 129–34.
3 Haller, *Nikolaus I. und Pseudoisidore*: "wohl der zynischste politische Aktenstück dieser ruchlosen Zeit," 69. Haller suspected Pope Nicholas I would have known about it.
4 Staubach, *Herrscherbild*, 241–5. Cf. Böhringer, *De Divortio*, 18.
5 Heidecker, *The Divorce of Lothar II*, 45.

even if its details were not circulated. Rather, it was signaling to the bishops and aristocrats of Lothar II's kingdom – none of whom was invited – that they needed to start preparing now for regime change if they wanted a political future.

Unfortunately, the exact date of the Metz oath is uncertain. The text was copied into a medieval manuscript that is now lost, but the oath was included in an early modern edition of texts by the renowned Jesuit scholar Jacques Sirmond, which preserved it for us. There it is clearly dated to 868, a date that has been accepted by several historians.[6] However, in the *Annals of St-Bertin*, Hincmar of Reims mentions that Charles met with Louis at Metz in April or May 867, "to hold discussions with his brother Louis king of Germany," leading some historians to suggest that this meeting provided the occasion for the oath.[7] In the absence of any manuscript evidence, the question is all but impossible to resolve. Whatever its exact date, though, the oath was bad news for King Lothar II.

Translation[8]

In the year of our Lord 868, first indiction, in the city of Metz by St-Arnulf, these agreements were made between the glorious kings Louis and Charles, in the presence of these people: Archbishop Hincmar,[9] Archbishop Liutbert,[10] Bishop Altfrid,[11] again Bishop Hincmar,[12] Bishop Witgar,[13] Bishop Odo,[14] in the twenty-ninth year of the reign of the glorious king Charles.

From now and henceforth, according to the will of God, and for the restoration and honor and defense of the holy church, and the shared

---

6 For instance Goldberg, *Struggle for Empire*, 294; Nelson, *Charles the Bald*, 217; Grotz, *Erbe wider Willen*, 199.
7 *Annals of St-Bertin*, trans. Nelson, 138. Dating the oath to this moment: Staubach, *Herrscherbild*, 151 (with n242) and 241; and Haller, *Nikolaus I.*, 69.
8 Edition: *Capitularia regum Francorum*, ed. Boretius and Krause, 2:167–8 (http://www.mgh.de/dmgh/resolving/MGH_Capit._2_S._167).
9 Reims (West Francia).
10 Mainz (East Francia).
11 Hildesheim (East Francia).
12 Laon (West Francia).
13 Augsburg (East Francia).
14 Beauvais (West Francia).

honor, safety, advantage, protection, and peace of the Christian people committed to us, I [Louis] shall be a faithful assistant to my brother Charles in advice and aid, as far as God grants me to understand and act, in true brotherhood.

And if God should grant to us something more from the kingdoms of our nephews, I shall be a true assistant and cooperator to him, in both acquiring and dividing, as either we or our shared faithful followers, whom we shall choose by common consent, establish most equally; and in agreeing and having and keeping and defending this division, both in what we already have, and in what the Lord might concede to us from these kingdoms, without trickery or deceit or misrepresentation, as a true brother owes to his brother by right; provided that he observes these things similarly with me.

We shall both equally preserve the protection and defense of the holy church of Rome, provided that the Roman popes observe the honor owed to us, as their predecessors observed for our predecessors.[15] Thus may God and these saints help me.[16]

And Charles swore similarly to Louis.

19. KING LOTHAR II WRITES TO ARCHBISHOP ADO OF VIENNE, JULY 869

In the summer of 869, Lothar II traveled to the south of Italy, hoping for a breakthrough, in changed and potentially more promising circumstances. The intransigent Pope Nicholas I had died on November 13, 867, perhaps only in his late forties; the new pope, Hadrian (or Adrian) II, seemed more open-minded. A window of opportunity had appeared, and Lothar II acted decisively to take advantage. He sent Theutberga to Rome, where she confirmed to the pope in person that she wished to separate. Then he visited his brother Emperor Louis II in southern Italy, where Louis was conducting military operations against the Muslim emirate of Bari. Louis II was not prepared to break off his siege, but his wife Empress Angilberga accompanied Lothar II for talks

---

15 Note the conditionality of obedience to the popes that is expressed here.
16 "These saints" suggests that the oath was sworn over holy relics.

with the new pope at the ancient hilltop monastery of Monte Cassino in early July.[1]

As we have seen, Lothar II was by this point in a grave position, with his uncles holding a meeting in his own kingdom to discuss how to divide it. Yet, in a brief and businesslike letter that he wrote to Archbishop Ado of Vienne (near Lyon) shortly after the Monte Cassino summit, Lothar II strikes an optimistic, even cheery note. He had persuaded his brother Louis II to appoint one of his own court notaries, Berner, as the new bishop of Grenoble, a see that formed part of Louis II's realm, and he now instructed Ado to carry out the formalities. In other words, Lothar II was still confidently making arrangements for the future and acting effectively as a patron to appoint someone he trusted to a leadership role. Lothar II also hinted to Ado that his meeting with the pope had gone well, which, up to a point, it had, despite some concern in Rome about going too far to meet Lothar's and Louis's demands.[2] Lothar II's letter ended with an instruction for Ado to come to meet him at the monastery of St-Maurice of Agaune, on the king's way home. This was a ruler who had by no means given up the struggle.

However, whether Lothar II realized it or not, Archbishop Ado was not the most committed of his followers. His archdiocese had been part of Lothar II's realm only since 863, when Lothar inherited this part of Charles of Provence's kingdom. Ado had strong connections with Pope Nicholas, and he carefully collected correspondence with the pope.[3] It is possible that Ado had anonymously sent one of the versions of the Aachen council held in April 862 to Nicholas, asking the pope what he made of it and warning Nicholas not to trust the good faith of Lothar II's circle: "they seek their own interests, not those of Jesus Christ."[4] In a brief historical chronicle that he finished after Lothar II's death, Ado

---

1 *Annals of St-Bertin*, trans. Nelson, 154. Louis II had already offered some support for Lothar II in 864: see Buc, "Text and Ritual in Ninth-Century Political Culture," on the ambiguities of what happened.
2 Evidence for this concern is a speech edited in *Die Konzilien der karolingischen Teilreiche 860–874*, ed. Hartmann, 366–71, which argues against an amnesty for Archbishop Gunthar of Cologne, though it says little directly about Lothar II's marriage. The speech was delivered to an assembly of bishops; whether it was given by Pope Hadrian II, or someone else, is disputed. According to Gunthar himself, Pope Hadrian II had made promises about restoring him to office (*Epistolae Colonienses*, 246).
3 Preserved in the manuscript Vatican, Biblioteca Apostolica Vaticana, Vat. Reg. Lat. 566.
4 *Epistolae variorum 798–923*, ed. Schröder, Epistola no. 12, 108–14; cf. Nicholas, *Reg.*, 580. The precise context for this fragmentary and cryptic letter has not been fully established.

was strongly critical of the king, writing that, "deceived by wicked counselors, he aroused almost the whole church against him by hesitating about marriage with two women," and expressing relief that Lothar II's attempts to win over Pope Hadrian II had been cut short.[5]

Whether Ado would have shared these views with the king at St-Maurice, and what the king would have told him about his meeting with Pope Hadrian II, we shall never know, for Lothar II did not make it there. After a brief visit to Rome, he died from a fever on his way home on August 8, 869. His body was quickly buried in the church of Sant'Antonino in the town of Piacenza in Lombardy, and those of his entourage who survived the diseases of the Italian summer hastened back into the turmoil of Lotharingia, a kingdom now bereft of its king, to be involved in whatever would happen next.

The unfortunate king was not wholly forgotten. Not long after his death, an aristocrat named Wicbert made a donation to the monastery of Tournus in Francia for the soul of the king, "who was like a father to me."[6] The canons of Sant'Antonino also received two donations of land in the king's memory. One was from his cousin, Charles the Fat, who passed through Piacenza in 880. The other, more remarkably, was from the person whom Lothar II had done most to harm in his lifetime, Queen Theutberga, and who only a year before his death had attested that she was terrified Lothar II wanted to kill her.[7] She gave two estates to the canons so that they might pray for Lothar II's soul for eternity, an act all the more extraordinary as we know of no other widowed Carolingian queen who did likewise for her husband.[8]

---

5 Ado of Vienne, *Chronicon*, 323: "At Lotharius rex, frater ejus, a pravis consiliariis deceptus, diu de duarum feminarum connubio vacillando pene totam ecclesiam contra se concitavit." On Ado's chronicle, see Raisharma, "Much Ado about Vienne?"

6 "qui mihi et pater extitit," *Histoire de l'abbaye royale et de la ville de Tournus*, ed. Chifflet, Preuves, 212. Wicbert's (or Wigbert's) mother was a daughter of Lothar I, making him Lothar II's cousin. He may be the *Uuipert* mentioned in the *Liber Memorialis* list discussed in Document 4, p. 49. He played some role in protecting Lothar II's son Hugh, who, however, killed him around 883 (Regino of Prüm, *Chronicle*, trans. MacLean, 189).

7 *Die Konzilien der karolingischen Teilreiche 860–874*, ed. Hartmann, 370; Theutberga swore in Rome that she would rather flee to the pagans than return to Lothar II, on account of *timorem mortis* ("fear of death").

8 Theutberga's charter unfortunately does not survive, but it is mentioned in another document issued by Emperor Charles the Fat around 881; it must have been issued before Theutberga's own death, thought to be c. 875. The unique nature of her grant is pointed out by Hartmann, *Die Königin im frühen Mittelalter*, 130.

Unlike the rest of Lothar II's surviving correspondence, including several letters addressed to Nicholas, the survival of his letter to Ado has nothing to do with Bishop Adventius of Metz. It seems rather to have been kept by its recipient, Ado, who had it copied along with similar letters from Louis II and Charles the Bald onto a blank page at the end of a manuscript of canon law (Paris, Bibliothèque nationale de France, MS Lat. 1452, fol. 196v). The letter is undated, but Ado took a note of when it arrived. Berner was indeed appointed as bishop of Grenoble, so Lothar II got his way on this matter, albeit posthumously.[9]

Translation[10]

In the name of our Lord Jesus Christ eternal God, Lothar, by command of divine providence king, greetings to our faithful follower Ado, venerable archbishop.

Concerning our journey, you should know that we happily reached our dearest brother the emperor [Louis II], and we discussed our case with the apostolic Hadrian, which we shall explain to you and our other faithful followers in due course. For now, we order that you should know we have given the bishopric of Grenoble to our faithful follower Berner, with the consent of our brother the emperor. When he comes to you, receive him as one of our faithful followers, and ordain him bishop of Grenoble. We have already made arrangements about this cleric for you, which the venerable archbishop Remigius and the illustrious count Gerard will tell you about, and inform you of our will.[11]

Farewell, and come to meet us at St-Maurice.

Received at Vienne on August 1.

---

9 Berner is attested as bishop of Grenoble at various church councils, among others the one at Mantailles in 879 that elected Boso, nephew of Queen Theutberga, as the first non-Carolingian king in Francia since 751. On this Boso (a relative of the husband of Engeltrude), see MacLean, "The Carolingian Response to the Revolt of Boso."

10 Edition: *Epistolae variorum inde a secolo novo*, ed. Dümmler, 175–6 (http://www.mgh.de/dmgh/resolving/MGH_Epp._6_S._175).

11 Archbishop Remigius of Lyon and Count Gerard of Vienne.

20. POPE HADRIAN II WRITES TO THE ARISTOCRATS OF LOTHAR'S KINGDOM, SEPTEMBER 5, 869

Lothar II's sudden death in Italy had many consequences. Both Waldrada and Theutberga entered convents, perhaps of their own free will, though there were not many other options open to either of them. Theutberga went to St-Glossinde in Metz and Waldrada to Remiremont in the Vosges mountains.[1] The question of who would succeed to Lotharingia was now urgent. Lothar II and Waldrada's children, including their son Hugh, remained at large, but it seems Hugh was too young to stake a serious claim to his father's kingdom.[2]

Pope Hadrian II had, as we have seen, shown some indications of flexibility toward Lothar II compared to the harsh line that his predecessor Nicholas I had taken.[3] He had released Waldrada from her excommunication in February 868, had met with Lothar II in the summer of 869, and had planned a fresh church council on a matter that his predecessor Nicholas had pronounced closed. It seems likely that this softening of position was partly a result of pressure from Lothar's brother, Emperor Louis II. And indeed, after Lothar II died, Hadrian weighed in heavily on Louis II's behalf. On September 5, 869, soon after hearing of Lothar II's death, Hadrian sent a number of letters to parties over the Alps, insisting that Louis II was the rightful heir to his brother's kingdom.

One of these letters, translated below, was addressed to the aristocrats of Lothar's former kingdom. The letter offers two different perspectives on this kingdom. On the one hand, Pope Hadrian II treats it as a going concern and threatens swift retribution on any "tyrant" who might invade it. The very existence of the letter implies that Lothar II's aristocrats still constituted a meaningful political community, even after

---

1 Theutberga would eventually be buried at St-Glossinde: "quae etiam ibi quiescit," *Translationes sanctae Glodesindis*, col. 232. She was still alive in 875, when she is mentioned as a beneficiary in a Frankish will, receiving a book of medicine (see Bricout, "Note sur deux laïcs," 458–9). Waldrada's death is recorded in the *Liber Memorialis* of Remiremont as taking place on April 9, but the year is not mentioned.
2 On Hugh's rather grim later history, culminating in his being blinded in 885, see Airlie, *Making and Unmaking*, 189–90; McDougall, *Royal Bastards*, 84–6; and in more detail, Wittkamp, "Schicksal."
3 For an introduction to Hadrian II, see Squatriti, "Hadrian II, Pope."

their king had died: Hadrian II may have had particular individuals in mind, but he addressed the kingdom's elite as a group. Lotharingia, in other words, lived on. On the other hand, Hadrian II deliberately associated the kingdom with the realm of the former emperor Lothar I, in order to make Louis II seem its natural heir, ready to reconstitute the former Middle Frankish kingdom that had been created in 843. In Hadrian II's letter, Louis II's claim was based on his descent from Lothar I, and not on his brotherhood with Lothar II. Perhaps Louis II had never fully come to terms with the Treaty of Orbe in 856; perhaps too Lothar II's plight meant his kingdom was not seen as a durable entity.

In his September letters, Hadrian II did not mince his words. His full-throated support of Louis II's claim to inherit Lotharingia reflected not only Louis II's intrinsically stronger inheritance rights but also the pope's reliance on the emperor, in the face of Muslim military pressure on southern Italy. It also indicates a different and somewhat more accommodating attitude to the nature of the imperial office from that of the combative and assertive Pope Nicholas. Hadrian II saw the emperor as more of an equal partner than Nicholas seems to have done, and he frames Louis II's claim to Lotharingia as a realization of his imperial authority as well as a result of kinship.[4] It is significant in this regard that the envoys who carried Hadrian II's letters north were accompanied by a high-ranking envoy from Louis II himself, in what was effectively a joint embassy.[5]

Yet for all the threats it contained, Hadrian II's intervention had no impact whatsoever on the fate of Lothar II's kingdom. This might be in part because of the sheer pace of events; as we shall see, Charles the Bald had invaded before Hadrian II even wrote his letters, let alone before they arrived across the Alps in November, by which point Charles had already been crowned king. Those of Lothar II's followers who had offered resistance to Charles were swiftly dispossessed of their lands.[6] In practice, it was never easy for popes to assert their authority over distant Frankish kings and their followers. Lothar II's vulnerability to papal injunctions had been the result of the particular circumstances of

---

[4] As Grotz, *Erbe wider Willen*, 287, put it, they had "an extraordinarily high regard for each other" ("eine ausserordentliche Hochachtung füreinander").

[5] *Annals of St-Bertin*, trans. Nelson, 165.

[6] *Annals of Fulda*, trans. Reuter, 61.

the moment. In contrast, when relations between Charles the Bald and Pope Hadrian II deteriorated, over Lotharingia as well as other matters, King Charles – once so attentive to papal sentiments – brusquely brushed off Hadrian II's reprimands with ringing declarations of royal sovereignty; Hadrian II backed down.[7]

Pope Hadrian II's letter to the Lotharingian aristocrats survives in a ninth-century manuscript, Paris, Bibliothèque nationale de France, MS Lat. 1557, fols. 90v–91v (next to similar letters he sent to Charles the Bald's followers and bishops). As already mentioned, this manuscript is associated with Bishop Hincmar of Laon in West Francia, who had connections with Lothar II's kingdom, and who may have opposed his king's takeover bid. The letter itself may have been drafted on Hadrian II's behalf by Anastasius "the Librarian," a prominent Roman cleric who also drafted a letter in Louis II's name, discussed in Document 22, pp. 182–200.

Translation[8]

Bishop Hadrian, servant of the servants of God, to all the leaders and glorious counts residing in the kingdom of the former great lord Emperor Lothar, father of the lord Emperor Louis.[9]

It is without doubt a good act of perfect love to *Rejoice with them that rejoice; weep with them that weep* [Rom. 12:15], following the Apostle. Since your former king Lothar left this world by divine command, we know that you are greatly saddened by his death, and as his faithful followers, are filled with an immensely bitter and sorrowful loss, and that you now weep for his passing with human emotion. Our apostolic spirit sympathizes and grieves with you, and we pray to the Lord unceasingly and tearfully, as is fitting, not only for Lothar's eternal rest and salvation, but also for your present consolation, and for peace, concord, and unity, which you may seek with your whole heart and embrace with every faithful devotion, as limbs of Christ, having no stain which could inflict upon you a present or future death. Every day, we beseechingly pray that by the grace of merciful consolation, God may deign to give

---

7 Nelson, "'Not Bishops' Bailiffs'"; and Pecksmith, "A King Praises Himself."
8 Edition: Hadrian II, *Epistolae*, no. 19, ed. Perels, 721–3.
9 That is, Emperor Lothar I, father of Emperor Louis II of Italy as well as of Lothar II.

and inspire eternal life to him who died in the flesh, and the mood and desire for peace and concord to you. For it is he who with a fatherly love chastises us with the rod of justice and afflicts us with cleansing sorrow, and he who mercifully consoles us in all our tribulation, so we can keep going and never give up.

We act on behalf of the prince of the apostles through heavenly grace, bearing responsibility and care for all God's churches, given to us by the Lord before all others, and owe the heaviest duty to the authority of the apostolic see. Therefore, dearest sons, before the ancient enemy, our adversary, corrupts your minds with the secret and wicked tricks of his evil, wounding you with an incurable disease, we must hasten, armed with divine weapons, to warn you with health-giving precepts. If you humbly follow them, you may be saved, like all those who have pleased God from the beginning, as the Lord says in the Gospel, *If any one love me, he will keep my word, and my Father will love him, and we will come to him, and will make our abode with him* [John 14:23].

Therefore, with the apostolic trumpet we warn and with celestial authority we advise Your Loves, most beloved of the Lord's Son, that for the stability of the realm you should now generally take great care to act in all matters concerning our most beloved and spiritual son, the august lord emperor Louis, with the same faith and sincerity of mind which you preserved in your pure hearts for the former emperor Lothar I his father. May no mortal man, no matter what his dignity or glory, be able to call you back by any means or argument from the precept and healthy counsel of the apostolic see, or turn you aside from the path of truth. Nor may you hasten to listen eagerly to anyone's precepts more than to those of the Apostle Peter, pronounced by our lips, which are more useful to you.

This kingdom is owed to Louis by paternal and hereditary right, according to law and reason, and it absolutely belongs to him through the succession of paternal inheritance. For his aforementioned father the former emperor made him emperor, and raised him up as the heir of his whole kingdom above all his other children.[10] Just as Isaac formerly blessed his son Jacob and made him master over Esau,[11] so the

---

10 Louis II had been crowned by Pope Leo IV as coemperor in Rome in April 850, at Emperor Lothar I's command.
11 A reference to Genesis 27.

empire was wholly conceded to Louis by his father before all others, who wished him to rule while he was still alive, and agreed in unity with you[12] that he should be crowned with a diadem by the apostolic see, and equipped with a scepter that was certainly imperial.

Therefore, we warn Your Nobility and we implore in the Lord's name, that you may be tempted by no promises or threats to divide and separate yourselves from our august spiritual son. But may you rather obey him in all things, as long as heaven grants him life, as your own lord, your own emperor, and the rightful heir to the kingdom, and keep your faith to him intact in customary fashion. And may you always work with wise endeavor to deserve the grace of almighty God and St Peter, and our own full blessing and membership of the apostolic communion. For if we perceive that any one of you is striving against these things, despising the warnings of the apostolic see in contempt of St Peter the apostle and keyholder of the celestial kingdom, and is seeking to join another side, then we shall treat him as not only alienated from our apostolic communion, as an unfaithful person and an enemy to ecclesiastical peace and salvation, but we shall also ensure that he be rightly and justly bound with the chains of anathema.

According to the privilege of apostolic dignity and power, we hold, and will hold while he lives, our spiritual son, the most excellent and august lord emperor Louis, to be the king, lord, and emperor of the kingdom of this province, that is of all Gaul, as it is known he was already preordained to be by God, and as may be seen through many proofs to have been decreed by our predecessors the holy popes.[13] If any tyrant dares to invade this kingdom, against divine and apostolic will, he will without delay suffer the censure of apostolic retribution.

May Your Nobility persist in single-minded devotion, and remain linked together with the unbreakable chain of love.

---

12 An interesting indication that Hadrian II had in mind King Lothar II's aristocracy as an abstract group, since by 869 many would have had nothing to do with Louis II's coronation some twenty years previously.

13 The notion that Louis II was preordained (*praeordinatum*) to be emperor over the kingdom is striking. It is unclear what "proofs" Hadrian II is referring to.

21. THE SACRAMENTARY OF METZ, c. 869

News of King Lothar II's death reached King Charles the Bald on August 23, 869 while he was staying at Senlis, north of Paris. Within a fortnight, Charles was in Metz, three hundred kilometers to the east, where on September 9 he had himself ceremonially crowned as king of Lothar II's realm, with the participation of four of Lothar II's former bishops.[1] His lightning-fast reaction, and his apparent confidence in receiving a welcome in Lotharingia, led the German historian Nikolaus Staubach to suggest that Charles had already planned to invade and depose Lothar II while he was in Italy, and that Lothar's unforeseen death simply expedited matters.[2]

A remarkable manuscript now held in the Bibliothèque nationale in Paris with the shelf mark MS Lat. 1141, and known as the Sacramentary of Metz, has long been associated with Charles's coronation as king in 869 (King Charles is known to have had a taste for commissioning expensive manuscripts).[3] A sacramentary is a liturgical book designed for bishops, recording the prayers for the Mass over the liturgical year. This particular manuscript is actually only the first section of a sacramentary, containing the so-called "canon of the Mass," that is, the liturgical prayer at the heart of the Mass. Its final folio is blank. Yet despite its apparently unfinished state, the manuscript's stunning calligraphy and ornamentation have long ensured its renown. Its ten pages are beautifully written in gold ink and accompanied with gorgeous illustrations, making it among the most impressive and luxurious of Carolingian manuscripts.

It is also, however, one of the most enigmatic. Much debate has focused on the image presented below, which shows a Frankish king, flanked by two bishops holding books, being crowned by a heavenly

---

1 Adventius of Metz, Hatto of Verdun, Arnulf of Toul, and Franco of Liège. The ceremony is detailed in *Annals of St-Bertin*, trans. Nelson, 158–62; the liturgical *ordo* of the coronation itself, written by Hincmar, also survives: *Capitularia regum Francorum*, ed. Boretius and Krause, 2:456–8.
2 Staubach, *Herrscherbild*, 245 (describing it as a *Blitzaktion*); Koziol, *Politics of Memory*, 108–10. Charles had already considered deposing his nephew Charles of Provence in 861: see Document 4, pp. 47–8.
3 McKitterick, "Charles the Bald and His Library." The manuscript can be viewed online and in color on the Gallica website of the Bibliothèque nationale de France (https://gallica.bnf.fr/ark:/12148/btv1b53019391x).

hand.[4] Though the king's depiction is broadly comparable to other images of rulers from the period, there are some jarring details, such as his calf-length boots instead of the more usual shoes. To include a picture of a royal coronation in a sacramentary is also strange in itself, given the nature of the sacramentary as a book for church Masses, and one reason why the manuscript has been connected to Charles's coronation. Unusual too is the decision to depict the coronation as bestowed directly by God, whose hand is shown placing the crown on the king's head, while two bishops merely observe these events.

Because the manuscript is unfinished, there is no label or indication of who these three figures are supposed to represent. Could this king be Charles the Bald, flanked by Archbishop Hincmar of Reims and Bishop Adventius of Metz? It was these two bishops who played the key roles in the ceremony for Charles's Metz coronation, according to the version of events in the *Annals of St-Bertin*. But if so, why are they shown with round nimbuses or halos, at this time usually reserved for the holy dead? And why is the king depicted as a young, beardless man, when Charles at this point was in his mid-forties, and in other images sported a full moustache? An alternative suggestion is that the king is not Charles but his distant ancestor King Clovis (d. 511), the first Christian Frankish king, supported by the sainted bishops Remigius of Reims and Arnulf of Metz. Clovis, Arnulf, and Remigius were all mentioned in Charles's coronation ceremony.[5] In this reading, Charles's coronation was being represented as something of a reenactment of Clovis's royal coronation some four and a half centuries earlier.

However we choose to interpret it, the coronation image in the Sacramentary of Metz stands as a powerful visualization of late Carolingian rulership, in which royal power was exercised by God's will and with the support of the episcopate. The image and the manuscript in which it appears were probably only one part of a coordinated effort by Charles to project an image of Christian kingship as a means through which to exert both symbolic and actual authority in Lothar II's kingdom. It

---

4 Still the fullest discussion is in Mütherich, *Sakramentar von Metz*, which includes a beautiful facsimile. For a concise discussion, see Garipzanov, *Symbolic Language*, 93–4 and 252–3.

5 *Annals of St-Bertin*, trans. Nelson, 161.

Figure 7. Sacramentary of Metz (Paris, Bibliothèque nationale de France, MS Lat. 1141, fol. 2v). The reversed text visible in the box beneath the figures is showing through from the previous page and is not part of the image.

has been suggested that Charles might have also commissioned a history book for the occasion, gathering together older works to represent himself as the culmination of Frankish history.[6]

Yet the takeover was not quite so serene and smooth for Charles as his image-making might suggest. For although his older brother Louis the German, who was recovering from a serious illness, was slower off the mark on the news of Lothar II's death, he refused to accept Charles's fait accompli and made it clear that he expected some of the spoils of their nephew's kingdom. Charles consolidated his position by marrying a woman named Richildis, whom he summoned to his side on October 12 (just three days after hearing of his wife Ermentrude's death), before in January 870 making her his wife. Richildis was the niece of Theutberga and the daughter of Bivin, mentioned above in connection to the monastery of Gorze.[7] This relationship connected Charles to powerful Lotharingian families. In the end, however, Charles decided to settle with Louis diplomatically rather than on the battlefield, perhaps out of fear of his more militarily experienced brother. On August 8, 870, at the palace of Meerssen, the two kings shared out Lotharingia, which at this point ceased to exist as a regnal community, though it would never be entirely forgotten.[8] The rights of other claimants, notably Lothar II's young son Hugh and his brother Emperor Louis II of Italy, were simply ignored.

22. EMPEROR LOUIS II OF ITALY WRITES TO EMPEROR BASIL I OF BYZANTIUM, EARLY 871

King Lothar II's older brother, Louis II, had been coemperor since 850 and had held Italy following their father Lothar I's death in 855. Throughout his reign, as Clemens Gantner has shown, Emperor Louis

---

6 On this manuscript, Vienna, Österreichische Nationalbibliothek, Cod. 473, see McKitterick, *History and Memory*, 120–32.
7 *Annals of St-Bertin*, trans. Nelson, 164, with n31.
8 For the treaty, see Schulz, "Überlegungen zum Vertrag von Meerssen," and, for visualizations, Schneider, "Spatializing Meersen." On the later uses of Lotharingia, see MacLean, "Who Were the Lotharingians?"

II prioritized Italian affairs.[1] In particular, he was determined to extend his influence further south. Since Charlemagne's conquest of the kingdom of Italy in 774, the Carolingian rulers had controlled the northern half of the peninsula, leaving the southern part dominated by independent Lombard princes, whose realms surrounded enclaves still ruled from Constantinople. From the ninth century, matters were further complicated by the appearance of Muslim raiders from Aghlabid North Africa and Sicily. They laid siege to Rome in 846, and around the same time one group of them captured the port city of Bari, some four hundred kilometers southeast of Rome.[2]

In 867, Emperor Louis II traveled south and besieged Bari, by this point an independent emirate. It seems he saw its capture as the first step in the assertion of his authority in southern Italy, and then even over Sicily.[3] However, Louis did not have warships at his disposal, which meant that Bari was difficult to take, since it could receive reinforcements and supplies by sea. For this reason, Louis entered into negotiations for naval assistance from the Eastern Roman Empire, which historians conventionally call Byzantium, ruled since late 867 by Emperor Basil I.[4] Basil eventually sent a fleet in late 870, which Louis II regarded as too late.[5] Nevertheless, Bari finally fell in February 871, its emir Sawdan was captured, and Louis II claimed the credit.

---

1 Gantner, *Worthy of Heaven*.
2 On these raids, see Gantner, "New Visions of Community in Ninth-Century Rome"; and for the view from the south itself, Whitten, "Franks, Greeks, and Saracens." On Bari in its Islamic context, see Bondioli, "Islamic Bari between the Aghlabids and the Two Empires," who dates the initial Muslim capture of Bari to 840 rather than the traditional 847.
3 For Louis II's uncompromising hostility to the Muslim emirates in southern Italy, see Ottewill-Soulsby, *The Emperor and the Elephant*, 272–81.
4 On Basil, see Tobias, *Basil I*, esp. 158–65. On Louis II's relations with Byzantium more broadly, see Gantner, "'Our Common Enemies Shall Be Annihilated!'" The modern terminology here is awkward, since as we shall see, Basil I considered himself not a "Byzantine" ruler, but a Roman emperor. But so did Louis II. The term "Eastern Roman Empire" is in some ways more accurate, but again not contemporary. For this reason, I keep the conventional "Byzantium" to describe the former eastern half of the empire after it emerged transformed from the seventh-century Islamic conquests.
5 It should be noted that this chronology is not supported by the *Annals of St-Bertin*, which suggest that Basil's fleet arrived at Bari already in 869 (trans. Nelson, 163); but it is possible that the author of the annals at this point, Hincmar of Reims, was wrong about the date (the alternative is that there were several fleets, which seems unlikely). For more details, see Kislinger, "Erster und zweiter Sieger."

When Basil wrote to Louis II, apparently to put him in his place, Louis II responded in the early summer of 871 with the remarkable letter of remonstration that is translated below. Besides setting the record straight about exactly what had happened at Bari, the letter reveals some of the ideological and intellectual differences between the Frankish and the Byzantine rulers, both heirs to ancient Rome but in distinctive ways.[6] For Louis II, for instance, dynastic legitimacy was of immense importance, both in anchoring his own claim to the imperial title and in unifying a Francia that was in practice divided into rival kingdoms. Louis II also portrayed a world in which the ethnic identity of kin-based peoples (labeled in Latin as *gentes*, as opposed to the more neutral term *populi*), including the Franks, was central to the religious and political order. Neither of these concepts would have resonated in a Byzantium in which dynasty formally counted for very little and where the key division was drawn between imperial "Romans" and (barbarian) kin-based groupings, perceived as two different kinds of community.[7]

The letter was ghostwritten for Louis II by the influential Roman cleric Anastasius "the Librarian," who had himself recently visited Constantinople.[8] This may account in part for the emphasis the letter places on papal authority, but there is nevertheless no reason to suppose that the letter does not reflect Louis II's own position. We do not know for certain how the letter was received in Constantinople, but it has been suggested that it contributed to a reexamination (and intensification) of Byzantium's links to the classical Roman past at this time.[9]

All this might seem remote from Lothar II's divorce case, beyond shedding further light on Frankish conceptions of authority and dynasty. Indeed, Louis II does not mention his recently deceased brother anywhere in the letter. Nor is there any evidence that Louis II ever went

---

6 For a thorough analysis of the letter, see Có, *Vescovi, re, imperatori*, 209–63; and the older but still useful Fanning, "Imperial Diplomacy." For an overview of relations between the Franks and Byzantium in the period, see Wickham, "Ninth-Century Byzantium through Western Eyes"; and in general, Sarti, *Orbis Romanus*.
7 For more on this important problematic, see Pohl, "Christian and Barbarian Identities"; and Heydemann, "People of God." For conceptions of Roman identity in Byzantium, see Stouraitis, "Byzantine Romanness."
8 On Anastasius's complicated career, see the summary in Gantner, "Ad utriusque imperii unitatem?" 36–53. On Anastasius's role in writing this letter, see Có, *Vescovi, re, imperatori*, 94–102 and 255–6. For Anastasius's general attitude to the Byzantines, see Forrai, "Sacred Nectar."
9 Chitwood, *Byzantine Legal Culture*, 21–2.

north of the Alps after 856. Focused on southern Italy though he was, however, Louis II was not oblivious to events farther north. He had obtained lands from Lothar II in 859 and had insisted on his share of the kingdom of their deceased brother Charles of Provence in 863. He had perhaps regularized his relationship with his wife Angilberga in 860 in reaction to his brother's plight.[10] He had offered Lothar II some intermittent support, chiefly by putting pressure on the popes, notably in 864.[11] And as we have seen, Louis II considered that he had a strong claim to inherit Lothar II's kingdom and repeatedly sent envoys and messengers across the Alps to make that point.

In this light, it is intriguing that the *Annals of St-Bertin* state that in 869, Louis II abandoned the siege of Bari and headed north, but that the Muslims of Bari sallied out to attack his departing forces and to ravage the area; after this, he seems to have returned to the siege.[12] We are not told why Louis II suddenly broke off the siege that he had begun years previously in 867, and that he had been unwilling to pause while his brother visited in June 869, nor the exact date at which he did so. But is it possible that Louis II was intending to head north to press his claims in person to his brother's kingdom against those of his uncles, until urgent military developments pulled him southward again? If so, then the fate of Lothar II's kingdom was unwittingly shaped by Sawdan, the emir of Bari, since in Louis II's physical absence, his uncles paid scant attention to his hereditary claims to Lotharingia. This would be a striking demonstration of how the history of the Frankish lands north of the Alps was entangled with the Mediterranean world.

Unfortunately for him, Louis II's decision to prioritize the Italian south over the Frankish lands to the north did not bear fruit, for only a short while after dispatching this letter, he was himself captured and imprisoned: not by Muslim forces, but by a Lombard prince, alarmed by the growing success and momentum of the emperor's campaigns.[13]

---

10 See on this Gantner, "'Our Common Enemies Shall Be Annihilated!'"; as well as Heidecker, *The Divorce of Lothar II*, 117.
11 On this, see Buc, "Text and Ritual in Ninth-Century Political Culture."
12 *Annals of St-Bertin*, trans. Nelson, 162: "Louis left off his siege of the Saracens and returned from the region of Benevento, whereupon those Saracens came out from Bari and pursued Louis's army from behind."
13 The event was commemorated in a poem, the "Rhythmus on Emperor Louis's Captivity." For a detailed analysis of the sources for the event, which differ significantly over its details, see Granier, "La captivité."

Though Louis II was soon released, his authority in the south never recovered, and Bari was handed over to the Byzantines in 876.

Louis II's reply to Basil I is preserved only in the *Chronicle of Salerno*, a history written in the tenth century, whose earliest surviving copy is in a thirteenth-century manuscript, Vatican, Biblioteca Apostolica Vaticana, Vat. Lat. 5001, where the letter is copied at folios 60r–67v.[14] Sadly, Basil's original letter to which Louis was responding is lost, but it is reasonably straightforward to reconstruct its thrust.

Translation[15]

In the name of our Lord, Jesus Christ the eternal God. Louis, by the working of divine providence august emperor of the Romans, to our most beloved and spiritual brother[16] Basil, the equally most glorious and most pious emperor of new Rome.

It is certainly a good thing and praiseworthy for someone to be kindled to the flame of love by the advice of brothers, as if by puffs of air. But it is even better to be eagerly set alight to this flame by the actions of one's own spontaneous will. And it is best of all for someone to take the path of virtue and to climb higher and higher, with great success. For that soldier who bravely assaults the enemy's forces after a late arrival is always more loved by the commander than those who arrive speedily, yet do nothing or at least very little afterward.[17]

Following this rule, and from the day in which it planted the root of love for Your Fraternity in its heart, our divinely raised rule [*imperium*] has not ceased to bring forth many fruits, attending to and defending your interests as much as our own. Although you boast of what you did for our envoys for the sake of friendship and kindness, it is clear that we

---

14 On this manuscript, see Pohl, "Historiography of Disillusion."

15 Edition: Louis II, *Letter to Basil I*, ed. Henze, 385–94 (http://www.mgh.de/dmgh/resolving/MGH_Epp._7_S._385), on which my paragraph structures are based (though I have divided up the longer paragraphs for convenience). I have also drawn on the Italian translations by Matarazzo, *Chronicon* and (better) by Arnaldi, "Impero d'occidente e impero d'oriente." Key words (notably *gens*, meaning people, and *imperium*, meaning empire or imperial rulership) are given in Latin, to help keep conceptual clarity.

16 The letter repeatedly uses a language of brotherhood to stress the bonds of equality between the two rulers.

17 Note how Louis II quickly brings in the issue of military valor.

did the same earlier for John the most celebrated officer [*patricius*],[18] whom in truth we treated and loved not like a friend or like the follower of our brother, that is of your rulership [*imperium*], but rather as if he was our kinsman, and the offspring of Your Excellence. While he was with us, neither lateness of the hour nor intimacy of space excluded him from our personal chambers.[19]

And we are amazed that Your spiritual Fraternity argumentatively uses so many long-winded phrases. This goes against the Apostle, who said, *if any man wishes to be contentious, we have no such custom, nor does the church of God* [1 Cor. 11:16]. For the dignity of rule [*imperium*] stands with God not in word or name but in the glorious heights of piety. And we should not care what we are called: it is what we are that should be considered. However, since you wrote a great deal to us about the imperial title, we are obliged to respond to your letters, in case if we remain silent on the matter, we should be thought by the foolish to be silent not to avoid dispute, but as if proved wrong by reason.

Your Love indicates that you fear the curse of the law, and therefore you refuse to move the eternal boundaries, or to change and overturn the decrees of the ancient emperors, against canonical and paternal precepts.[20] And yet you do not openly explain which boundaries, which ancient decrees, which canonical and paternal precepts these are, or when or how they were established, unless perhaps you wish all these things to be implied in the title of emperor. Over here with us, in truth, many books have been read, and many are tirelessly being read, yet never have we found that boundaries were set out, or that decrees or precepts were established, that no one is to be called *basileus*[21] except whoever happens to hold the helm of rule [*imperium*] in the city of Constantinople.

Indeed, setting aside for the moment the records of particular peoples [*singulares gentes*], the sacred histories show us very plainly that

---

18 A senior Byzantine officer.
19 In other words, the Byzantine envoy John was granted easy access to Emperor Louis II, rather than being kept at arm's length.
20 Here we are given a flavor of Basil I's original letter, in which he apparently presented himself as the custodian of ancient tradition. The "eternal boundaries" is a nod to Deuteronomy 19:14. It seems likely that Basil I was reluctant to call Louis II an emperor or *basileus* (βασιλεύς); indeed, most ninth-century Byzantine sources termed him a king (ῥήγα).
21 The Greek word for emperor (plural: *basileis*). The word is written here in Latin script but correctly inflected in Greek (here as *basilea*, the accusative form).

many have been called *basileis*, including not only some of the elect, such as Melchizedek and David, but also the reprobate, such as the leaders of the Assyrians, the Egyptians, and the Moabs, and other nations which it would be tedious to list. Since things are so, Your Prudence will understand that it is pointless to argue that none should be called *basileis* apart from yourself, unless you think that the books of all the world should be erased, in which the leaders of almost all the peoples from ancient times and thenceforth are found to be called *basileis*.

Indeed, leaving Latin books to one side, if you consider Greek books that have been recently issued,[22] you will find without any doubt that many people are called by such a name there, and that not only the leaders of the Greeks were honored with the appellation of βασιλεῖς,[23] but also those of the Persians, the Hepierotae, the Indians, the Bithynians, the Parthians, the Armenians, the Saracens, the Ethiopians, the Vandals, the Goths, and other peoples. Look into this, brother, and consider how in various times, in various places, and from various peoples, many were or are still called *basileis*. And do not begrudge us what we are called, or usurp for yourself alone what you share not only with us, but also with many leaders of other peoples. Pride in an individual dignity is a serious vice: who first sought this, or what happened to him who sought such things, we are unwilling to bring to your attention here, lest Your Fraternity think it brought up to cause you offense.[24]

You also say that the four patriarchal sees[25] have a tradition handed down from the God-bearing apostles[26] to commemorate a single empire during Mass, and you say we should persuade them that they should call us emperors. But neither does reason demand this, nor does it need to be done. Firstly, since it is not fitting for us to instruct others on what we should be called. Secondly, because we know that, without any persuasion on our part, both patriarchs and all other people under this heaven, both officeholders and private citizens, except Your Fraternity,

---

22 This might refer to books that Anastasius, the ghostwriter of the letter, had himself seen in Constantinople during his visit in the spring of 870.
23 *Basileis*, written in Greek script (here, in the inflected form βασιλέων). Anastasius "the Librarian" was competent in Greek and translated several works into Latin: see Forrai, "Sacred Nectar."
24 A cryptic reference, presumably to an episode in the Bible.
25 Constantinople, Alexandria, Antioch, and Jerusalem.
26 *Deiferis apostolis*, an odd term in Latin and probably a translation of a Greek phrase.

do call us by this title, as often as we receive letters and writings from them. And we find that our uncles, glorious kings,[27] call us emperor without any envy and say without any doubt that we are the emperor, not taking age into account – for they are older than us – but instead considering anointing and the blessing by which, through the laying on of hands and prayer of the highest pontiff, we are divinely raised to this height, and the rulership of the Roman principality [*Romani principatus imperium*], which we hold by heavenly permission.[28] However this may be, if the patriarchs do make mention of a single empire during the holy sacraments, then they should be praised as acting entirely appropriately. For there is indeed one empire of the Father, the Son, and the Holy Ghost, of which the church on earth is a part. But God has not granted this church to be steered by either me or you alone, but so that we should be bound to each other with such love that we cannot be divided, and should seem to exist as one.[29]

And we do not believe that the most holy patriarchs commemorate you in such a way that they should pass over mentioning other rulers, let alone us. For the Apostle commanded that we should pray even for those who persecute the church, that they may lead a secure and peaceful life, with all piety. And especially since we do not doubt that they pray for the impious under whose rule they live, just as the people led into Babylon were commanded by Jeremiah to pray for the king of Babylon.[30] For in their peace, the faithful also placed their own peace.

We are justified in feeling some astonishment that Your Serenity believes we are aspiring to a new or recent title. For as much as it pertains to the lineage of our descent [*genus*], it is neither new nor recent, for it comes from our great-grandfather of glorious memory.[31]

---

27 Kings Charles the Bald and Louis the German. Given that they had just ignored Louis II in dividing up Lotharingia, his statement here about the respect in which they held him is not altogether convincing.
28 Note the importance that Louis II here places on anointing by the pope. Byzantine rulers were not anointed.
29 This is the last explicit Carolingian reference to the notion of a joint Roman *imperium* (I am grateful to Laury Sarti for pointing this out).
30 The cities of the patriarchs of Jerusalem, Antioch, and Alexandria had been conquered by the Muslims in the seventh century. In other words, Louis II expects that the patriarchs of these Christian churches prayed for the caliph of Baghdad who ruled over them, just like the people of Israel prayed for the Babylonians during the Babylonian Captivity, so why should they not also pray for him?
31 That is, Charlemagne.

He did not usurp it, as you maintain, but, by the will of God and the judgment of the church, received the imposition of hands and anointing from the highest pontiff, as you will easily find written in your books.[32] Anyway, what would be surprising if it were new? For all old things have their beginning in some novelty, and not the new from the old. When the first Roman rulers began to rule [*imperare*], that too was a novelty which in the passing of time acquired antiquity. Not every novelty is a fault, but only the novelty that is reprehensible. For the Apostle, writing to his beloved disciple, did not say, "shun the words that are new," but rather *shun the new words that are profane* [1 Tim. 6:20]. Indeed, no one who is aware that we are the successor of ancient emperors, and who knows the wealth of divine piety, doubts that the dignity of our empire is ancient. For what is surprising if at the end of time, God shows openly what in previous times he predestined in secret counsel?[33]

But it is equally surprising that you assert that the ruler of the Arabs is called a *protosimbolus*, since nothing of the sort is found in our books, and your books sometimes call him *architon*, sometimes king, and sometimes other names. We prize beyond all other books the holy scriptures, in which David says that the kings, not the *protosimboloi*, of the Arabs and of Saba are setting out.[34] And we find that the leader of the Avars is called the Khan, but not those of the Khazars nor of the Northmen. Nor is the leader of the Bulgars called a "prince," but rather the king or lord of the Bulgars. We say all this so that through reading Greek books, you may realize that things are not as you have written. For you insist that they are satisfied with their titles, but you do not yourself remember their appropriate titles. When you craftily take the title of *βασιλεύς* from all these rulers so that it remains to you alone, you interpret violently, not appropriately.

---

32 The Latin here is a little hard to construe. Perhaps a reference to the *Chronographia* of George the Synkellos and Theophanes, which was completed around 815, and which discussed Charlemagne's coronation. Anastasius certainly knew the work since he translated it into Latin, a version known as the *Historia Tripartita*. On the *Chronographia*, see now Torgerson, *Chronographia*. For the Byzantine perception of Charlemagne's rulership, see Sarti, *Orbis Romanus*.

33 That is, the Carolingian empire might be chronologically new, but it is rooted in God's plan for the world.

34 A reference to Psalm 71:10 ("the kings of the Arabians and of Saba shall bring gifts").

It is only right to laugh at what you said about the imperial name being neither hereditary nor appropriate for a people [*gens*].[35] How is it not hereditary, since it was hereditary for our grandfather? In what way is it inappropriate for a people, since we know – mentioning only a few for the sake of brevity – that Roman emperors were raised from the people [*gens*] of Hispania, of Isauria, and of Khazaria?[36] And though you cannot truthfully assert that these nations are more outstanding in religion or virtues than the people of the Franks, yet you do not refuse to include them nor disdain to talk of emperors coming from them.

Further, o brother, accept this as a short response to your comment that we do not rule [*imperare*] in all Francia. Indeed we do rule in all Francia, since beyond all doubt we hold whatever they hold with whom we are one flesh and blood, and by this one spirit through the Lord.[37]

Your beloved Fraternity, moreover, indicates you are surprised that we are called emperor of the Romans, not of the Franks. But you should know that if we were not emperor of the Romans, we would not be emperor of the Franks either. We derive this title and dignity from the Romans, among whom the first summit of the glorious title shone out, whose people [*gens*][38] and whose city we divinely received to govern, and whose church, the mother of all the churches of God, we received to defend and raise up. From this church the ancestors of our family took up the authority first of ruling as kings [*regendi*], and then of ruling as emperors [*imperandi*].

For the rulers of the Franks were first called kings, then emperors, those, that is, who had been anointed for this purpose with holy oil by the Roman pontiff. It was Charles the Great, our great-grandfather, who first from our people and from our stock [*genealogia*] received this anointing through the highest pontiff, such was his piety, and who was

---

35 The Byzantines in the ninth century did not regard themselves as a people (*gens* or γένος), a concept that they reserved for the "barbarian" groups whom they considered were biological rather than truly political units. The Franks, in contrast, perceived the whole world as divided into *gentes*. See Stouraitis, "Byzantine Romanness"; and Pohl, "Christian and Barbarian Identities."
36 These details may have been taken from the *Chronographia* of George the Synkellos and Theophanes (my thanks to Mirela Ivanova for pointing this out).
37 This peremptory claim about Frankish unity on the basis of kinship is a stretch, yet Lothar II's divorce case shows how interconnected the kingdoms were.
38 Note that for Louis II, the Romans are just another *gens*, like the Franks.

called emperor and made the anointed of the Lord.[39] This is especially important since often some have been called to imperial rule who have acquired it without any divine working channeled through the ministry of pontiffs, but only by the senate and the people, without this causing concern. And many indeed did not even have this much, but were simply acclaimed and set up in their rule by soldiers, and indeed some were promoted to the scepter of the Roman empire by women, and others by various means.[40]

Now, if you incriminate the Roman pontiff for what he did,[41] you must also incriminate Samuel, who rejected Saul whom he had anointed with his own hands, and did not scruple afterward to anoint David as king.[42] Truly, if there is someone who dares to grumble against the pope on this matter, he will not lack a response. But in the meantime, if you turn the pages of the Greek annals and consider what troubles the Roman popes have suffered from others without any defense from you, and indeed from you yourselves, you will find at once that you cannot justly criticize them. Indeed they would readily have considered these matters being done abroad as of little importance, had they not also discovered the attempts of those seeking by means of various heresies to destroy from within.[43] So it was with merit that the popes abandoned the apostates – for what communication is there between Christ and Belial?[44] – and they cleaved to the people which cleaves to God,[45] and which brings forth the fruits of his kingdom. For the Lord shows no partiality, but as the great Apostle says, *in every people anyone who fears him is acceptable to him* [Acts 10:35]. Since things are so, and since in every people anyone who fears God is acceptable to him, why do you take such effort to criticize us because we come from the Franks and have charge of the reins of the Roman empire?

For the elder Theodosius and his sons Arcadius and Honorius, and Theodosius the younger, the son of Arcadius, were raised from Spaniards

---

39 That is, Charlemagne, here called *Karolus Magnus*.
40 A general point about Byzantine history, but perhaps also a specific jab at Basil I, whose elevation to the imperial throne had not been smooth.
41 That is, in anointing Charlemagne as emperor in 800.
42 A reference to 1 Kings 15.
43 That is, the Byzantine rulers who had sometimes sought to intervene on doctrinal matters.
44 A reference to 2 Corinthians 6:15.
45 That is, the Franks.

to the summit of the Roman empire.[46] And we do not find that anyone complained or grumbled that Theodosius was not a Roman but a Spaniard, nor did they try to prevent or prohibit his sons from succeeding to their father's place and honor, just as now, we say with respect, Your Fraternity, which we love and support, appears to be attempting to do. As if the people of the Franks do not belong to that inheritance, about which the Father said to the Son, *Ask of me, and I will make the peoples your inheritance* [Ps. 2:8] and so on, and elsewhere, *I will honor those who honor me* [1 Kings 2:30],[47] and in innumerable other places.

So, dearest brother, cease to be so quarrelsome, cease to bend the ears of Your Purity to flatterers. For the people of the Franks [*gens Francorum*] have brought many and most fertile fruits to God, not only by quickly converting themselves, but by converting many others to salvation. And God's law says to you, *The kingdom of God will be taken away from you, and given to a people that produces the fruits of the kingdom* [Matt. 21:43]. Just as God was able to lift up the sons of Abraham from the rocks, so he was able to raise the successors of the Roman empire from the hardness of the Franks. And just as, according to the Apostle, if we are Christians we are the seed of Abraham, so if we are Christians we have through his grace all those things that those who are Christians have. And just as we are the seed of Abraham through the faith of Christ, and the Jews ceased to be the sons of Abraham because of their treachery,[48] so we took up the rule of the Roman empire on account of our good belief and orthodoxy; while the Greeks ceased to be emperors of the Romans because of their kacodoxy [*kacodosia*], that is their bad belief.[49] And so they have not only left the city and the seat of empire but also the Roman people, and have entirely lost the language itself, and have migrated in all things to another city, seat, people, and language.[50]

---

46 Emperor Theodosius I ("the elder") ruled from 379 to 395.
47 Note that this passage of the Bible is quoted in other texts about Carolingian kingship (Document 3, p. 44, and Document 6, p. 94).
48 A reference to the Christian view that the Jews had broken their pact with God by failing to acknowledge Jesus Christ. For a specific study of Carolingian anti-Jewish sentiment, see Liu, "Agobard, Deuteronomic Curses, and an Anti-Jewish Exegetical Discourse."
49 The term *kacodosia* as an opposite of orthodoxy is coined here. This letter was written in the context of considerable tension between the Roman Church and the Byzantine Empire, embodied in the so-called Photian schism. On this, see Dvornik, *Photian Schism*; as well as Chrysos, "Rome and Constantinople in Confrontation."
50 A very strong challenge to the Byzantines' sense of themselves as the heirs of Rome.

But o beloved brother, so that sadness does not fill your heart, hear what follows: *God has not rejected his people whom he foreknew [...] I say therefore, Have they so stumbled, that they should fall? May it not be so. But their crime is become*[51] our honor, and their loss has become our plenitude. When the branches were broken, we were grafted onto them; when we were wild olives, we were joined to their roots and became fat with olives.[52] We say therefore that the branches were broken so that we might be grafted on. Good: they were broken for their wrong beliefs alone; we stand through our faith.[53] *Who has ears for hearing, let him hear* [Matt. 11:15].

You say that there was a moment when, as you promised to Our Fraternity, we might have gained that title, if God had wished to carry to its conclusion that on which we were advised.[54] About that advice which you mention: what we said then, we say now. We do not change our mind between yes and no, nor do we slip to the left or the right of our words, but we unchangingly maintain them. Up till now, neither we nor our fathers are recognized to have had that title through our flesh and blood, and we rightly disdain to have it in this way. For we are accustomed to be honored through our fathers, not through our sons, and among us, glory does not derive from sons to the father, but from fathers to sons. That which we took from the Father of Light, from whom all good things and every gift is given, we wish to take neither from a son, nor through any other man, or from men.

Finally, you should know that whoever calls someone a "rix" does not know what he is saying.[55] Even if you spoke all languages in the fashion of the apostles or like angels, you would not be able to say what language "rix" comes from, or to what dignity that barbarian sound refers. There is none, unless perhaps you intended that "rix" means king [*rex*], treated in the idiom of your language. But since this is Latin,

---

51 Romans 11:2, 11.
52 Cf. Romans 11:17. Note how this biblical metaphor is used to express a kind of imperial continuity with ancient Rome.
53 Cf. Romans 11:19.
54 This is a reference to a proposed marriage between Louis II's daughter Ermengard and Basil I's son. By implication, Basil had suggested that Louis II's status would rise through his daughter's marriage.
55 This paragraph mocks the misspelling of the Latin word for king, *rex*, in Basil's letter.

not barbarian, it is fitting that it should be translated properly into your own language when it comes into your hands. And if this were done, how else would it be rendered other than as βασιλεύς [*basileus*]? As indeed all the translators of the Old and also of the New Testament attest. And if you hate this word used of other peoples, then hurry and erase the name of king or βασιλεύς from all books, Latin and Greek. For king means in Latin nothing other than what βασιλεύς means in Greek.

Having considered these points, we are astonished at what Your Serenity goes on to say: that your forces, that is the Greeks, assaulted Bari and fought to destroy it, and that our men offered no assistance, and either just stared or were left dissolute through feasting, and so there was no way to capture the city. Rather, our men, whether by staring alone, or feasting, or doing whatever, and while few in number and overstretched, fought and captured it with divine help.[56] Your men appeared like caterpillars in their numbers, and gave their first assault like locusts, in that they showed their effort in the first attack, but then were overcome by fear and weakened. And so like locusts they jumped forward, but then exhausted as if from the effort of flying they fell back. And so neither staring, nor feasting, nor conquering, nor with any other sign of triumph, they retreated immediately and in secret, and returned ineffectively to their home with just a few Christian captives. So, brother, do not mock the Franks, since even in the face of death they take the effort to have feasts and every sign of charity for their neighbors, and yet do not slacken from their undertaking. For according to the Apostle, they know how *to suffer abundance and penury, to be bloated and to fast*, and, in brief, they can do all things in him who strengthens them [Phil. 4:12–13].

What surprises you about the paucity of numbers, if they were few but brought back so much booty? And indeed we have already indicated to Your Love why they were so few.[57] But since you have criticized us on that issue for a second time, then accept our response for a second time. When the fleet of Your Fraternity had long delayed, and we no longer anticipated its arrival, we thought that nothing could be done that year for the siege of Bari, and so we let

---

56 The city of Bari was captured by the Franks in February 871, after the Byzantine fleet had departed.
57 A reference to now lost earlier correspondence.

all our men return to their homes, keeping back only those whom we thought sufficient to prevent the city receiving provisions.[58] And so it was that your fleet unexpectedly arrived and found us few in number. Yet it was these few, and in fact even fewer for some were sickened with various diseases, who before Bari was captured destroyed three squadrons, a numerous multitude of Saracens, who were ravaging Calabria, and brought great solace to your populace through God's right arm. Thus not only was there a mighty diminution in the number of the Calabrian Ishmaelites, but also a great dissolution of the power of the men of Bari, so that it was made easier to capture. We suppose that your men brought trophies of this deed to your empire and spoke wonderfully of the works of God which ought not to be passed over.

Moreover, we request the love of Your Fraternity not to bring any harm to bear on the *patricius* Nicetas because of how he so insolently offended our spirits.[59] For although he was so reckless and contumacious concerning our rule [*imperium*] that a great number of our faithful men would have attacked him, had we not calmed the matter down for the sake of your honor and the love we bear you; nevertheless, we do not and should not return evil for evil. So we demand that if any threats loom over him by your power, that they should swiftly be removed by your hand for the sake of our love.

As for the papal apocrisiaries, neither their profession nor their learning nor their previous behavior shows them to be men such as are described in those letters Your Fraternity sent to us. For our spiritual father the highest pontiff, and the whole church, sent on the request of your empire (may God preserve it) chosen and approved men who are experienced in knowledge and strenuous in the matters of ecclesiastical correction. And so it would have befitted Your Excellence to send them back guarded in such a way that they would not have been attacked by pirates or other wicked people. For a serious complaint about this is rising against you, from both our spiritual father the apostolic pope and from the whole of the Roman Church, that you sought

---

58 A reminder that the Carolingian rulers did not have a salaried army at their disposal (unlike the Byzantine rulers).
59 Nicetas (or Niketas) Ooryphas had been tasked with escorting Louis II's daughter Ermengard to Constantinople in 869, but the marriage alliance was called off.

these men from the apostolic see with enthusiasm but sent them back without proper attention.[60]

And Nicetas the *patricius*, with the fleet of the lieutenant Hadrian, took advantage of the opportunity, and seized much booty from the Slavs, and destroyed some of their fortresses and took their men captive.[61] And nor has what the apocrisiaries lost been returned to them so far.[62] We do not wish Your spiritual Fraternity to be unaware that we are more angry than words can say about the destruction of our fortresses and about so many of our peoples [*populi*] of our *Sclavenia* being led away in captivity without any mercy.[63] For it was not appropriate that while these Slavs of ours were at Bari in their boats, ready for battle for the common good and thinking that there was no danger from other quarters, their homes were wickedly ravaged, and things took place which if they had known about in advance, they would have avoided. So we advise and recommend to Your Fraternity that you order this to be corrected, and those captives to be returned to their lands with their belongings, if you wish the bond of love between us not to be broken. For no one can remember such things having been done to our empire [*imperium*] before. And unless some correction is carried out by your order, our vengeance will quickly follow on, and what was done with such boldness in contempt of us will not remain unpunished.

And we declare that we were equally astonished to hear what the letters of Your Sweetness intimated to us about our envoys, indicating that they walked around without order and with unsheathed swords, and that they killed not only beasts but men. If this had been so, Our Mildness would have been very upset, and we wished very much to find out the truth of this. They were carefully questioned by us, and they have denied that they had acted in this way. And since there is no one

---

60 The papal envoys were captured by pirates as they sailed back from Constantinople in early 870 after attending the Eighth Ecumenical Council, as noted by the *Liber Pontificalis*, trans. Davis, 287–8. See Bobrycki, "A Hypothetical Slave in Constantinople," 64.
61 This damage was carried out in the course of freeing the papal envoys.
62 In particular this may refer to the authenticated copy of the Eighth Ecumenical Council of Constantinople that the papal envoys had just attended, a manuscript that the *Liber Pontificalis* (trans. Davis, 288) notes was taken from them as they travelled back home.
63 Probably a reference to the Croats, led at the time by Duke Domagoj. See Majnarić, "In the Shadows of Empires."

who accuses them of this to their face, and they have neither been convicted nor have they confessed, there is nothing to be done in terms of correcting them. Indeed, we have not taught or instructed them that they should fall into the actions you claim, and so we do not think it easy to believe this of them. And it sounds distasteful too that Your Fraternity claims your men would have wounded our envoys not with their swords but with their teeth, had they not been barely restrained for fear of you. For if they had not been in your empire [*imperium*], they would not have sought such protection, and nor when in your kingdom [*regnum*][64] would any of our men have been at all afraid: for they are unafraid of men in such numbers or indeed even of more, thanks be to God.

Finally, Your Fraternity wrote to us about Naples, saying that we had sent our people [*populus*] to cut down trees and burn the harvest, in order to subject the city to our rule.[65] Although it always used to be ours, and paid tribute to the pious emperors our ancestors, we have demanded nothing beyond the customary assistances from its citizens, except to their own benefit: that they should abandon pestilential contact with the wicked and cease attacking the Christian people. For they hand over arms and food and other help to the infidel, and lead them through the shores of our whole empire, and with them they secretly try to ravage the entire territory of the apostles of St Peter, so that Naples seems to have become Palermo or Africa. And when our men attack the Saracens, they flee to Naples so that they can escape. They do not need to reach Palermo but only Naples, and hide there as long as they like, until they return unexpectedly to their work of destruction.

We warned the Neapolitans many times about this, but our warning only made them worse, to the extent that they threw out their own bishop because he was advising them to avoid consorting with the wicked, and they tied up important and worthy citizens with chains. So, if they will not dissolve their association with the infidel, according to the Apostle who says, *Do not lead the yoke with nonbelievers* [2 Cor. 6:14], and they will not receive back their own shepherd and bishop, we shall place their lot with those whose union they embrace so willingly. And

---

64 Note the description of the Byzantine Empire as a "kingdom."
65 At this time, Naples, under the rule of Duke Sergius II, had made agreements with the Aghlabid rulers of North Africa.

we shall weigh them both in one balance, since the already mentioned eminent Apostle judges to be worthy of death not just those who do wicked things, but those who consent that they be done. Especially since they bear arms against Christians and fight them, and if they can capture any of the faithful, they pass them into the hands of the Saracens and go to war along with them in a single charge.

As for the rest, dearest brother, you will know that with the help of the great Creator, our army has submitted Bari to our triumph in the way described above, and has wonderfully and quickly humiliated and shattered the Saracens of Taranto and of Calabria. And with God's help they would soon be destroyed, if from the sea they were prohibited from receiving provisions of food or even numerous boats from Palermo or Africa. Since the forces of our peoples [*populi*] are seldom or never lacking on dry land in both Taranto and Calabria, let Your Fraternity send a fleet sufficient to prevent them from taking food from the sea, and so that if it happens that more battalions of that dreadful people should arrive, as is often announced, it will be easier to resist them with a divinely strengthened arm. For the *stratigos*[66] George, though he keeps watch carefully and fights as hard as he can, will not be able to cope if many boats of the enemy should appear from whichever direction, since he has only a few warships.

And since some of the thieving Saracens of Palermo are ravaging through the Tyrrhenian Sea on their boats, supported by the aid and hospitality of the Neapolitans, it is befitting that a fleet of yours be sent out at once to capture them. For it is these who indefatigably offer assistance to the Saracens of Calabria and provide daily help to those at Palermo. And if they were captured, the boats of most of the Saracens, both of Palermo and Calabria, would be restricted. Once Calabria has been cleansed, thanks to God, we have decided to restore Sicily to its former freedom, according to our shared wish.[67] The faster they are weakened by the capture of their boats and their thieves through the divine right hand, the easier both these tasks will be. Let there be no

---

66 A senior Byzantine military officer.
67 *Commune placitum*, which might imply a joint agreement. Louis II seems to be discussing the possibility of a joint military expedition to recapture Sicily, as an incentive for the Byzantines to provide greater assistance. Sicily had been under Byzantine control until Muslim Aghlabid forces from North Africa began a campaign of gradual conquest in 827.

delay, dearest brother, and no slowness in sending a fleet, lest their forces are not weakened but are rather strengthened through receiving an abundance of provisions by sea, or by the reinforcement of a fleet of the Hagarenes[68] – and so strengthened that they can be weakened afterward only with more difficulty. Our men will tirelessly take to battle on dry land in vain, if they obtain either provisions or stronger reinforcements from the sea.

Finally, we have sent to Your beloved Fraternity Auprand, a faithful and trusted follower of ours, who will tell you in person certain things which are not in this letter about your empire (may God protect it). We ask that once he has been received kindly by Your Fraternity beloved by us in Christ, he should be kept for no longer than eight days, but with Christ's help let him quickly be sent back to us without any further delay as is fitting.

---

[68] A term used by Christians for Muslims.

Conclusion

With its wealth of royal palaces, bishoprics, and monasteries, Lotharingia was not an intrinsically weak kingdom, and it was not doomed from the outset in 855. Its failure was both historically contingent and enormously significant. The existence of a robust middle Frankish kingdom in the 870s and the 880s would have fundamentally changed European politics of the time, and subsequently too. Similarly, had Lothar II managed to secure his divorce from Theutberga, a major precedent would have been established for putting aside a queen as wife, even in the teeth of papal opposition. This book has presented a set of contemporary sources to allow readers to trace how these possibilities were closed down.

True, a case can be made that what ultimately destroyed Lotharingia was not Lothar II's divorce case but simply the premature death from sudden illness that snatched him away at Piacenza in 869 in his mid-thirties. His son and presumed heir was still young, and the succession of a child-king in the ruthless Carolingian dynastic context was fraught with risk. On the other hand, Carolingian child-kings had succeeded before, notably Hugh's uncle Charles of Provence. Charles had been only around ten years old when he became king, and was sickly too; but unlike Hugh, his dynastic legitimacy was unquestioned, and he enjoyed powerful support from major aristocratic backers, in his case Count Gerard of Vienne.[1] Thanks to Lothar II's marriage controversies, Hugh was in a weaker position.

---

[1] See Airlie, *Making and Unmaking*, 114; and Offergeld, *Reges pueri*, 330–7.

In any case, it is worth considering whether, given the political circumstances, Lothar II's premature death – itself a direct consequence of the risk he took in rushing to southern Italy in the dangerous heat of the summer – merely spared him from a fate similar to that of his older cousin, King Pippin II. As the son of the short-lived Pippin I and, like Lothar II, a grandson of Emperor Louis the Pious, Pippin II ruled Aquitaine in what is now western France as an independent kingdom for a decade or so between 839 and 848. He issued charters for several monasteries and minted coins, much like his cousin Lothar II. Under constant pressure from his uncle Charles the Bald, however, Pippin II's support began to dry up. He finally wrecked his political reputation by allying with viking raiders from 857 and was even accused of following their religious customs.[2] Pippin II's inherent dynastic legitimacy enabled him to limp on for a few years, but he was captured and imprisoned by Charles in 864, and he subsequently vanished. To be sure, Lothar II held a stronger hand of cards than Pippin II, but it is not clear that he played them any better. Had Lothar II survived his illness at Piacenza, his deposition, and Lotharingia's dismemberment, would still have been in the cards, because of the damage years of unsuccessful wrangling over his marriage had inflicted on his kingship.

What Lothar II's case – and for that matter Pippin II's too – shows us is that the Frankish kings in the mid-ninth century could be powerful and dynamic, but also that their rule was fundamentally unstable. In concert with their bishops, they creatively drew on the precedents set by Charlemagne and, perhaps still more so, Louis the Pious, in using the institutions and rituals of Christianity to consolidate their power, appropriating and manipulating a public representation of kingship. A king who grasped and embodied the evolving obligations of Christian kingship within this framework was well placed to prosper alongside, and maybe at the expense of, his royal relatives. But a king could lose control of this slippery discourse, and if he did, there were no limits to how far he might fall.

To complicate matters, the parameters within which Lothar II and his royal uncles and brothers operated were changing. Military

---

[2] On Pippin II, see Airlie, *Making and Unmaking*, 192–204. On his alleged conversion, see Hack, *Von Christus zu Odin*; and Bauduin, *Le monde franc et les Vikings*. Both suggest that it is unlikely Pippin II actually renounced Christianity.

incursions from Northmen along the coasts and down the rivers, and Muslim raiding in southern Italy, with consequent pressures on Rome, presented new challenges and opportunities that needed to be taken into account. At the same time, Frankish bishops were increasingly self-conscious about their collective obligations and did not always agree among themselves about how they should relate to the kings with whom they jointly led Frankish society, conceived as the *ecclesia*. Meanwhile, the pope in Rome, while still tied into a Mediterranean framework, displayed a renewed interest in intervening in Frankish affairs north of the Alps.

All these issues played into the politics of Lothar II's attempt to make Waldrada his queen. On the basis of the material that has been presented here, readers can make up their own minds about what drove the crisis that engulfed his kingdom, and at what point (if any) it became impossible for Lothar II to escape the net being woven around him. However, in this complex and hotly contested environment, where the rules of the game were themselves uncertain and negotiable, this book suggests that the young Lothar II and his advisers – among whom we should certainly count Waldrada herself – made three key mistakes. They failed to appreciate how sensitive marriage had become within the Carolingian ideology of kingship, and thus how carefully it needed to be handled in the face of internal and external opposition to Lothar II's plans; they failed to predict Pope Nicholas I's capacity to disrupt the traditional partnership of a king and his bishops; and they failed to realize how tenacious Theutberga would prove in the face of intimidation and threats.

These miscalculations left Lothar II and his kingdom dangerously exposed and vulnerable by the time of the king's death, and made a smooth transfer of power to his son utterly impossible. Yet though Lothar II certainly made mistakes, they can be understood only in the wider context of continuous competition for power in mid-Carolingian Francia, a struggle that was articulated not despite but through ideologies of Christian rulership. At its heart, the failure of Lothar II and his court was a failure to grasp fully how these ideologies were evolving. Far from representing a tragic quirk of fate or an aberration, the fall of Lothar II's kingdom demonstrates how the highly fluid dynamics of Carolingian Francia entangled politics, law, and religion, and in so doing enduringly shaped Europe's cultural and political landscape.

Bibliography

Websites

Capitularia Project, Nordrhein-Westfälischen Akademie der Wissenschaften und der Künste, https://capitularia.uni-koeln.de/en/project/definition/

Codices Vossiani Latini, https://primarysources.brillonline.com/browse/vossiani-latini/

Epistolae: Medieval Women's Letters, Columbia University Libraries, Columbia University, https://epistolae.ctl.columbia.edu/

Monumenta Germanie Historica, www.dmgh.de

Manuscripts

Leiden, University Library, MS Voss. Lat. O 92
Paris, Bibliothèque nationale de France, MS Lat. 1141
Paris, Bibliothèque nationale de France, MS Lat. 1452
Paris, Bibliothèque nationale de France, MS Lat. 1557
Paris, Bibliothèque nationale de France, MS Lat. 5095
Rome, Biblioteca Angelica, MS 10
Rome, Biblioteca Vallicelliana, MS D 38
Rome, Biblioteca Vallicelliana, MS I 76
Vatican, Biblioteca Apostolica Vaticana, Pal. Lat. 576
Vatican, Biblioteca Apostolica Vaticana, Reg. Lat. 11
Vatican, Biblioteca Apostolica Vaticana, Reg. Lat. 566
Vatican, Biblioteca Apostolica Vaticana, Vat. Lat. 4493
Vatican, Biblioteca Apostolica Vaticana, Vat. Lat. 4982
Vatican, Biblioteca Apostolica Vaticana, Vat. Lat. 5001
Vienna, Österreichische Nationalbibliothek, Cod. 473

Edited Primary Sources

Sources are listed by their author whenever this is known, followed by the title of their work, in its most common form in scholarship. For each entry, I provide reference both to the standard edition of the original Latin and to a published English translation where one is available, to help readers connect different versions of the sources. Collections of sources are provided when these have been cited in footnotes, chiefly for anonymous and untitled sources.

Ado of Vienne. *Chronicon*. Edited by G.H. Pertz. *Scriptores*. MGH Scriptores 2:317–23. Hannover: Hahn, 1828.

Adventius of Metz. *Letters*. Edited by Ernst Dümmler. *Epistolae ad divortium Lotharii regis pertinentes. Epistolae Karolini aevi 4*. MGH Epistolae 6, pt. 1, 205–40. Berlin: Weidmann, 1902. Some individual letters and extracts translated in Paul Dutton. *Carolingian Civilization: A Reader*. 2nd ed. Peterborough, ON: Broadview, 2004; and in David d'Avray. *Dissolving Royal Marriages: A Documentary History, 860–1600*. Cambridge: Cambridge University Press, 2014.

———. *Mandement*. Edited by Daniel Misonne. "Mandement inédit d'Adventius de Metz à l'occasion d'une incursion normande (mai–juin 867)." *Révue Bénédictine* 93, nos. 1–2 (1983): 71–9.

Ambrose of Milan. *Commentary on the Gospel according to Luke*. Edited by Karl Schenkl. *Sancti Ambrosii Opera pars 4. Expositio evangelii secundum Lucam*. CSEL 32, pt. 4. Vienna: Tempsky, 1902. Translated by Ide Ní Riain. *Commentary of Saint Ambrose on the Gospel according to Saint Luke*. Dublin: Halycon, 2001.

Annales Xantenses. Edited by Bernhard von Simson. *Annales Xantenses et Annales Vedastini*. MGH SS rer. Germ. 12. Hannover: Hahn, 1909.

Annals of Fulda. Edited by Friedrich Kurze. *Annales Fuldenses sive Annales regni Francorum orientalis*. MGH SRG 7. Hannover: Hahn, 1891. Translated by Timothy Reuter. *Annals of Fulda*. Manchester: Manchester University Press, 1992.

Annals of St-Bertin. Edited by Félix Grat. *Annales de Saint-Bertin*. Paris: Klincksieck, 1964. Translated by Janet L. Nelson. *Annals of St-Bertin*. Manchester: Manchester University Press, 1991.

Ansegis. *Collectio capitularium*. Edited by Gerhard Schmitz. *Die Kapitulariensammlung des Ansegis*. MGH Capitularia regum Francorum, n.s. 1. Hannover: Hahn, 1996.

Augustine. *Adulterous Marriages*. Edited by Joseph Zycha. *Sancti Aureli Augustini*. CSEL 41:347–410. Vienna: Tempsky, 1900. Translated by Ray Kearney. *Marriage and Virginity*. Works of Saint Augustine: A Translation for the 21st Century, pt. 1, 9:142–91. New York: New City Press, 1999.

———. *On the Good of Marriage*. Edited by Joseph Zycha. *Sancti Aureli Augustini*. CSEL 41:187–231. Vienna: Tempsky, 1900. Translated by Ray Kearney. *Marriage and Virginity*. Works of Saint Augustine: A Translation for the 21st Century, pt. 1, 9:33–61. New York: New City Press, 1999.

———. *On the Sermon on the Mount*. Edited by Almut Mutzenbecher. *Sancti Aurelii Augustini de sermone domini in monte libri duos*. CCSL 35. Turnhout: Brepols, 1967. Translated by William Findlay. *Saint Augustine*. Nicene and Post-Nicene Fathers, ser. 1, vol. 6, 1–63. Buffalo: Christian Literature Publishing Company, 1888.

Bede. *Marci euangelium expositio*. Edited by David Hurst. CCSL 120. Turnhout: Brepols, 1960.

Capitularia regum Francorum. Vol. 2. Edited by Alfred Boretius and Viktor Krause. MGH Leges. Hannover: Hahn, 1897.

Cartulaire de l'Abbaye de Cysoing et de ses dépendences. Edited by I. de Coussemaker. Lille: Impr. Saint-Augustin, 1884.

Cartulaire de l'Abbaye de Gorze, MS 826 de la Bibliothèque de Metz. Edited by A. d'Herbomez. Paris: Klincksieck, 1898–1905.

Chartae Latinae Antiquiores: Facsimile-Edition of the Latin Charters. 2nd Series: Ninth Century. Vol. 93. Edited by Cristina Mantegna. Zürich: Urs Graf, 2014.

Die Konzilien der karolingischen Teilreiche 843–859. Edited by Wilfried Hartmann. MGH Concilia 3. Hannover: Hahn, 1984.

Die Konzilien der karolingischen Teilreiche 860–874. Edited by Wilfried Hartmann. MGH Concilia 4. Hannover: Hahn, 1998.

Die Urkunden Lothars I und Lothars II. Edited by Theodor Schieffer. MGH Diplomata Karolinorum 3. Hannover: Hahn, 1966.

Ekkehard of St Gall. *Fortune and Misfortune at Saint Gall*. Edited and translated by Emily Albu and Natalie Lozovsky. Cambridge, MA: Harvard University Press, 2021.

Epistolae Colonienses. Edited by Ernst Dümmler. *Epistolae Karolini aevi 4*. MGH Epistolae 6, pt. 1, 243–56. Berlin: Weidmann, 1902.

Epistolae variorum 798–923. Edited by Isolde Schröder. *Epistolae Karolini aevi 7*. MGH Epistolae 9. Wiesbaden: Harrassowitz, 2022.

Epistolae variorum inde a seculo novo. Edited by Ernst Dümmler. *Epistolae Karolini aevi 4*. MGH Epistolae 6:127–206. Berlin: Weidmann, 1925.

Flodoard. *Historia Remensis ecclesiae*. Edited by Martina Stratmann. MGH Scriptores 36. Hannover: Hahn, 1998.

Gregory the Great. *Forty Gospel Homilies*. Edited by Raymond Etaix. *Homiliae in evangelia*. CCSL 141. Turnhout: Brepols, 1999. Translated by David Hurst. *Forty Gospel Homilies*. Kalamazoo: Cistercian Publications, 1991.

———. *Homilies on the Prophet Ezekiel*. Edited by Marcus Adriaen. *Homiliae in Hiezechihelem prophetam*. CCSL 132. Turnhout: Brepols, 1971. Translated by Theodosia Tomkinson. *The Homilies of St. Gregory the Great on the Book of the Prophet Ezekiel*. Etna, CA: Center for Traditionalist Orthodox Studies, 2008.

———. *Letters*. Edited by Dag Norberg. *Gregorii Magni Registrum epistularum*. CCSL 140. Turnhout: Brepols, 1982. Translated by John Martyn. *Letters of Gregory the Great*. 3 vols. Toronto: Pontifical Institute of Mediaeval Studies, 2004.

———. *Morals on the Book of Job*. Edited by Marcus Adriaen. *Moralia in Iob*. CCSL 143. Turnhout: Brepols, 1979. Translated by John Parker. *Morals on the Book of Job*. London, 1844.

Hadrian II. *Epistolae*. Edited by Ernst Perels. *Epistolae Karolini aevi 4*. MGH Epistolarum 6:691–765. Berlin: Weidmann, 1925.

Hincmar of Reims. *On the Divorce of King Lothar and Queen Theutberga*. Edited by Letha Böhringer. *De Divortio Lotharii regis et Theutbergae reginae*. MGH Concilia 4, suppl. 1. Hannover: Hahn, 1992. Translated by Rachel Stone and Charles West. *The Divorce of King Lothar and Queen Theutberga: Hincmar of Rheims's* De Divortio. Manchester: Manchester University Press, 2016.

———. *On the Governance of the Palace*. Edited by Thomas Gross and Rudolf Schieffer. *De ordine palatii*. MGH Fontes Iuris 3. Hannover: Hahn, 1980. Translated by Paul Dutton. *Carolingian Civilization: A Reader*, 516–32. 2nd ed. Peterborough, ON: Broadview, 2004.

Histoire de l'abbaye royale et de la ville de Tournus. Edited by Pierre Chifflet. Dijon, 1664.

Innocent I. *Epistolae*. Edited by J.-P. Migne. *Patrologia Latina*, vol. 20, col. 463–611. Paris, 1844–55.

Jerome. *Commentary on Matthew*. Edited by David Hurst. *Commentariorum in Matheum libri IV*. CCSL 77. Turnhout: Brepols, 1969. Translated by Thomas Scheck. *Commentary on Matthew: Saint Jerome*. Fathers of the Church 117. Washington, DC: Catholic University of America Press, 2008.

———. *Letters*. Edited by Isidorus Hilberg. *Sancti Eusebii Hieronymi Epistolae*. CSEL 54–6. Vienna: Tempsky, 1910–18. Translated by W. Fremantle. *The Principal Works of St. Jerome*. Nicene and Post-Nicene Fathers, ser. 2, vol. 6, 1–298. Oxford: Parker and Company, 1893.

Jonas of Orléans. *De laicali institutione*. Edited and translated (in French) by Odile Dubreucq. *Jonas d'Orléans: Instruction des laïcs*. 2 vols. Paris: Les Éditions du Cerf, 2012–13.

Leo I. *Letters*. Edited by J.-P. Migne. *Patrologia Latina*, vol. 54, col. 581–1218. Paris, 1841–64. Translated by Charles Feltoe. *The Letters and Sermons of Leo the Great*. Nicene and Post-Nicene Fathers, ser. 2, vol. 12. Oxford, 1894.

Liber Memorialis von Remiremont. Edited by Eduard Hlawitschka, Karl Schmid, and Gerd Tellenbach. 2 vols. MGH Libri Memoriales 1. Zurich: Weidmann, 1970.

Liber pontificalis. Edited by Louis Duchesne. *Le Liber pontificalis: Texte, introduction et commentaire*. 2 vols. Paris: E. Thorin, 1886–92. Translated by Raymond Davis. *Lives of the Ninth-Century Popes (Liber pontificalis): The Ancient Biographies of Ten Popes from A.D. 817–891*. Liverpool: Liverpool University Press, 1995.

Louis II. *Letter to Basil I.* Edited by Walter Henze. *Ludovici II imperatoris epistola ad Basilium imperatorem Constantinopolitanum missa.* Epistolae Karolini aevi 5. MGH Epistolarum 7, 385–94. Berlin: Weidmann, 1928. Translated (in Italian) by Raffaele Matarazzo. *Chronicon: Anonimo salernitano*, 154–75. Naples: Arte tipografica, 2002. Also translated (in Italian) by Girolamo Arnaldi. "Impero d'occidente e impero d'oriente nella lettera di Ludovico II a Basilio I." *La Cultura. Rivista di Filosofia, Letteratura e Storia* 1 (1963): 404–24.

Nicholas I. *Epistolae.* Edited by Ernst Perels. *Epistolae Karolini aevi* 4. MGH Epistolae 6, 267–690. Berlin: Weidmann, 1925.

Regino of Prüm. *Chronicle.* Edited by Friedrich Kurze. *Reginonis abbatis Prumiensis Chronicon cum continuatione Treverensi.* MGH SSRG 50. Hannover: Hahn, 1890. Translated by Simon MacLean. *History and Politics in Late Carolingian and Ottonian Europe: The Chronicle of Regino of Prüm and Adalbert of Magdeburg.* Manchester: Manchester University Press, 2009.

"Rhythmus on Emperor Louis's Captivity." Edited and translated by Luigi Berto. *Italian Carolingian Historical and Poetic Texts*, 108–11. Pisa: Pisa University Press, 2016.

Sedulius Scottus. *On Christian Rulers.* Edited and translated by R.W. Dyson. *Sedulius Scottus: On Christian Rulers.* Woodbridge: Boydell and Brewer, 2010.

Translationes sanctae Glodesindis. Edited by J.-P. Migne. *Patrologia Latina*, vol. 137, cols. 219–40. Paris, 1841–64.

Historiography

Airlie, Stuart. "'For It Is Written in the Law.' Ansegis and the Writing of Carolingian Royal Authority." In *Early Medieval Studies in Memory of Patrick Wormald*, edited by Stephen Baxter, Catherine E. Karkov, Janet L. Nelson, and David Pelteret, 219–36. Aldershot: Ashgate, 2009.

———. *Making and Unmaking the Carolingians, 751–888.* London: Routledge, 2021.

———. "Private Bodies and the Body Politic in the Divorce Case of Lothar II." *Past and Present* 161 (1998): 3–38.

———. "Unreal Kingdom: Francia Media under the Shadow of Lothar II." In *De la mer du Nord à la Mediterranée: Francia Media, une région au coeur de l'Europe (c.840–c.1050): Actes du colloque international (Metz, Luxembourg, Trèves, 8–11 février 2006)*, edited by Michèle Gaillard, Michel Margue, Alain Dierkens, and Hérold Pettiau, 339–56. Luxembourg: CLUDEM, 2011.

Althoff, Gerd. *Rules and Rituals in Medieval Power Games: A German Perspective.* Leiden: Brill, 2019.

Bartlett, Robert. *Trial by Fire and Water: The Medieval Judicial Ordeal.* Oxford: Clarendon, 1986.

Bauduin, Pierre. *Le monde franc et les Vikings: VIIIe–Xe siècle.* Paris: Albin Michel, 2009.

Belletzkie, Robert Joseph. "Pope Nicholas I and John of Ravenna: The Struggle for Ecclesiastical Rights in the Ninth Century." *Church History* 49, no. 3 (1980): 262–72.

Blanc, William, and Christophe Naudin. *Charles Martel et la bataille de Poitiers: De l'histoire au myth identitaire.* 2nd ed. Paris: Editions Libertalia, 2022.

Bobrycki, Shane. "The Flailing Women of Dijon: Crowds in Ninth-Century Europe." *Past and Present* 240, no. 1 (2018): 3–46.

———. "A Hypothetical Slave in Constantinople: Amalarius's Liber Officialis and the Mediterranean Slave Trade." *Haskins Society Journal* 26 (2014): 47–67.

Bof, Riccardo, and Conrad Leyser. "Divorce and Remarriage between Late Antiquity and the Early Middle Ages: Canon Law and Conflict Resolution." In *Making Early Medieval Societies: Conflict and Belonging in the Latin West, 300–1200*, edited by Kate Cooper and Conrad Leyser, 155–80. Cambridge: Cambridge University Press, 2016.

Böhringer, Letha. "Das Recht im Dienst der Machtpolitik? Anmerkungen zu einer Neuerscheinung über die Scheidungsaffäre König Lothars II." *Mitteilungen des Instituts für Österreichische Geschichtsforschung* 119 (2011): 146–54.

———. *De Divortio Lotharii regis et Theutbergae reginae.* MGH Concilia 4, suppl. 1. Hannover: Hahn, 1992.

———. "Gunthar Erzbischof von Köln." Portal Rheinische Geschichte. LVR. 2017. http://www.rheinische-geschichte.lvr.de/Persoenlichkeiten/gunthar/DE-2086/lido/57c8146c997093.53178933.

Bondioli, Lorenzo M. "Islamic Bari between the Aghlabids and the Two Empires." In *The Aghlabids and Their Neighbours: Art and Material Culture in Ninth-Century North Africa*, edited by Glaire D. Anderson, Corisande Fenwick, and Mariam Rosser-Owen, with Sihem Lamine, 470–90. Leiden: Brill, 2018.

Booker, Courtney M. *Past Convictions: The Penance of Louis the Pious and the Decline of the Carolingians.* Philadelphia: University of Pennsylvania Press, 2009.

Bouchard, Constance. "The Bosonids or Rising to Power in the Late Carolingian Age." *French Historical Studies* 15, no. 3 (1988): 407–31.

Bougard, François. "Composition, diffusion et réception des parties tardives du *Liber pontificalis* romain (VIIIe–XIe siècles)." In *Liber, Gesta, Histoire. Écrire l'histoire des évêques et des papes, de l'Antiquité au XXIe siècle*, edited by François Bougard and Michel Sot, 127–52. Turnhout: Brepols, 2009.

———. "En marge du divorce de Lothaire II: Boson de Vienne, le cocu qui fut fait roi?" *Francia* 27, no. 1 (2000): 33–51.

Bricout, Sébastian. "Note sur deux laïcs carolingiens et la médicine au IXe siècle." *Latomus* 65, no. 2 (2006): 458–61.

Buc, Philippe. "Text and Ritual in Ninth-Century Political Culture: Rome, 864." In *Medieval Concepts of the Past: Ritual, Memory, Historiography*, edited by Gerd Althoff, Johannes Fried, and Patrick J. Geary, 123–38. Cambridge: Cambridge University Press, 2002.

Burbank, Jane, and Frederick Cooper. *Empires in World History: Power and the Politics of Difference*. Princeton: Princeton University Press, 2010.

Butz, Eva-Maria. "Das Königtum Lothars II: im Spiegel der Gedenkbuchüberlieferung." In *D'un regnum à l'autre: La Lotharingie, un espace de l'entre-deux? Vom Regnum zum Imperium: Lotharingien als Zwischenreich?* edited by Tristan Martine and Jessika Nowak, 19–36. Nancy: Presses universitaires de Nancy, 2021.

———. "Von Namenlisten zu Netzwerken? Waldrada, Lothar II. und der lothringische Adel im Spiegel der Gedenküberlieferung. Überlegungen zur Anwendung der Netzwerkmethode in der Gedenkbuchforschung." In *Von Gruppe und Gemeinschaft zu Akteur und Netzwerk? Netzwerkforschung in der Landesgeschichte: Festschrift für Alfons Zettler zum 60. Geburtstag*, edited by Erik Beck and Eva-Maria Butz, 105–18. Ostfildern: Thorbecke, 2019.

Butz, Eva-Maria, and Alfons Zettler. "The Making of the Carolingian *Libri Memoriales*: Exploring or Constructing the Past?" In *Memory and Commemoration in Medieval Culture*, edited by Elma Brenner, Meredith Cohen, and Mary Franklin-Brown, 79–92. London: Routledge, 2013.

Campbell, Darryl. "The *Capitulare de villis*, the *Brevium exempla*, and the Carolingian Court at Aachen." *Early Medieval Europe* 18, no. 3 (2010): 243–64.

Carvajal Castro, Álvaro, and Carlos Tejerizo-García. "The Early Medieval State: A Strategic-Relational Approach." *Journal of Historical Sociology* 35, no. 4 (2022): 547–66.

Chitwood, Zachary. *Byzantine Legal Culture and the Roman Legal Tradition, 867–1056*. Cambridge: Cambridge University Press, 2017.

Chrysos, Evangelos K. "Rome and Constantinople in Confrontation: The Quarrel over the Validity of Photius's Ordination." In *Byzantium in Dialogue with the Mediterranean: History and Heritage*, edited by Daniëlle Slootjes and Mariëtte Verhoeven, 24–46. Leiden: Brill, 2019.

Có, Giulia. *Vescovi, re, imperatori: Anastasio Bibliotecario fra Occidente e Oriente*. Bologna: Società editrice Il mulino, 2019.

Cooijmans, Christian. *Monarchs and Hydrarchs: The Conceptual Development of Viking Activity across the Frankish Realm (c. 750–940)*. London: Routledge, 2020.

Cook, Michael. "Comparing Carolingians and 'Abbasids." In *The 'Abbasid and Carolingian Empires: Comparative Studies in Civilizational Formation*, edited by Deborah G. Tor, 191–223. Leiden: Brill, 2017.

Costambeys, Marios, Matthew Innes, and Simon MacLean. *The Carolingian World*. Cambridge: Cambridge University Press, 2011.

Coupland, Simon. "Boom and Bust at Ninth-Century Dorestad." In *Dorestad in an International Framework: New Research on Centres of Trade and Coinage in*

Carolingian Times. Proceedings of the first Dorestad Congress held at the National Museum of Antiquities, Leiden, the Netherlands, June 24–27, 2009, edited by Annemarieke Willemsen and Hanneke Kik, 95–103. Turnhout: Brepols, 2010.

———. "Denare Lothars II. (855–869) aus Niederlahnstein und die Münzen von Köln im 9. Jahrhundert." *Numismatisches Nachrichtenblatt* 5 (2022): 181–6.

———. "Der Karolingerschatz von Bassenheim." *Numismatisches Nachrichtenblatt* 4 (2019): 144–9.

———. "The Frankish Tribute Payments to the Vikings and Their Consequences." *Francia* 26, no.1 (1999): 57–75.

d'Avray, David. *Dissolving Royal Marriages: A Documentary History, 860–1600.* Cambridge: Cambridge University Press, 2014.

———. *Papacy, Monarchy and Marriage, 860–1600.* Cambridge: Cambridge University Press, 2015.

———. *Papal Jurisprudence, 385–1234: Social Origins and Medieval Reception of Canon Law.* Cambridge: Cambridge University Press, 2022.

de Jong, Mayke. "Carolingian Monasticism: The Power of Prayer." In *The New Cambridge Medieval History*, vol. 2, edited by Rosamond McKitterick, 622–53. Cambridge: Cambridge University Press, 1995.

———. "Ecclesia and the Early Medieval Polity." In *Staat im frühen Mittelalter*, edited by Stuart Airlie, Walter Pohl, and Helmut Reimitz, 113–26. Vienna: Verlag der Österreichischen Akademie der Wissenschaften, 2006.

———. "The Empire That Was Always Decaying: The Carolingians, 800–888." *Medieval Worlds* 2 (2015): 6–25.

———. *The Penitential State: Authority and Atonement in the Age of Louis the Pious, 814–840.* Cambridge: Cambridge University Press, 2009.

———. "The Sacred Palace, Public Penance, and the Carolingian Polity." In *Great Christian Jurists and Legal Collections in the First Millennium*, edited by Philip L. Reynolds, 155–81. Cambridge: Cambridge University Press, 2019.

Diesenberger, Maximilian. "Making the Past in Late and Post-Carolingian Historiography." *Medieval Worlds* 10 (2019): 2–16.

Dohmen, Linda. "Der König und die Seinen: Ein Blick auf die Herrschaft Lothars II: im Spiegel der Urkunden." In *D'un regnum à l'autre: La Lotharingie, un espace de l'entre-deux? Vom Regnum zum Imperium: Lotharingien als Zwischenreich?* edited by Tristan Martine and Jessika Nowak, 37–54. Nancy: Presses universitaires de Nancy, 2021.

———. *Die Ursache allen Übels: Untersuchungen zu den Unzuchtsvorwürfen gegen die Gemahlinnen der Karolinger.* Ostfildern: Thorbecke, 2017.

Dorofeeva, Anna. "Miscellanies, Christian Reform and Early Medieval Encyclopaedism: A Reconsideration of the Pre-Bestiary Latin *Physiologus* Manuscripts." *Historical Research* 90, no. 250 (2017): 665–82.

Ducourthial, Cyrille. "Géographie du pouvoir en pays de Savoie au tournant de l'an mil." In *Le royaume de Bourgogne autour de l'an mil*, edited by Christian Guilleré, 207–46. Chambéry: Université de Savoie, 2008.

Dupraz, Louis. "Deux préceptes de Lothaire II (867 et 868) ou les vestiges diplomatiques d'un divorce manqué." *Zeitschrift für schweizerische Kirchengeschichte* 59 (1965): 193–236.

Dvornik, Francis. *The Photian Schism: History and Legend*. Cambridge: Cambridge University Press, 1948.

Fanning, Steven. "Imperial Diplomacy between Francia and Byzantium: The Letter of Louis II to Basil I in 871." *Cithara* 34 (1994): 3–17.

Fees, Irmgard, and Yanick Strauch, eds. *Die Regesten Karls des Kahlen, 840 (823)–877*, Lieferung 2, Abschnitt 1, *849–859*. Mainz: 2022.

Firey, Abigail. *A Contrite Heart: Prosecution and Redemption in the Carolingian Empire*. Leiden: Brill, 2009.

Forrai, Réka. "The Sacred Nectar of the Deceitful Greeks. Perceptions of Greekness in Ninth-Century Rome." In *Knotenpunkt Byzanz: Wissensformen und kulturelle Wechselbeziehungen*, edited by Andreas Speer and Philipp Steinkrüger, 71–84. Berlin: De Gruyter, 2012.

Fouracre, Paul. *The Age of Charles Martel*. London: Longman, 2000.

———. "Carolingian Justice: The Rhetoric of Improvement and Contexts of Abuse." *La giustizia nell'alto medioevo, secoli V–VIII*, 771–803. Spoleto: CISAM, 1995.

———. "Lights, Power and the Moral Economy of Early Medieval Europe." *Early Medieval Europe* 28, no. 3 (2020): 367–87.

Gaillard, Michèle. *D'une réforme à l'autre (816–934): Les communautés religieuses en Lorraine à l'époque carolingienne*. Paris: Éditions de la Sorbonne, 2006.

———. "Un évêque et son temps, Advence de Metz (858–875)." In *Lotharingia. Eine europäische Kernlandschaft um das Jahr 1000*, edited by Hans-Walter Herrmann and Reinhard Schneider, 89–119. Saarbrücken: Saarbrücker Druckerei und Verlag, 1995.

Gantner, Clemens. "Ad utriusque imperii unitatem? Anastasius Bibliothecarius as a Broker between Two Cultures and Three Courts in the Ninth Century." *Medieval Worlds* 13 (2021): 36–53.

———. "A King in Training? Louis II of Italy and His Expedition to Rome in 844." In *After Charlemagne: Carolingian Italy and Its Rulers*, edited by Walter Pohl and Clemens Gantner, 164–81. Cambridge: Cambridge University Press, 2020.

———. "New Visions of Community in Ninth-Century Rome: The Impact of the Saracen Threat on the Papal World View." In *Visions of Community in the Post-Roman World: The West, Byzantium and the Islamic World, 300–1100*, edited by Walter Pohl, Clemens Gantner, and Richard Payne, 403–21. Farnham: Ashgate, 2012.

———. "'Our Common Enemies Shall Be Annihilated!' How Louis II's Relations with the Byzantine Empire Shaped His Policy in Southern Italy." In *Southern Italy as Contact Area and Border Region during the Early Middle Ages: Religious-Cultural Heterogeneity and Competing Powers in Local, Transregional and Universal Dimensions*, edited by Kordula Wolf and Klaus Herbers, 295–314. Cologne: Böhlau, 2018.

———. *Worthy of Heaven: The Dynamics of Italy at the Time of Louis II (840–875)*. Forthcoming.

Garipzanov, Ildar H. *The Symbolic Language of Authority in the Carolingian World (c. 751–877)*. Leiden: Brill, 2008.

Garver, Valerie L. *Women and Aristocratic Culture in the Carolingian World*. Ithaca: Cornell University Press, 2009.

Gillis, Matthew. *Heresy and Dissent in the Carolingian Empire: The Case of Gottschalk of Orbais*. Oxford: Oxford University Press, 2017.

Glansdorff, Sophie. *Diplômes de Louis le Germanique (817–876)*. Limoges: Presses universitaires de Limoges, 2009.

———. "L'évêque de Metz et archichapelain Drogon (801/802–855)." *Revue belge de philologie et d'histoire* 81, no. 4 (2003): 945–1014.

Goldberg, Eric J. *In the Manner of the Franks: Hunting, Kingship, and Masculinity in Early Medieval Europe*. Philadelphia: University of Pennsylvania Press, 2020.

———. "'A Man of Notable Good Looks Disfigured by a Cruel Wound': The Forest Misadventure of Charles the Young of Aquitaine (864) in History and Legend." In *Historiography and Identity 3: Carolingian Approaches*, edited by Rutger Kramer, Helmut Reimitz, and Graeme Ward, 355–86. Turnhout: Brepols, 2021.

———. "*Regina nitens sanctissima Hemma*: Queen Emma (827–876), Bishop Witgar of Augsburg, and the Witgar-Belt." In *Representations of Power in Medieval Germany: 800–1500*, edited by Björn Weiler and Simon MacLean, 57–95. Turnhout: Brepols, 2006.

———. *Struggle for Empire: Kingship and Conflict under Louis the German, 817–876*. Ithaca: Cornell University Press, 2006.

Granier, Thomas. "La captivité de l'empereur Louis II à Bénévent (13 août–17 septembre 871) dans les sources des IXe–Xe siècles." In *Faire l'événement au Moyen Âge*, edited by Claude Carozzi and Huguette Taviani-Carozzi, 13–39. Aix: Publications de l'Université de Provence, 2007.

Grondeux, Anne. "Le rôle de Reichenau dans la diffusion du *Liber glossarum*." *Dossiers d'HEL* 8 (2015): 79–93.

Grotz, Hans. *Erbe wider Willen. Hadrian II. (867–872) und seine Zeit*. Vienna: Böhlau, 1970.

Haack, Christoph. *Die Krieger der Karolinger: Kriegsdienste als Prozesse gemeinschaftlicher Organisation um 800*. Berlin: De Gruyter, 2020.

Hack, Achim Thomas. *Von Christus zu Odin: Ein Karolinger bekehrt sich*. Stuttgart: Franz Steiner, 2014.

Hadley, Dawn M., and Julian D. Richards. *The Viking Great Army and the Making of England*. London: Thames & Hudson, 2021.

Haller, Johannes. *Nikolaus I. und Pseudoisidore*. Stuttgart: Cotta, 1936.

Halsall, Guy. *Warfare and Society in the Barbarian West*. London: Routledge, 2003.

Hartmann, Martina. *Die Königin im frühen Mittelalter*. Stuttgart: Kohlhammer, 2009.

Heidecker, Karl. *The Divorce of Lothar II: Christian Marriage and Political Power in the Carolingian World.* Translated by Tanis M. Guest. Ithaca: Cornell University Press, 2010.

———. *Kerk, huwelijk en politieke macht: De zaak Lotharius II, 855–869.* Amsterdam, 1997.

Herbers, Klaus, ed. *Die Regesten des Kaiserreiches unter den Karolingern, 751–918.* Band 4, *Papstregesten 800–911*, Teil 2, *844–872.* Lieferung 2, *858–867 (Nicolaus I.).* Vienna: Böhlau, 2012.

Heydemann, Gerda. "Bibelexegese und rechtlicher Diskurs in der Karolingerzeit: Der Matthäuskommentar des Paschasius Radbertus." In *The Politics of Interpretation: The Bible and the Law in the Early Middle Ages*, edited by Gerda Heydemann and Rosamond McKitterick. Sigmaringen: Thorbecke, forthcoming.

———. "The People of God and the Law: Biblical Models in Carolingian Legislation." *Speculum* 95, no. 1 (2020): 89–131.

Hoffmann, Hartmut, and Rudolf Pokorny. "Ratramnus von Corbie, De propinquorum coniugiis: Ein zweites Blatt des fragmentarischen Briefgutachtens." *Deutsches Archiv für Erforschung des Mittelalters* 67, no. 1 (2011): 1–18.

Howe, John. *Before the Gregorian Reform: The Latin Church at the Turn of the First Millennium.* Ithaca: Cornell University Press, 2016.

Hunter, David G. "The Significance of Ambrosiaster." *Journal of Early Christian Studies* 17 (2009): 1–26.

Hyam, Jane. "Ermentrude and Richildis." In *Charles the Bald: Court and Kingdom. Papers Based on a Colloquium Held in London in April 1979*, edited by Margaret T. Gibson and Janet L. Nelson, 153–68. Oxford: Oxford University Press, 1981.

IJssennagger, Nelleke L. "Between Frankish and Viking: Frisia and the Frisians in the Viking Age." *Viking and Medieval Scandinavia* 9 (2013): 69–98.

Jasper, Detlev, and Horst Fuhrmann. *Papal Letters in the Early Middle Ages.* Washington, DC: Catholic University of America Press, 2001.

Joye, Sylvie. "Carolingian Rulers and Marriage in the Age of Louis the Pious and His Sons." In *Gender and Historiography: Studies in the Earlier Middle Ages in Honour of Pauline Stafford*, edited by Janet L. Nelson, Susan Reynolds, and Susan M. Johns, 101–14. London: University of London Press, Institute of Historical Research, 2012.

———. "Family Order and Kingship according to Hincmar." In *Hincmar of Rheims: Life and Work*, edited by Rachel Stone and Charles West, 190–210. Manchester: Manchester University Press, 2015.

———. "Le rapt de Judith par Baudoin (862): Un clinamen sociologique?" In *Les élites au haut Moyen Âge: Crises et renouvellements*, edited by François Bougard, Laurent Feller, and Régine le Jan, 361–80. Turnhout: Brepols, 2006.

Karras, Ruth Mazo. *Unmarriages: Women, Men, and Sexual Unions in the Middle Ages.* Philadelphia: University of Pennsylvania Press, 2012.

Kershaw, Paul J.E. "Eberhard of Friuli, a Carolingian Lay Intellectual." In *Lay Intellectuals in the Carolingian World*, edited by C. Patrick Wormald and Janet L. Nelson, 77–105. Cambridge: Cambridge University Press, 2007.

Kessler, Herbert L. "A Lay Abbot as Patron: Count Vivian and the First Bible of Charles the Bald." *Committenti e produzione artistico-letteraria nell'alto medioevo occidentale: 4–10 aprile 1991*, edited by Ovidio Capitani, 647–76. Spoleto: Presso la Sede del Centro, 1992.

Kislinger, Ewald. "Erster und zweiter Sieger. Zum byzantinisch-karolingischen Bündnis bezüglich Bari 870–871." *Zbornik radova Vizantoloskog Instituta* 50 (2013): 245–58.

Kornbluth, Genevra. "The Seal of Lothar II: Model and Copy." *Francia* 17, no. 1 (1990): 55–68.

Koziol, Geoffrey. *The Politics of Memory and Identity in Carolingian Royal Diplomas: The West Frankish Kingdom (840–987)*. Turnhout: Brepols, 2012.

Kramer, Rutger. "Monasticism, Reform, and Authority in the Carolingian Era." In *The Cambridge History of Medieval Monasticism in the Latin West*, vol. 2: *The Carolingians to the Eleventh Century*, edited by Isabelle Cochelin and Alison Beach, 432–49. Cambridge: Cambridge University Press, 2020.

———. "Order in the Church: Understanding Councils and Performing *Ordines* in the Carolingian World." *Early Medieval Europe* 25, no. 1 (2017): 54–69.

Kuchenbuch, Ludolf. *Versilberte Verhältnisse: Der Denar in seiner ersten Epoche (700–1000)*. Göttingen: Wallstein, 2016.

La Rocca, Cristina. "Angelberga, Louis's II Wife, and Her Will (877)." In *Ego Trouble: Authors and Their Identities in the Early Middle Ages*, edited by Richard Corradini, Matthew Gillis, Rosamond McKitterick, and Irene van Renswoude, 221–6. Vienna: Verlag der Österreichischen Akademie der Wissenschaften, 2010.

La Rocca, Cristina, and Luigi Provero. "The Dead and Their Gifts. The Will of Eberhard, Count of Friuli, and His Wife Gisela, Daughter of Louis the Pious (863–864)." In *Rituals of Power: From Late Antiquity to the Early Middle Ages*, edited by Frans Theuws and Janet Nelson, 225–80. Leiden: Brill, 2000.

Lebecq, Stéphane. "Le testament d'Evrard et Gisèle de Cysoing. Présentation et traduction." In *Splendor Reginae: Passions, genre et famille. Mélanges en l'honneur de Régine Le Jan*, edited by Laurent Jégou, Sylvie Joye, Thomas Lienhard, and Jens Schneider, 59–68. Turnhout: Brepols, 2015.

Le Jan, Régine. "Douaires et pouvoirs des reines en Francie et en Germanie (VIe–Xe siècle)." In *Dots et douaires dans le haut Moyen Âge*, edited by Régine le Jan, Laurent Feller, and François Bougard, 457–98. Rome: Ecole française de Rome, 2002.

Leyser, Conrad. "The Memory of Gregory the Great and the Making of Latin Europe, 600–1000." In *Making Early Medieval Societies: Conflict and Belonging in the Latin West, 300–1200*, edited by Kate Cooper and Conrad Leyser, 181–201. Cambridge: Cambridge University Press, 2016.

Liu, Yin. "Agobard, Deuteronomic Curses, and an Anti-Jewish Exegetical Discourse in Carolingian Lyon." *Viator* 51, no. 1 (2020): 205–39.

MacLean, Simon. "The Carolingian Response to the Revolt of Boso, 879–887." *Early Medieval Europe* 10, no. 1 (2001): 21–48.

———. *Kingship and Politics in the Late Ninth Century: Charles the Fat and the End of the Carolingian Empire*. Cambridge: Cambridge University Press, 2003.

———. "Queenship, Nunneries and Royal Widowhood in Carolingian Europe." *Past and Present* 178 (2003): 3–38.

———. "Royal Adultery, Biblical History and Political Conflict in Tenth Century Francia: The Lothar Crystal Reconsidered." *Francia* 49 (2022): 1–26.

———. "Shadow Kingdom: Lotharingia and the Frankish World, C.850–C.1050." *History Compass* 11, no. 6 (2013): 443–57.

———. "Who Were the Lotharingians? Defining Political Community After the End of the Carolingian Empire." In *Historiography and Identity 4: Writing History across Medieval Eurasia*, edited by Walter Pohl and Daniel Mahoney, 247–74. Turnhout: Brepols, 2021.

Majnarić, Ivan. "In the Shadows of Empires: Early Medieval Croatia in the Ninth and Tenth Centuries." *History Compass* 16, no. 7 (2008): 1–11.

McCormick, Michael. *Eternal Victory: Triumphal Rulership in Late Antiquity, Byzantium, and the Early Medieval West*. Cambridge: Cambridge University Press, 1987.

———. *Origins of the European Economy: Communications and Commerce, AD 300–900*. Cambridge: Cambridge University Press, 2002.

McDougall, Sara. *Royal Bastards: The Birth of Illegitimacy, 800–1230*. Oxford: Oxford University Press, 2017.

McKitterick, Rosamond. "Charles the Bald and His Library: The Patronage of Learning." *English Historical Review* 95 (1980): 28–47.

———. *History and Memory in the Carolingian World*. Cambridge: Cambridge University Press, 2004.

Melve, Leidulf. "'Even the Very Laymen Are Chattering about It': The Politicization of Public Opinion, 800–1200." *Viator* 44, no. 1 (2013): 25–48.

Miller, Maureen C. *Clothing the Clergy: Virtue and Power in Medieval Europe, c. 800–1200*. Ithaca: Cornell University Press, 2014.

Mistry, Zubin. "Ermentrude's Consecration (866): Queen-Making Rites and Biblical Templates for Carolingian Fertility." *Early Medieval Europe* 27, no. 4 (2019): 567–88.

Mütherich, Florentine. *Sakramentar von Metz: Fragment. MS Lat. 1141, Bibliothèque nationale, Paris. Vollständige Faksimile-Ausg*. Graz: Akademische Druck- und Verlagsanstalt, 1972.

Nelson, Janet L. "The Carolingian Moment." In *Debating Medieval Europe: The Early Middle Ages, c. 450–c. 1050*, edited by Stephen Mossman, 63–96. Manchester: Manchester University Press, 2020.

———. "Carolingian Oaths." In *Le sacré et la parole: Le serment au Moyen Âge*, edited by Martin Aurell, Jaume Aurell i Cardona, and Montserrat Herrero López, 33–56. Paris: Classiques Garnier, 2018.

———. *Charles the Bald*. London: Routledge, 1992.
———. "Early Medieval Rites of Queen-Making and the Shaping of Medieval Queenship." In *Queens and Queenship in Medieval Europe*, edited by Anne J. Duggan, 301–15. Woodbridge: Boydell & Brewer, 1997.
———. "England and the Continent in the Ninth Century: 2, The Vikings and Others." *Transactions of the Royal Historical Society* 13 (2003): 1–28.
———. "Kingship and Royal Government." In *The New Cambridge Medieval History*, vol. 2: *c.700–c.900*, edited by Rosamond McKitterick, 381–430. Cambridge: Cambridge University Press, 1995.
———. "'Not Bishops' Bailiffs but Lords of the Earth.' Charles the Bald and the Problem of Sovereignty." In *The Church and Sovereignty c.590–1918: Essays in Honour of Michael Wilks*, edited by Diana Wood, 23–34. Oxford: Blackwell, 1991.
Nelson, Janet L., and Patrick Wormald, eds. *Lay Intellectuals in the Carolingian World*. Cambridge: Cambridge University Press, 2007.
Nightingale, John. *Monasteries and Patrons in the Gorze Reform: Lotharingia c.850–1000*. Oxford: Oxford University Press, 2001.
Noble, Thomas. "Pope Nicholas I and the Franks: Politics and Ecclesiology in the Ninth Century." In *Religious Franks: Religion and Power in the Frankish Kingdoms: Studies in Honour of Mayke de Jong*, edited by Rob Meens, 472–88. Manchester: Manchester University Press, 2016.
O'Brien, Conor. *The Rise of Christian Kingship, 400–850*. Oxford: Oxford University Press, forthcoming.
Offergeld, Thilo. *Reges pueri: Das Königtum Minderjähriger im frühen Mittelalter*. Hannover: Hahn, 2001.
Ottewill-Soulsby, Samuel. *The Emperor and the Elephant: Christians and Muslims in the Age of Charlemagne*. Princeton: Princeton University Press, 2023.
Panczer, Gérard, Geoffray Riondet, Lauriane Forest, Michael S. Krzemnicki, Davy Carole, and Florian Faure. "The Talisman of Charlemagne: New Historical and Gemological Discoveries." *Gems & Gemology: The Quarterly Journal of the Gemological Institute of America* 55, no. 1 (2019): 30–46.
Patzold, Steffen. *Episcopus: Wissen über Bischöfe im Frankreich des späten 8. bis frühen 10. Jahrhunderts*. Ostfildern: Thorbecke, 2008.
———. "Verhandeln über die Ehe des Königs. Das Beispiel Lothars II." In *Herstellung und Darstellung von Entscheidungen: Verfahren, Verwalten und Verhandeln in der Vormoderne*, edited by Barbara Stollberg-Rilinger and André Krischer, 391–410. Berlin: Duncker & Humblot, 2010.
Pecksmith, Robert. "A King Praises Himself: The Letters of Charles the Bald to Pope Hadrian II." *English Historical Review*, forthcoming.
Petry, Klaus, and Stefan Wittenbrink. *Der karolingiche Münzschatzfund von Pilligerheck*. Münster: Verein der Münzfreunde für Westfalen und Nachbargebiete, 2021.
Pezé, Warren. "Doctrinal Debate and Social Control in the Carolingian Age: The Predestination Controversy (840s–60s)." *Early Medieval Europe* 25, no. 1 (2017): 85–101.

Pohl, Walter. "Christian and Barbarian Identities in the Early Medieval West: Introduction." In *Post-Roman Transitions: Christian and Barbarian Identities in the Early Medieval West*, edited by Walter Pohl and Gerda Heydemann, 1–46. Turnhout: Brepols, 2013.

———. "Historiography of Disillusion: Erchempert and the History of Ninth-Century Southern Italy." In *Historiography and Identity 3: Carolingian Approaches*, edited by Rutger Kramer, Helmut Reimitz, and Graeme Ward, 319–54. Turnhout: Brepols, 2021.

Pohl, Walter, and Veronika Wieser, eds. *Der frühmittelalterliche Staat: Europäische Perspektiven*. Vienna: Verlag der österreichischen Akademie der Wissenschaften, 2009.

Pokorny, Rudolf. "Sirmonds verlorener Lütticher Codex der Hinkmar-Schriften: Ein erhaltenes Inhaltsverzeichnis." *Deutsches Archiv für Erforschung des Mittelalters* 66 (2010): 511–35.

Pössel, Christina. "Authors and Recipients of Carolingian Capitularies, 779–829." In *Texts and Identities in the Early Middle Ages*, edited by Richard Corradini, Rob Meens, Christina Pössel, and Philip Shaw, 253–76. Vienna: Verlag der österreichischen Akademie der Wissenschaften, 2006.

Raisharma, Sukanya. "Much Ado about Vienne? A Localizing Universal *Chronicon*." In *Historiography and Identity 3: Carolingian Approaches*, edited by Rutger Kramer, Helmut Reimitz, and Graeme Ward, 271–90. Turnhout: Brepols, 2021.

Rampton, Martha. "Love and the Divorce of Lothar II." In *On the Shoulders of Giants: Essays in Honor of Glenn W. Olsen*, edited by David F. Appleby and Teresa Olsen Pierre, 91–115. Toronto: Pontifical Institute of Mediaeval Studies, 2015.

———. *Trafficking with Demons. Magic, Ritual, and Gender from Late Antiquity to 1000*. Ithaca: Cornell University Press, 2021.

Rennie, Kriston. *The Foundations of Medieval Papal Legation*. London: Palgrave MacMillan, 2013.

Reuter, Timothy. "'You Can't Take It with You.' Testaments, Hoards and Moveable Wealth in Europe, 600–1100." In *Treasure in the Medieval West*, edited by Elizabeth M. Tyler, 11–24. York: York Medieval Press, 2000.

Reynaud, Jean-François. *À la recherche d'un Lyon disparu: Vie et mort des édifices religieux du IVe au XXe siècle*. Lyon: Alpara, 2021.

Reynolds, Philip. *Marriage in the Western Church: The Christianization of Marriage during the Patristic and Early Medieval Periods*. Leiden: Brill, 1994.

Riché, Pierre. "Trésors et collections d'aristocrates laïques carolingiens." *Cahiers archéologiques. Fin de l'antiquité et Moyen Âge* 22 (1972): 39–46.

Rosenwein, Barbara H. *Negotiating Space: Power, Restraint, and Privileges of Immunity in Early Medieval Europe*. Manchester: Manchester University Press, 1999.

Sarti, Laury. *Orbis Romanus: Byzantium and the Roman Legacy in the Carolingian World*. Oxford: Oxford University Press, forthcoming.

Schäpers, Maria. *Lothar I. (795–855) und das Frankenreich*. Vienna: Böhlau, 2018.

Schmid, Karl. "Ein karolingischer Königseintrag im Gedenkbuch von Remiremont." *Frühmittelalterliche Studien* 2, no. 1 (1968): 96–134.

Schneider, Jens. "Spatializing Meersen: Monasteries in Jurassian Burgundy (6th–9th c.)." *Bulletin du centre d'études médiévales d'Auxerre* 22, no. 1 (2018).

Schulz, Julien. "Überlegungen zum Vertrag von Meerssen (870)." *Francia* 43 (2016): 333–52.

Screen, Elina. "Coining It? Carolingian Rulers and the Frankish Coinage, c. 750–900." *History Compass* 17, no. 9 (2019): 1–15.

———. "The Importance of the Emperor. Lothar I and the Frankish Civil War, 840–843." *Early Medieval Europe* 12, no. 1 (2003): 25–51.

Smith, Julie Ann. "The Earliest Queen-Making Rites." *Church History* 66, no. 1 (1997): 18–35.

Squatriti, Paolo. "Hadrian II, Pope." In *Medieval Italy: An Encyclopedia*, edited by Christopher Kleinherz, 486–7. New York: Routledge, 2004.

Staubach, Nikolaus. *Das Herrscherbild Karls des Kahlen: Formen und Funktionen monarchischer Repräsentation im früheren Mittelalter.* Münster, 1981.

———. "'Quasi semper in publico.' Öffentlichkeit als Funktions- und Kommunikationsraum karolingischer Königsherrschaft." In *Das Öffentliche und Private in der Vormoderne*, edited by Gert Melville and Peter von Moos, 577–608. Cologne: Böhlau, 1998.

Stone, Rachel. "'Bound from Either Side': The Limits of Power in Carolingian Marriage Disputes, 840–870." *Gender and History* 19, no. 3 (2007): 467–82.

———. "Introduction: Hincmar's World." In *Hincmar of Rheims: Life and Work*, edited by Rachel Stone and Charles West, 1–45. Manchester: Manchester University Press, 2015.

———. *Morality and Masculinity in the Carolingian Empire.* Cambridge: Cambridge University Press, 2012.

Stouraitis, Ioannis. "Byzantine Romanness: From Geopolitical to Ethnic Conceptions." In *Transformations of Romanness: Early Medieval Regions and Identities*, edited by Walter Pohl, Clemens Gantner, Cinzia Grifoni, and Marianne Pollheimer-Mohaupt, 123–42. Berlin: De Gruyter, 2018.

Tessera, Miriam Rita. "Milano, gli irlandesi e l'impero carolingio nel IX secolo: Intrecci politici e culturali intorno al divorzio di Lotario II." *Mélanges de l'Ecole française de Rome: Moyen Âge* 130, no. 1 (2018): 245–59.

Tobias, Norman. *Basil I, Founder of the Macedonian Dynasty: A Study of the Political and Military History of the Byzantine Empire in the Ninth Century.* Lewiston: The Edwin Mellen Press, 2007.

Torgerson, Jesse W. *The Chronographia of George the Synkellos and Theophanes: The Ends of Time in Ninth-Century Constantinople.* Leiden: Brill, 2022.

Treggiari, Susan. *Roman Marriage: Iusti Coniuges from the Time of Cicero to the Time of Ulpian.* Oxford: Oxford University Press, 1991.

Ubl, Karl. "Der Entwurf einer imaginären Rechtsordnung im 9. Jahrhundert: Die Kapitulariensammlung des Benedictus Levita." In *La productivité d'une crise: Le règne de Louis le Pieux (814–840) et la transformation de l'Empire carolingien (Relectio, 1)*, edited by Philippe Depreux, 185–204. Ostfildern: Thorbecke, 2018.

———. *Inzestverbot und Gesetzgebung: Die Konstruktion eines Verbrechens (300–1100)*. Berlin: De Gruyter, 2008.

Unger, Veronika. *Päpstliche Schriftlichkeit im 9. Jahrhundert: Archiv, Register, Kanzlei*. Vienna: Böhlau, 2019.

Vanderputten, Steven. *Dark Age Nunneries: The Ambiguous Identity of Female Monasticism, 800–1050*. Ithaca: Cornell University Press, 2018.

Vanderputten, Steven, and Charles West. "Inscribing Property, Rituals, and Royal Alliances: The 'Theutberga Gospels' and the Abbey of Remiremont." *Mitteilungen des Instituts für Österreichische Geschichtsforschung* 124 (2016): 296–321.

van Doren, Jan. "*De Divortio* and *de Resignatione*: A Case of Carolingian Legal Precedent?" In *Law, Book, Culture in the Middle Ages*, edited by Thom Gobbitt, 149–71. Leiden: Brill, 2021.

van Espelo, Dorine. "Rulers, Popes and Bishops: The Historical Context of the Ninth-Century Cologne Codex Carolinus Manuscript (Codex Vindobonensis 449)." In *Religious Franks: Religion and Power in the Frankish Kingdoms: Studies in Honour of Mayke de Jong*, edited by Rob Meens, 455–71. Manchester: Manchester University Press, 2016.

van Rhijn, Carine. *Leading the Way to Heaven: Pastoral Care and Salvation in the Carolingian Period*. London: Routledge, 2022.

———. "Royal Politics in Small Worlds: Local Priests and the Implementation of Carolingian correctio." In *Kleine Welten: Ländliche Gesellschaften im Karolingerreich*, edited by Thomas Kohl, Steffen Patzold, and Bernhard Zeller, 237–52. Ostfilden: Thorbecke, 2019.

Vocino, Giorgia. "Framing Ambrose in the Resources of the Past: The Late Antique and Early Medieval Sources for a Carolingian Portrait of Ambrose." In *The Resources of the Past in Early Medieval Europe*, edited by Clemens Gantner, Rosamond McKitterick, and Sven Meeder, 135–54. Cambridge: Cambridge University Press, 2015.

———. "A *Peregrinus*'s Vade mecum: MS Bern 363 and the 'Circle of Sedulius Scottus.'" In *The Annotated Book in the Early Middle Ages: Practices of Reading and Writing*, edited by Mariken Teeuwen and Irene van Renswoude, 87–123. Turnhout: Brepols, 2017.

West, Charles. "'And How, If You Are a Christian, Can You Hate the Emperor?' Reading a Seventh-Century Scandal in Carolingian Francia." In *Criticising the Ruler in Pre-Modern Societies – Possibilities, Chances and Methods*, edited by Karina Kellermann, Alheydis Plassmann, and Christian Schwermann, 411–30. Bonn: Bonn University Press, 2019.

———. "Between the Flood and the Last Judgment: Hincmar of Rheims and the Trial by Ordeal." In *Beyond Time and Space: Medieval Studies by and in Memory of Miriam Czock*, edited by Matthew Gillis, Anja Rathmann-Lutz, and Laury Sarti. Forthcoming.

———. "Carolingian Kingship and the Peasants of Le Mans: The *Capitulum in Cenomannico pago datum*." In *Charlemagne: Les temps, les espaces, les hommes. Construction et déconstruction d'un règne*, edited by Rolf Grosse and Michel Sot, 227–44. Turnhout: Brepols, 2018.

———. "'Dissonance of Speech, Consonance of Meaning': The 862 Council of Aachen and the Transmission of Carolingian Conciliar Records." In *Writing the Early Medieval West*, edited by Elina Screen and Charles West, 169–82. Cambridge, Cambridge University Press, 2018.

———. "Knowledge of the Past and the Judgement of History in Tenth-Century Trier: Regino of Prüm and the Lost Manuscript of Bishop Adventius of Metz." *Early Medieval Europe* 24, no. 2 (2016): 137–59.

———. "Pope Leo of Bourges, Clerical Immunity and the Early Medieval Secular." *Early Medieval Europe* 29, no. 1 (2021): 86–108.

Whitten, Sarah. "Franks, Greeks, and Saracens: Violence, Empire, and Religion in Early Medieval Southern Italy." *Early Medieval Europe* 27, no. 2 (2019): 251–78.

Wickham, Chris. "Consensus and Assemblies in the Romano-Germanic Kingdoms: A Comparative Approach." In *Recht und Konsens im frühen Mittelalter*, edited by Verena Epp and Christoph Meyer, 389–424. Ostfildern: Thorbecke, 2017.

———. "Ninth-Century Byzantium through Western Eyes." In *Byzantium in the Ninth Century: Dead or Alive? Papers from the Thirtieth Spring Symposium on Byzantine Studies, Birmingham, March 1996*, edited by Leslie Brubaker, 245–56. Aldershot: Ashgate, 1998.

Winder, Simon. *Lotharingia: A Personal History of Europe's Lost Country*. London: Penguin, 2019.

Wittkamp, Thomas. "Das Schicksal Hugos, Sohn Lothars II., und die Normannenpolitik der Lotharlinie." In *D'un regnum à l'autre: La Lotharingie, un espace de l'entre-deux? Vom Regnum zum Imperium: Lotharingien als Zwischenreich?* edited by Tristan Martine and Jessika Nowak, 97–124. Nancy: Presses universitaires de Nancy, 2021.

Woods, David. "Valentinian I, Severa, Marina and Justina." *Classica et Mediaevalia* 57 (2006): 173–87.

Worm, Peter. *Karolingische Rekognitionszeichen: Die Kanzlerzeile und ihre graphische Ausgestaltung auf den Herrscherurkunden des achten und neunten Jahrhunderts*. Marburg: Universitätsbibliothek Marburg, 2004.

Zielinksi, Herbert. *Die burgundischen Regna 855–1032: Niederburgund bis zur Vereinigung mit Hochburgund (855–940)*. Regesta Imperii 1.3/4. Cologne: Böhlau, 2013.

Index

Page numbers in italics refer to figures.

Aachen, 14, 14n11. *See also* Council(s) of Aachen (860); Council of Aachen (862)
Adalard (son of Eberhard and Gisela), 116, 116n12, 118, 119–20, 121
Adalroch (nephew of Eberhard and Gisela), 121
Ado of Vienne (archbishop), 123n7, 171–2, 173
Adrian II (pope). *See* Hadrian II (pope)
Adventius of Metz (bishop)
  coronation of Charles the Bald as king of Lotharingia and, 179n1, 180
  Council of Aachen (860) and, 53n7
  Council of Aachen (862) and, 53, 55, 56–60
  Gorze monastery reforms and, 106–8, 108–12, 111n26
  letter from Lotharingian bishops to West Frankish bishops and, 131
  letter to Nicholas I, 123–4, 124–9, 125nn14–15
  letter to Theutgaud of Trier, 99–101, 101–2
  ordination as bishop, 126n21
  prayers organized against Northmen, 164–7
  Savonnières summit and, 89, 89n17
  St-Glossinde convent and, 141n6
  Theutgaud's deposition and, 100n3
Aeneas of Paris (bishop), 24
Aethicus Ister
  Cosmography, 119
African Council, 67, 67n57, 79
Alcuin, 120
Altfrid of Hildesheim (bishop), 89, 89n15, 169, 169n11
Althoff, Gerd, 99
Ambrose of Milan, 73–5
  On Various Sermons, 119, 119n32
Ambrosiaster (Pseudo-Ambrose), 59–60, 59n27, 59n30, 65–6, 65n49, 70, 70n67
Anastasius the Librarian, 184, 188n22, 190n32
Angilberga (empress, wife of Louis II of Italy), 137, 170–1, 185

Arduicus (Hartwig) of Besançon (archbishop), 56n16
aristocracy, 87–8, 112–13, 114–15, 130
Arnulf of Metz (bishop), 180
Arnulf of Toul (bishop), 56, 179n1
Arsenius of Orte (bishop), 134–5, 140, 160n16
Augustine, 71–2, 75–9, 76n82, 80–1, 80n89, 84, 120
  Enchiridion, 120
  On Adulterous Marriages, 75
  On Drunkenness, 120
  On the City of God, 119
  On the Good of Marriage, 84
  On the Words of the Lord, 119
Auprand (envoy of Louis II of Italy), 200
Avernus Lake, 101n11

Balaam, 158, 158n9
Baldwin (count), 47n5, 86, 91, 91n34
Bari, 183, 183n2, 183n5, 185–6, 185n12, 195–6, 195n56, 199
basileus (emperor), use of term, 187–93, 187nn20–1, 188n23, 195
Basil I (Byzantine emperor)
  Bari siege and, 183, 195–6
  elevation to imperial throne, 192n40
  letter from Louis II of Italy, 184, 186–200, 186nn16–17
  letter to Louis II, 184, 187, 187n20
  proposed marriage between Basil's son and Louis II's daughter, 194, 194n54
  self-perception as Roman emperor, 183n4
Bassenheim hoard, 18
Bede, 73, 119n36
Berengar (son of Eberhard and Gisela), 116, 117–18, 119, 121, 121n47
Berner of Grenoble (bishop), 173, 173n9

Berta (daughter of Lothar II and Waldrada), 103
Betto (abbot of Gorze), 106, 110, 110n23, 111, 123, 128n26
Bibles, 119n29
bishops. *See* Church; Quierzy Letter, to Louis the German; *specific bishops*
Bivin of Gorze, 106, 107, 108, 110, 110n22, 182
Böhringer, Letha, 7n12
Bondioli, Lorenzo M., 183n2
Boso (husband of Engeltrude), 86, 86n6, 90, 90n28
Boso (nephew of Theutberga), 161n20, 173n9
Bosonid family, 3, 113, 161, 161n20
Bougard, François, 137
Breviary of Alaric (book of Anianus), 120, 120n39
bribery, 37, 37n48
Byzantium (Eastern Roman Empire), 183–4, 183n4, 191n35, 192n43, 193, 193n50, 196n58. *See also* Basil I (Byzantine emperor)

Calabria, 196, 199
Canons of the Apostles, 79, 79n85
capitularies, 30, 30n27
Carloman (son of Charles the Bald), 150, 150n12
Carolingian empire
  aristocracy, 87–8, 112–13, 114–15, 130
  child-kings, 201
  defense of against Basil I, 187–95, 190n33
  dynastic nature of rule, 150, 150n11
  fragmentation of, 1, 2–3
  Frankish unity via kinship, 184, 191, 191n37
  map, *4*
  military, 196n58
  political instability, 202–3

publics within, 87–8
queens, 141, 157n7
summits between kings, 85, 85n1, 86–7
See also kings and kingship; Lotharingia
cartularies, 108
Catholic Church. *See* Church
celibacy, 62n38, 67n60
Charlemagne
  Carolingian empire established by, 1
  Church and, 32
  coinage, 17
  conquest of Italy, 183
  as emperor, 189–90, 191–2, 192n39, 192n41
  prayers before battle, 166
Charles (son of Charles the Bald), 147, 150, 150n13
Charles Martel, 31–2, 31n34
Charles of Provence (king of Provence)
  death and burial, 102, 104
  Lothar II's family tree, place in, *6*
  map of kingdom, *4*
  mentioned in *Liber Memorialis* of Remiremont, 49
  reign, 3, 102, 201
  threat from Charles the Bald, 48, 48n8, 179n2
  Treaty of Orbe and, 11
Charles the Bald (king of West Francia)
  anointed as king, 42, 42n57
  bishops' protection of in Quierzy Letter, 42–3, 43n59
  coronation as king in Lotharingia, 179, 179n1
  Eigil of Sens and, 47
  epithet, 2n3
  Ermentrude's coronation as queen and, 146, 147–8, 150, 153n20
  Hadrian II and, 176

Hubert (brother of Theutberga) and, 106n6
invasion by Louis the German, 19, 113, 132, 132n9
kingdom of, 2, *4*
letter from Nicholas I, 154–7, 157–63
letter to Nicholas I on Adventius's behalf, 123–4
Lothar II and, 7, 47, 47n6
Lothar II's family tree, place in, *6*
Lotharingia divided with Louis the German, 182
Louis II of Italy and, 189, 189n27
marriage to Richildis, 148, 182
Metz oath and, 168–9, 169–70, 170nn15–16
as Nicholas I's intermediary, 155–6, 162, 162n22
royal emissaries, 41n53
Sacramentary of Metz and, 179–82, *181*
Savonnières summit (862) and, 85–6, 88, 88n12, 89–95, 96–7, 98, 98n46
summits with brothers, 33–4, 34nn41–2
Theutberga and, 5, 47, 47n5, 154, 157, 157n7, 182
as threat to Charles of Provence, 48, 48n8, 179n2
as threat to Lothar II, 7, 129–30, 132, 132n8
Charles the Fat, 49, 172, 172n8
charters
  about, 11–12, 13
  donation to St-Pierre convent, 103, 104–5
  Gorze monastic reforms, 106–8, 108–12, 111n26
  land granted to Theutberga, 135–7, 137–9, 137n10, 138n15, 138nn19–20, *139*, 139n22
  to Winebert, 12–13, 14, 14n14, 15–16, 15n18, *16*

chastity, 62n38
child custody, 75, 75n80
christianitas (Christendom, Christianity), 30n32. *See also* Church
Christian of Auxerre (bishop), 89, 89n23
Chrodegang of Metz (bishop), 106, 110, 110n20
Chronicle of Salerno, 186
Chronographia (George the Synkellos and Theophanes), 190n32, 191n36
Church
  call to protect in Quierzy Letter, 29–33
  church property allocated to secular aristocrats, 30–1, 31n33
  clerical vs. secular offices, 43, 43nn60–1
  emperors anointed by popes, 189, 189n28
  episcopal authority and hierarchy, 99
  four patriarchal sees on empire, 188–9
  holy cross, 117, 117n18
  intervention in Frankish affairs, 203
  letter from Lotharingian bishops to West Frankish bishops, 129–31, 131–4, 131n5, 131n7
  oaths and, 43–4, 43n62
  papal judicial authority, 159–60, 159n14
  Photian schism, 193n49
  rulers commemorated by four patriarchal sees, 189n30
  secular vs. spiritual authority, 45, 45n64, 61, 61n34
  synods, 30, 30n30
  See also Adventius of Metz (bishop); excommunication; Gunthar of Cologne (archbishop); Hadrian II (pope); Hincmar of Reims (archbishop); monasteries and convents; Nicholas I (pope); Quierzy Letter, to Louis the German; Theutgaud of Trier (archbishop)
Clovis (king), 33n40, 180
coinage, 16–18, 17n3, *19*, 118n27
Conrad (cousin of Charles the Bald), 87, 98n45
convents. *See* monasteries and convents
coronation, of Queen Ermentrude, 146–9, 149–53, 149n8, 150n14, 153n19
Costambeys, Mario, 7
Council(s) of Aachen (860)
  confirmed by Council of Aachen (862), 58, 58n25
  double transmission of acts, 53, 53n7
  Eigil of Sens and, 47
  referenced at Council of Aachen (862), 62, 62n36, 63, 63n43, 64n47
  Theutberga's "voluntary" confession at, 3, 46, 64
Council of Aachen (862), 52–85
  about, 52–3
  bishops present, 56, 56n16
  double transmission of acts, 53, 67–8, 68n61
  Lothar II's divorce from Theutberga and marriage to Waldrada, 53, 57–60, 62–3, 62n35, 64–7, 66nn55–6, 67n59, 80–5, 100
  Nicholas I and, 91–2, 92n36, 100, 171
  Text A (Acts of the Council (Adventius's version?)), 53, 55, 56–60, 58n24
  Text B (Booklet of Complaint of Lothar II), 52, 55, 61–3, 61n33, 64n44

Index

Text C (Acts of the Council (Gunthar's version?)), 53, 55, 63–8, 63n42, 81n91
Text D (A Treatise on Marriage), 54–5, 68–85, 68nn62–3
Council of Agde (506), 60, 60n32, 65, 65n48, 81, 81n91
Council of Antioch, 126
Council of Carthage (419), 159n14
Council of Epaon (517), 60n32
Council of Estinnes (743), 32, 32n36
Council of Lérida (546), 58–9, 58n26, 65n48
Council of Metz (863)
 acts of, 105–6
 Adventius's charter on Gorze monastic reforms and, 112n29
 annulled by Nicholas I, 5, 121–2, 123, 156
 Lothar II's marriage to Waldrada and, 5, 55, 100, 103
 monastic reforms and, 107–8, 109, 109n17
 references to in Adventius's letter to Nicholas I, 126, 126n19, 128, 128n25
Council of Paris (829), 45n64
Council of Tusey (860), 90, 90n27
Council of Valence, 66–7, 66n56, 67n57
Coupland, Simon, 164
Croats, 197n63
cross, holy, 117, 117n18

Dacheriana canon law collection, 58n26
dagger (*facilus*), 117, 117n16
dalmatic, 117, 117n19, 118
d'Avray, David, 159n14
De Jong, Mayke, 52
Diesenberger, Maximilian, 129n1
diplomas. *See* charters
Diso (witness to Eberhard and Gisela's will), 121

divorce, 73n74, 74n78, 152, 152n18, 201. *See also* marriage; marriage crisis (Lothar II and Theutberga)
Doda (stepmother of Lothar II), 50
Dohmen, Linda, 11
Domagoj (Croat duke), 197n63
Dorestad, 18
Drogo of Metz (archbishop), 15, 15n16, 109, 109n15, 110
Drumar (witness to Eberhard and Gisela's will), 121
Duchesne, André, 149n8

Eastern Roman Empire (Byzantium), 183–4, 183n4, 191n35, 192n43, 193, 193n50, 196n58. *See also* Basil I (Byzantine emperor)
East Francia. *See* Louis the German
Ebbo of Reims (archbishop), 47, 146
Eberhard of Friuli, and wife Gisela
 land and estates, 113–14, 115–17, 116n11
 library, 113, 119–20, 119n28, 120n41
 movable property, 113, 117–19, 117n21, 118n22
 political loyalty, 114–15
 remaining property, 120–1
 will, 113–14, 115–21
Eighth Ecumenical Council, 197n60, 197n62
Eigil of Sens (archbishop), 47, 47n3
emperor (*basileus*), use of term, 187–93, 187nn20–1, 188n23, 195
Engelhad (witness to Eberhard and Gisela's will), 121
Engeltrude (daughter of Eberhard and Gisela), 116, 118–19, 120, 121
Engeltrude (wife of Boso), 86, 86n6, 90–1, 90n28, 91n30, 127, 140

Ercambald (archchancellor), 105
Erchenrad of Châlons (bishop), 21, 22n7
Ermengard (daughter of Lothar II and Waldrada), 103
Ermengard (daughter of Louis II of Italy), 194n54, 196n59
Ermentrude (wife of Charles the Bald)
 coronation as queen, 146–9, 149–53, 149n8, 150n14, 153nn19–22
 mediation between Charles and Lothar II, 158n8
estates, royal, 39–41, 39n50
ethnic identity, 184, 191n35
Eucherius of Orléans, 31, 31n35
excommunication
 of Engeltrude, 90–1, 127
 as infectious, 91, 144n19
 Lothar II threatened with, 100, 100n4, 134, 145n26
 as papal prerogative, 145n26
 Quierzy Letter on calling excommunicated to repentance, 39
 of Waldrada, 140, 142, 144, 144nn19–21, 145, 145n23, 155, 162, 174

facilus (dagger), 117, 117n16
farm/household (*mansus*), 104, 104n11, 164
Field of Lies (June 833), 26n16
Franco of Liège (bishop), 56, 128n26, 179n1
Franks, 191, 191n35, 193, 195.
 See also Carolingian empire
Fredeco (witness to Eberhard and Gisela's will), 121
Fulgentius, 119, 120

Gaillard, Michèle, 48n11, 144n17
Gantner, Clemens, 182
garale (grail), 118, 118n25
Gelasius (pope), 45n64

gens/gentes (people), 184, 191, 191n35, 191n38
George (*stratigos*, senior Byzantine military officer), 199
George the Synkellos
 Chronographia (with Theophanes), 190n32, 191n36
Gerard of Vienne, 102, 173, 201
Gisela (daughter of Eberhard and Gisela), 116n15, 120, 120n45
Gisela (daughter of Lothar II and Waldrada), 103, 165
Gisela (wife of Eberhard). *See* Eberhard of Friuli, and wife Gisela
Godfrid (Northman, Lothar II's son-in-law), 165
Gorgon (martyr), 110, 110n20
Gorze Abbey, reforms, 106–8, 108–12, 111n26
Gottshalk of Orbais, 134n12
Gregory II (pope), 91, 91n32
Gregory the Great (pope), 37n48, 92, 127, 158, 158n10
 On the Prophet Ezechiel, 119, 119n37
Grimbland (scribe), 137n10, 138
Grondeux, Anne, 119n36
Grotz, Hans, 175n4
guesthouses, for pilgrims, 34–5
Gunthar of Cologne (archbishop)
 attempts to regain office, 155, 155n4, 171n2
 Council of Aachen (860) and, 53n7
 Council of Aachen (862) and, 53, 56, 63–8
 deposition of, 113n2, 121–2, 125–6, 126n18
 mentioned in Adventius's letter to Nicholas I, 125–6, 127
 Theutgaud's deposition and, 125n17

Hadrian II (pope)
 Charles the Bald and, 176

Gunthar of Cologne and, 171n2
letter to Lotharingian aristocrats in support of Louis II of Italy, 174–6, 176–8, 178n12
Lothar II and, 170–1, 173, 174
Louis II and, 175, 175n4
Haldin (abbot of Gorze), 110, 110n21
Haller, Johannes, 168n3
Hartwig (Arduicus) of Besançon (archbishop), 56n16
Hatto of Verdun (bishop), 56, 89, 89n18, 179n1
Heidecker, Karl, 7, 7n12, 53n5, 54, 55n13, 158n8, 167
Heilwich (daughter of Eberhard and Gisela), 116, 118–19, 120, 121
Herard of Tours (archbishop), 149n9
Herbers, Klaus, 123n6
Heribert (witness to Eberhard and Gisela's will), 121
Heydemann, Gerda, 54n10
Hildegar of Meaux (bishop), 23
Hincmar of Laon (bishop), 89, 89n21, 157, 169, 169n12
Hincmar of Reims (archbishop)
on agreement between Charles the Bald and Lothar II, 158n8
on Boso and Engeltrude's marriage, 86n6
call for Frankish synod, 42n56
coronation of Charles the Bald as king of Lotharingia and, 180
coronation of Ermentrude as queen and, 149, 149n9
council at St-Medard monastery (866) and, 146
ignored by Lothar II, 24
marriage crisis of Lothar II and Theutberga and, 55, 58n23, 91, 91n35, 93n38, 165
Metz oath and, 169
Nicholas I's circular letter on Council of Metz and, 123n7
proverb by, 22n10
Quierzy Letter and, 21, 26n17
Savonnières summit (862) and, 87, 89, 89n20, 98n45
Hispana canon law collection, 60n32
Holy Roman Empire. *See* Carolingian empire
honors, 28n22
hostels, for pilgrims, 34–5
household/farm (*mansus*), 104, 104n11, 164
Hraban Maurus of Mainz (archbishop), 12n4, 165n7
Hubert (brother of Theutberga), 3, 13, 106, 106n6, 136, 137, 138n20, 157
Hugh (aristocrat), 112–13, 113n2
Hugh (Hugo; son of Lothar II and Waldrada)
as claimant to Lotharingia, 5, 174, 182, 201
later history of, 174n2
mentioned in *Liber Memorialis* of Remiremont, 49, 50
public acknowledgment of in charter to St-Pierre convent, 103, 104
Wicbert and, 172n6
Hunger of Utrecht (bishop), 56, 56n16

imperium, joint Roman, 189, 189n29
incest, 30, 30n28, 54, 58–60, 64–5, 80–5, 83n96
incontinence, 57, 57n22, 62, 62n37
Innes, Matthew, 7
Innocent I (pope), 66, 66n56, 79–80
Isidore of Seville
Synonyms, 113n6, 119, 120
Italy, 183. *See also* Louis II of Italy

Jerome, 72–3
John (*patricius*, senior Byzantine officer), 187, 187nn18–19

John of Cambrai (bishop), 146n1
John of Cervia (bishop), 105, 107–8
Jonas of Orléans (bishop), 83n96
Judith (daughter of Charles the
    Bald), 47n5, 86, 91, 91n34, 149
Judith (daughter of Eberhard and
    Gisela), 116, 118–19, 120, 121

kacodosia, 193, 193n49
Karlman (son of Louis the German),
    49
kings and kingship
  anointed by popes, 189, 189n28
  aristocracy and, 87–8, 112–13,
      114–15, 130
  authority and, 52–3, 53n3
  child-kings, 201
  confiscation of property by, 116,
      116n14
  marriage and, 55, 203
  Quierzy Letter on, 20, 35–6, 36–9,
      37n47
  summits between kings, 85, 85n1,
      86–7
  See also Carolingian empire
Koblenz summit (860)
  about, 20, 85, 89n24
  Eberhard of Friuli at, 114
  mentioned during Savonnières
      summit (862), 87, 89, 89n25,
      90, 91n33, 94, 95, 96

Lanfrid (witness to Eberhard and
    Gisela's will), 121
Lebecq, Stéphane, 119n36
Le Jan, Régine, 136
Leo I (pope), 126, 151
Leo IV (pope), 177n10
liber memorialis, 48
Liber Memorialis of Remiremont,
    48–52, 48n11, *51*, 108
Liber Pontificalis (*Deeds of the Roman
    Pontiffs*), 119, 119n35
Liutbert of Mainz (archbishop),
    146n1, 169, 169n10

Lorraine, 5, 5n10
Lothar I (emperor)
  coinage, 17
  Doda (concubine) and, 50
  family tree, *6*
  Field of Lies (833) and, 26, 26n16
  kingdom and succession, 2, 11,
      11n1
  Louis II of Italy as coemperor,
      177n10
  mentioned in Hadrian's II letter,
      176, 176n9
  monasteries and, 33
  prayers before battle, 166
  summits with brothers, 33–4,
      34nn41–2
Lothar II (king of Lotharingia)
  ascent to throne, 11, 11n1
  birth, 3n5
  Booklet of Complaint at Council
      of Aachen (862), 52, 55, 61–3,
      61n33, 64n44
  Boso and Engeltrude and, 90n28
  Charles the Bald and, 7, 47, 47n6
  children and heir, 103
  coinage, 16–18, 17n3, *19*
  death, 168, 172, 174, 176–7, 201,
      202
  donation to St-Pierre convent,
      103–5, 104n10
  family tree, *6*
  kingdom, 3, *4*
  land granted to Theutberga,
      135–7, 137–9, 137n10, 138n15,
      138nn19–20, *139*, 139n22
  letters from Nicholas I to, 122,
      122n1, 154
  letter to Ado of Vienne, 171, 173
  Louis the German and, 3, 20, 21,
      42n55, 47–8, 97, 97n44
  marriage to Theutberga, 3
  marriage to Waldrada, 52, 52n1,
      53, 53n4
  mentioned in *Liber Memorialis* of
      Remiremont, 49

Metz oath and, 168–9
moral treatise given to, 12, 12n4
opposition to from within
  Lotharingia, 132, 132n10
political failure, 167–8, 203
protection against Northmen,
  164–7, 164n2
public acknowledgment of
  Waldrada and Hugh, 103, 104
public penance by, 52–3, 58,
  58n23, 64, 64nn45–6
residences, 14, 14n11
royal charters issued by, 12
royal charter to Winebert, 12–14,
  14n14, 15–16, 15n18, *16*
Savonnières summit (862) and,
  85–6, 88, 89, 97–8
succession after, 174
territorial acquisitions in
  Provence, 102–3
threat to excommunicate, 100,
  100n4, 134, 145n26
Vegetius and, 119n31
See also marriage crisis
Lotharingia
  about, 1–2, 8–9
  coronation of Charles the Bald as
    king, 179, 179n1
  divided between Charles the Bald
    and Louis the German, 182
  failure of, 5, 7–8, 201–3
  Hadrian II's letter to aristocrats
    in support of Louis II of Italy,
    174–6, 176–8, 178n12
  map, *4*
  See also Lothar II; marriage crisis
Louis (son of Louis the German),
  49
Louis II of Italy (emperor)
  Bari siege and, 183, 185, 185n12,
    195–6, 199
  as claimant to Lotharingia, 182,
    185
  coronation as coemperor, 177n10
  Hadrian II and, 175, 175n4

Hadrian II's support for claim to
  Lotharingia, 174, 175, 177–8,
  178n13
imprisonment by Lombard
  prince, 185–6, 185n13
kingdom, 2–3, *4*
letter to Basil I (Byzantine
  emperor), 184, 186–200,
  186nn16–17
Lothar II's family tree, place in, *6*
Metz oath and, 168
reign, 182–3
relations with Charles the Bald
  and Louis the German and,
  189, 189n27
self-perception as emperor,
  183n4
support for Lothar II, 170–1,
  171n1, 173, 174
territorial acquisitions in
  Provence, 102–3
Treaty of Orbe and, 11
Louis the German (king of East
  Francia)
  death, 25n14
  epithet, 2n3
  invasion of West Francia, 19–21,
    113, 132, 132n9
  kingdom, 2, *4*
  Lothar II and, 3, 7, 20, 21, 42n55,
    47–8, 97, 97n44
  Lothar II's family tree, place in, *6*
  Lotharingia divided with Charles
    the Bald, 182
  Louis II of Italy and, 189, 189n27
  mentioned in *Liber Memorialis* of
    Remiremont, 49
  Metz oath and, 168–9, 169–70,
    170nn15–16
  Savonnières summit (862) and,
    85, 88, 89, 95–6
  summits with brothers, 33–4,
    34nn41–2
  See also Quierzy Letter, to Louis
    the German

Louis the Pious (emperor)
  burial place, 14
  Carolingian empire and, 1, 2
  Church protected by, 32
  comparison to Louis the German in Quierzy Letter, 20, 25–6, 25n15, 26n16
  daughter Gisela married to Eberhard of Friuli, 114
  family tree, *6*
  public penance by, 47, 52
Louis the Stammerer, 147–8
love, Augustinian view of, 160n18
Loxus the doctor
  Physionomia, 120
Lupus of Ferrières
  On the Laws of the Franks, Ripuarians, Lombards, Alemans and Bavarians, 119, 119n30
luxuria, 83, 83n97, 85

MacLean, Simon, 7, 141
mancipia (peasants, slaves), 115, 115n10, 116, 121
mancuses, 118, 118n27
mansus (farm/household), 104, 104n11, 164
marriage
  concubinage vs., 62, 62n39
  Council of Aachen (862) on, 54–5, 58–60, 64–6, 68–85, 68n65, 74n78, 76n82
  kingship and, 55, 203
  See also divorce; incest
marriage crisis (Lothar II and Theutberga)
  about/overview, 3, 5
  accusation of incestuous adultery against Theutberga, 54, 64, 80, 80n88, 82–5, 160
  Adventius's claims to lack knowledge of, 123, 126–7, 126n21
  Council of Aachen (862) and, 53, 56–60, 62–3, 62n35, 64–7, 66nn55–6, 67n59, 80–5, 100

Council of Metz (863) and, 5, 55, 100, 103
land granted to Theutberga and, 135–7, 137–9, 137n10, 138n15, 138nn19–20, *139*, 139n22
letter from Lotharingian bishops to West Frankish bishops and, 129–31, 131–4, 131n5, 131n7
Lothar's claim of prior marriage to Waldrada and, 55n12, 105
Lothar's marriage to Waldrada and, 52, 52n1, 53, 53n4
Lothar's perseverance, 153–4
Nicholas I's letter on Waldrada and, 140–2, 142–6, 142n10, 143n11, 143n14, 145n25
Nicholas I's letter to Charles the Bald and, 154–7, 157–63
ordeals and trials for Theutberga, 20–1, 46, 154–5, 159, 159n12
political implications, 5, 7–8, 201
pressure on Theutberga to become a nun, 135, 135n5
Savonnières summit (862) and, 85–6, 88, 91–5, 95–6, 97–8
Theutberga's appeals to papacy, 122, 135n5, 148, 154, 170
Theutberga's fear of Lothar II, 172, 172n7
Theutberga's flight to Charles the Bald, 47, 47n5, 55n13, 157n7
Theutberga's restoration as queen, 134–5, 148
Theutberga's tenacity, 160, 160n16, 203
Theutberga's "voluntary" confession, 3, 46, 64
Martin of Braga
  On the Four Virtues, 119, 119n33
Matfrid (count), 116, 116n13
McCormick, Michael, 87
Meerssen summit (851), 22n9, 34, 34n42, 96
Metz, 15n16, 99, 109n15. *See also* Council of Metz (863)

Metz Cathedral, 109, 109n14
Metz oath, 168–9, 169–70, 170nn15–16
Misonne, Daniel, 166
Mistry, Zubin, 148
monasteries and convents
   call to support in Quierzy Letter, 33, 33n39, 34, 34n44
   estates and servants, 111, 111n28
   Gorze reforms, 106–8, 108–12, 111n26
   lay abbots, 33n39, 106, 106n6, 109, 109n19
   monastic life as spiritual warfare, 109, 109n13
   queens as patrons, 141, 157n7
Monte Cassino summit, 171
Muslims, in southern Italy, 166, 170, 183, 183n2, 185, 196, 198–200, 198n65, 199n67

Naples, 198–9, 198n65
Nicetas (Niketas) Ooryphas, 196, 196n59, 197
Nicholas I (pope)
   Adventius's letter to, 123–4, 124–9, 125nn14–15
   circular letter on Council of Metz, 123, 123n7, 124–5, 124n12
   communication challenges, 155–6
   Council of Aachen (862) and, 91–2, 92n36, 100, 171
   Council of Metz annulled by, 5, 121–2, 123, 156
   death, 170
   deposition of Theutgaud, 100n3
   letters on Lothar II's marriage crisis, 154
   letters to Lothar II, 122, 122n1, 154
   letter to bishops on Waldrada, 140–2, 142–6, 142n10, 143n11, 143n14, 145n25
   letter to Charles the Bald, 154–7, 157–63

   Lothar II's claim of marriage to Waldrada and, 105, 105n2, 107
   Metz oath and, 168n3
   monastic reforms and, 107, 109, 109n18, 112
   self-perceived authority, 122–3
   Theutberga's appeals to, 122, 135n5, 148, 154
   threat to excommunicate Lothar II, 100n4, 134, 145n26
Niederlahnstein hoard, 17n3, 18
Nightingale, John, 107
Northmen (vikings)
   call for Louis the German to drive away, 28–9
   impacts on Carolingian empire, 27, 27n20, 28nn23–4, 124, 124n13, 163–4, 164n4
   prayers organized against, 164–7

oaths
   bishops and, 43–4, 43n62
   Metz oath, 168–9, 169–70, 170nn15–16
Odo of Beauvais (bishop), 89, 89n22, 169, 169n14
Otpert (witness to Eberhard and Gisela's will), 121

pagi (regions), 135, 138n16
pallium, 118, 118n26
papacy. *See* Church; Hadrian II (pope); Nicholas I (pope)
papal apocrisiaries (envoys), 196–8, 197nn60–1
Parma, 137
passionaries, 120, 120n44
Paul Orosius
   Seven Books, 120
peasants (slaves, *mancipia*), 115, 115n10, 116, 121
penance, public, 47, 52–3, 58, 58n23, 64, 64nn45–6, 102, 102n13

people (*gens*), 191, 191n35, 191n38
Phineas, 146n27
Photian schism, 193n49
phylacteries, 117, 117n20
physiognomy, 120n41
pilgrims, guesthouses for, 34–5
Pilligerheck hoard, 17–18, *19*
Pippin II of Aquitaine, 202, 202n2
Pippin the Short, 32
Pokorny, Rudolf, 149n8
precaria grants, 32, 32n37
predestination, 134, 134n12
Provence, 3, 102–3, 185. *See also* Charles of Provence
pyx, 117, 117n17

queens
   as convent patrons, 141, 157n7
   Ermentrude's coronation, 146–9, 149–53, 149n8, 150n14, 153n19
Quierzy Letter, to Louis the German, 19–46
   about, 19–20, 21
   on advice's divine source, 22–3, 23n11
   bishops' apologies for meeting, 22
   bishops' position towards Louis, 41–2, 41n54, 44–6
   on bringing excommunicated to repentance, 39
   call to examine conscience, 24–5, 26–7
   call to improve situation, 27–8
   call to protect Church, 29–33
   call to support monasteries, 33, 33n39, 34, 34n44
   Charles the Bald under the bishop's protection, 42–3, 43n59
   comparison to letter from Lotharingian bishops to West Frankish bishops, 130
   criticism of Louis's army, 27, 27n19
   on driving away Northmen, 28–9
   on guesthouses for pilgrims, 34–5
   kingship advice, 20, 35–6, 36–9, 37n47
   Lothar II's marriage crisis and, 93n38
   on Louis's previous inattention, 23–4
   on oath-swearing by bishops, 43–4, 43n62
   preface, 21–2, 22n7
   on rebellions against Louis the Pious, 25–6, 25n15
   reminder of Louis's previous pledges, 33–4
   on royal estates, 39–41
   warning against advisors, 27, 45

Radbert (Paschasius) of Corbie (monk), 53n3, 54, 54n10
Radoald of Porto (bishop), 105, 107–8
Rathold of Strasbourg (bishop), 56, 56n16, 128n26
Ratramnus of Corbie (monk), 54
Regino of Prüm (monk), 7, 142, 142n8, 144n18, 144n20, 145n25
Remigius of Lyon (archbishop), 146n1, 173
Remigius of Reims (saint), 33, 33n40, 117n20, 118, 180
Remiremont convent, 48, 50, 141, 144n17, 174. *See also Liber Memorialis* of Remiremont
rex, 194–5, 194n55
Richildis (queen, wife of Charles the Bald), 148, 182
Rodmund (Hrodmund; royal notary), 12, 136, 138
Rodolph (son of Eberhard and Gisela), 116, 118, 120, 121
Rodulf (Northman), 164
Roman Church. *See* Church
Romans and Roman Empire, 191, 191n38, 192–3. *See also* Eastern Roman Empire
Rorik (Northman), 164, 166

Rosenwein, Barbara, 13
royal charters. *See* charters
royal estates, 39–41, 39n50

sacramentaries
  about, 179
  of Metz, 179–82, *181*
Salomon of Konstanz (bishop), 89, 89n16
Sant'Antonino (Piacenza church), 172
Savonnières summit (862), 85–98
  about, 85–8, 88n12, 98
  Charles the Bald's declarations, 96–7, 98, 98n46
  Charles the Bald's letter, 89–95, 90n26
  complaints against Lothar II, 85–6, 90–2
  demands for Lothar II, 93–5, 94nn39–40
  location, 85n2
  Lothar II's declaration, 97–8
  Louis the German's declaration, 95–6
Sawdan (emir of Bari), 183, 185
Schmid, Karl, 48n11, 49, 50
Sedulius Scottus, 86
Sergius II (duke of Naples), 198n65
Sicily, 183, 199, 199n67
Sirmond, Jacques, 169
slaves (peasants, *mancipia*), 115, 115n10, 116, 121
Smaragdus of St-Mihiel, 118, 118n23, 120
society, conception of, 61, 61n34
St-Arnulf monastery (Metz), 12, 13–14, 15, 15n18
Staubach, Nikolaus, 7n13, 168, 179
St-Felix convent (Zürich), 144n17
St-Glossinde convent (Metz), 141n6, 174, 174n1
St-Martin of Tours monastery, 106
St-Maurice monastery, 106
St-Nabor monastery, 16, 16n19

stofa, 15, 15n17
St-Pierre-aux-Nonnains convent (Metz), 144n17
St-Pierre des Terreaux convent (Lyons), 103–5, 104n10
Sulpicius Severus
  Life of Saint Martin of Tours, 119, 119n38
summits, between kings, 85, 85n1, 86–7
Susanna Crystal, 135
synods, 30, 30n30

Talisman of Charlemagne, 117n20
Theoderic of Cambrai (bishop), 56n16
Theodosius I (emperor), 192–3, 193n46
Theomar (abbot of Gorze), 111, 111n27
Theophanes
  Chronographia (with George the Synkellos), 190n32, 191n36
Theutberga (wife of Lothar II)
  Charles the Bald and, 5, 47, 47n5, 154, 157, 157n7, 182
  death, 174n1
  donation to Sant'Antonino in Lothar II's memory, 172, 172n8
  Ermentrude's coronation as queen and, 153n22
  Gorze monastic reforms and, 108
  land granted to, 135–7, 137–9, 137n10, 138n15, 138nn19–20, *139*, 139n22
  as "limb of the Lord's body," 145, 145n23
  marriage, 3
  Metz convent and, 141, 141n6
  Nicholas I's concern for, 160–1
  not mentioned in *Liber Memorialis* of Remiremont, 50
  as nun after Lothar's death, 174
  restoration as queen, 134–5, 148
  See also marriage crisis

Theutgaud of Trier (archbishop)
  Adventius's letter to, 99–101, 101–2
  Council of Aachen (862) and, 56
  deposition of, 100n3, 121–2, 125, 125nn16–17
  Lothar II's penance and, 57–8, 58n23
  Waldrada and, 141n4
Theuthild (abbess of Remiremont), 48, 50n18
Tironian notes, 105n12
Treaty of Orbe (856), 11, 11n2, 175
Treaty of Verdun (843), 19, 85
Trier, 99

Unruoch (Unroch; son of Eberhard and Gisela), 115–16, 117, 119, 120, 121, 121n46
Uto (witness to Eberhard and Gisela's will), 121
Utrecht, 164, 164n2

Valentinian I (Roman emperor), 8n15
Vegetius
  On Military Matters, 119, 119n31
vikings. *See* Northmen
Vulcan (god of fire), 101n9

Waldrada (queen, wife of Lothar II)
  background, 141n4
  children, 103
  as concubine, 58n23
  death, 174n1
  excommunication of, 140, 142, 144, 144nn19–21, 145, 145n23, 155, 162, 174
  Lothar's claim of prior marriage to, 55n12, 105
  Lothar's perseverance to recognize as wife, 153–4
  marriage crisis and, 3, 5
  marriage to Lothar II, 52, 52n1, 53, 53n4
  mentioned in *Liber Memorialis* of Remiremont, 49, 50
  Nicholas I's letter on, 140–2, 142–6, 142n10, 143n11, 143n14, 145n25, 162
  as nun at Remiremont after Lothar's death, 52, 174
  ongoing power and influence, 140–1, 143–4, 143n14, 143n16, 144n17
  public acknowledgment of in charter to St-Pierre convent, 103, 104
  summons to Rome, 135, 140, 143
Walter (count and advisor), 13, 13n6, 15, 50, 99–100, 102
wars (*werras*), first known use of term, 44, 44n63
wax tablets, 118, 118n24
Welfs, 87, 113n2
Wellebert (priest, witness to Eberhard and Gisela's will), 121
Wenilo of Rouen (archbishop), 21, 22n7, 24
Werimbert (witness to Eberhard and Gisela's will), 121
West Francia. *See* Charles the Bald
Wicbert (aristocrat), 172, 172n6
will, of Eberhard of Friuli, and wife Gisela, 113–14, 115–21
Willibert of Cologne (archbishop), 155n4
Winebert, royal charter to, 12–14, 14n14, 15–16, 15n18, *16*
Witgar of Augsburg (bishop), 169, 169n13

"Your Dominance," term of address, 22n8
youth, 82n94

Milton Keynes UK
Ingram Content Group UK Ltd.
UKHW021340051223
433832UK00004B/4